Assessing NAFTA: A Trinational Analysis

Assessing NAFTA: A Trinational Analysis

edited by
Steven Globerman and
Michael Walker

THE FRASER INSTITUTE

The Fraser Institute
Vancouver, British Columbia, Canada

Canadian Cataloguing in Publication Data

Globerman, Steven.

Assessing NAFTA

ISBN 0-88975-156-0

1. Canada. Treaties, etc. 1992 Oct. 7. 2. Free trade—North America. 3. North America—Commercial treaties. I. Walker, Michael, 1945– II. Fraser Institute (Vancouver, B.C.) III. Title.
HF1766.G66 1993 382′.71′097 C93–091231–4

Table of Contents

Introduction

THE CENTRAL PREOCCUPATION OF THE FRASER INSTITUTE and its research program is the solutions that markets provide for the economic problems that are mankind's constant companion. This research constantly encounters barriers to market operation which are imposed by government actions of one kind or another. While often enacted with the best of intentions, these impediments frequently injure those they are intended to help and benefit groups who in turn become the champions of the political support for the impediments. Protectionism is undoubtedly one of the more insidious of these anti-market devices. The beneficiaries of protection are often concentrated politically, highly motivated by substantial gains, and effective in pressing their case. The victims of protectionism—consumers of the protected product—are diffuse in their interest, unaware or unconcerned about their loss and disorganized in pressing their own interests in the matter. Because of this asymmetry, protectionism is often the outcome of political action and has been a constant source of economic loss.

This book contains a set of studies examining the content of the proposed North American Free Trade Agreement. It is part of an extensive program of research and other activities which the Fraser Institute has undertaken in conjunction with the Centre for International Studies at the University of Toronto, the Americas Program at Stanford University, the Hudson Institute, the Center for Strategic and International Studies, Political Economy Research Center, El Colegio de Mexico, and economists at many of the most prestigious universities on the continent. This four-year program of activity has been generously funded by the Lilly Endowment, Inc. of Indianapolis and we are pleased to acknowledge their wholehearted support and the encouragement and insights that have been provided by John Mutz and Gordon St. Angelo.

There can be no more important set of issues than those that relate to the establishment of one market for most products on the North American continent. The Fraser Institute has therefore been pleased to lend its support and assistance to the accomplishment of this program of research which reaches out for an understanding of how North America will be configured as we begin to recognize the opportunities of the next century. However, the authors in this book and in all of the other projects in the program of the Fraser Institute work independently and are subject to review only by independent referees and editors. In consequence, the conclusions to which they come are their own and may or may not reflect the view of the members or the Trustees of the Fraser Institute.

Michael A. Walker

Overview

THIS VOLUME CONTAINS, in the form of a series of independently conducted analyses, a comprehensive overview of the North American Free Trade Agreement (NAFTA)[1]. The agreement is a process by which Mexico, the United States and Canada have agreed to surrender their control or sovereignty over certain limited aspects of their trade policy. They have made this partial surrender of autonomy in order to achieve the benefits that are available from mutual relaxation of protectionism and the cementing of this resolve in the form of an international agreement.

Evaluation of the success of the trade negotiations which have produced this agreement should focus on the extent to which the countries have given up their ability to impede trade. That is to say, in a paradoxical way the country that "gave up the most" in terms of control over international trade is also the country that gained the most in terms of benefits. The apparently paradoxical nature of this statement is resolved with the recognition that protectionism does not benefit all of the citizens of a country but rather benefits one group—namely

---

1 The discussion in this book is based on the August, 1992 version of the agreement. While no substantial changes have been made, a new, slightly reorganized version of NAFTA was released the week this volume was sent to the printer. The only paper which has been revised to take this change into account is that by Leonard Waverman.

protected producers—at the expense of the consumers and other producers who must pay higher prices for the protected products. Protectionism is like a tax and expenditure program which taxes consumers and producers and conveys benefits to businesses and workers in the protected sector. Opening borders to foreign suppliers increases competition, removes the privilege enjoyed by protected producers and in consequence reduces prices.

Trade agreements like NAFTA also benefit competitive producers by giving them assured or improved access to the markets in the other countries which are part of the agreement.

There are of course "losers" in any liberalization. They are those who have been the beneficiaries of the protectionism. These losers can be expected to object to the signing of any such agreement and their opposition is quite understandable. The opposition of these losers to any trade liberalization usually takes the form of a claim that their interest is the same as the national interest. Therefore, what the U.S. textile producers and workers "lose" is portrayed as a loss for the U.S., or the "gain" of the Mexican auto industry is portrayed as a loss for Canada.

In evaluating NAFTA, the authors of this book have looked through the veil of apparent interest to the real motivations of the negotiating parties. They have revealed the strengths and weaknesses of the deal as it provides for the improvement of the standard of living for all three countries. The book is divided into three sections. The first provides an assessment, from the point of view of the three countries involved, of the overall impact of the agreement upon those countries. The second section deals with the impact on specific sectors that were of particular importance in the negotiations. It contains papers on automobiles, textiles, agriculture, financial services and energy. The third section provides a discussion of topics that were important in the negotiations and have an effect on many sectors. There are papers on the Rules of Origin and their importance, a review of the disputes settlement mechanisms agreed to, a treatment of the agreed regulations regarding Investment as well as a discussion of the environmental impact of the agreement.

Section One—The Country Assessments

The first section contains three papers which provide overviews from the point of view of the three countries as to the overall impact of the agreement. Since Professor Sidney Weintraub from the United States alone provides a comprehensive summary of the trade deal and since his paper therefore provides the best introduction to NAFTA, we made his the first chapter.

The Impact on the United States

In addition to an overview of the agreement, Weintraub provides an insight as to the U.S. objectives in approaching the negotiations and how the features of the deal meet these expectations. He also provides a very valuable survey of the economic impact analyses which have been conducted, concluding that the deal is likely to have modest short term consequence for the U.S. In assessing the evidence on the likely economic impact, Weintraub points out that, to the extent that the deal has negative consequences for employment and other aspects of labour markets, these effects would be forthcoming anyway. On the other hand, the deal will enable a restructuring of some industries, such as automobiles, that will make them more competitive and therefore more likely to survive global restructuring in the industry.

The economic evidence surveyed by Weintraub suggests that the pact will boost U.S. output by about 1 per cent and even more as time passes if the Mexican economy expands. According to Weintraub this positive assessment is the consensus of economists even though there are some dissenting views. Conclusions in one study that the deal will have strongly negative effects "are not well substantiated," according to Weintraub.

One development supporting the positive assessment of the deal is the recent expansion of U.S. exports to Mexico driven by the growth in the Mexican economy. This is likely to continue under the new arrangements and the U.S. is expected to enjoy a trade surplus with Mexico as that country's economy expands—a surplus lasting for several decades.

Weintraub brings to his paper much experience with the operation of the policy process in Washington and his insights about the micro politics of the deal are particularly interesting. The early opponents of the deal sided with trade-unionists and environmentalists concerned, respectively, about the lack of labour market provisions respecting worker safety and sanitation and about protection for the environment. Weintraub predicts that as the implementing legislation is submitted to the U.S. Congress, many of these Congressional opponents will be revealed as really opposing the deal because of anticipated impacts on industries in their districts.

Environmentalists have influenced the agreement in that it is the first such to include a comprehensive treatment of environmental issues. An additional measure in the form of a tri-national commission, proposed by President Clinton, is likely to be rejected by the other countries, in Weintraub's opinion. On the other hand, while labour conditions are not dealt with in the agreement, they are the subject of a consultative Commission established at the same time as the agreement was reached.

In some ways the most contentious issue of concern to opponents is the extent of support available to those who are displaced by the trade pact. President George Bush had already addressed this issue by proposing a worker adjustment initiative funded to the tune of $10 billion over five years but gave no indication of what should be dropped from the budget to accommodate this new program. Weintraub predicts that even though such an adjustment program is essential to get the support of organized labour, the pressure from other entitlement programs will make its realization difficult. In any event, as he notes, this is a matter for domestic U.S. policy and not for an international trade agreement.

The impact on Canada

The second paper, by Professor Leonard Waverman, Director of the University of Toronto's Centre for International Studies, discusses the impact of NAFTA for Canada.

In the course of his paper, Waverman provides a very valuable service for all who are interested in the issue of expanding trade in North America in that he faces directly an issue that has hung like a pall over the discussions, namely, the implication that the Canadia-U.S. Free Trade Agreement (FTA) has been a tremendous flop from Canada's point of view. As one wag put it, if the FTA has been a failure, why would we want to expand it to make it even more of a failure, and why would Mexico want to join in a practise that has been so bad for Canada.

Waverman surveys all of the studies that have been undertaken to assess the impact of the FTA. Some of the studies show a positive impact on employment and growth, some show a slight negative impact. The important thing is that none of the five studies show the sort of massive job loss that is sometimes claimed. Recession, global restructuring, adverse increases in the relative costs of manufacturing in Canada including higher rates of taxation and other factors seem to explain most of the job loss. At most, according to Waverman, 15 per cent of the job loss that has occurred since the FTA came into effect can be attributed to the agreement and these are related to the primary adjustment to the FTA. The longer term effects which will boost growth and employment have not had time to be fully felt.

One comprehensive study by Peter Pauly using the economic models in the United Nations Project Link shows that once all the other forces affecting the economy had been taken into account, even in the first two years of the agreement, the separate impact of the FTA was to boost Canadian output by nearly half of one per cent and to reduce the unemployment rate below what it would otherwise have been.

Waverman goes on to point out that the major future threat to Canadian employment is a general lack of competitiveness in a restructuring world. Canada cannot opt out of this process, and opening freer trade in North America is an essential response to what is happening. Moreover, as he notes, Mexico is going to open up to the U.S. and be admitted to the U.S. market with corresponding trade and investment diversion away from Canada, whether Canada is involved in NAFTA or not. By joining the agreement Canada stands to gain much better access to Mexico, and remains part of the emerging hemispheric trade area, thus enjoying, along with the other participants, the benefits of the largest marketplace in the world.

The impact on Mexico

The impact of NAFTA in Mexico is discussed in the third paper in the first section. Author Rogelio Ramirez De la O notes that Mexico's attempt to complete such a trade deal stems from a program of economic liberalization and stabilization which began in the mid 1980s. Currency stabilization, privatization of banks and other industries and a general climate which investors found reassuring led to a repatriation of capital by Mexicans and the beginning of economic restructuring. One result of this program was a dramatic increase in the amount of importation and a rapidly widening current account deficit corresponding to the capital inflow.

In the early stages of the restructuring, Mexico had little success in attracting the capital of non-residents. There was danger that the economic resurgence would come to a crashing halt owing to a capital shortage. Concern about this was heightened by the reunification of Germany and the impact this might have on the supply of capital in the western world. Finally, Mexico, like Canada before it, was impressed by the apparent world-wide trend toward regional trading blocks which might leave Mexico without an assured access to any market unless it could strike a deal with its closest and most important trading partner.

Ramirez De la O, president of the highly respected Mexico-based private consulting group Ecanal, expects that the NAFTA agreement will have exactly the effects that motivated the Mexican government to pursue it. He expects, even in the short run, a boost in Mexican incomes, wages and investment. He forecasts a significant further increase in imports and a swelling of the Mexican trade deficit as more capital floods into Mexico to take advantage of the opportunities available there. He has some claim to expertise in the area since he has more accurately forecasted the evolution of Mexican trade performance in the past few years than either the government or other private sector analysts.

Section II—Sectoral Impacts

The automotive sector

Arguably, the most important aspect of the North American Free Trade Agreement is its provisions regarding the automotive sector, which accounts for the largest share of continental trade flows. They are important because they make some changes to the Auto Pact between Canada and the United States, which was the kernel sectoral agreement that was the historical precedent for the comprehensive Free Trade

Agreement signed in 1988. They are also important because of the fundamental changes they will bring to the Mexican auto sector, which will, via the Agreement, be brought fully into the North American automobile market by the end of the transition period allowed for in the Agreement.

The auto provisions of the agreement are not something that a free trader would find very attractive. As in the textile sector, there are a mind-numbing array of rules and regulations concerning the regional value content of automobiles produced under the Agreement, a trilogy of regulations respecting the basis on which the content regulations will be applied, and a complex process of tracing this value content (which was contained in the original U.S./Canada Auto Pact but was dropped in the FTA).

On the other hand, NAFTA has some distinct advantages over the FTA in that it greatly reduces the amount of flexibility provided to customs officials in the determination of the eligibility of a particular product to be transported duty free across the borders of the participating countries. This ambiguity in the FTA led to a corresponding uncertainty as to how regional value content should be calculated and, therefore, a lack of predictability and precision in the entire regime.

In his masterful chapter on the subject, Jon Johnson, who is a lawyer with the Toronto firm of Goodman and Goodman, provides a thorough description of the way in which NAFTA will affect the evolution of the automotive sectors in all three countries. He shows that under NAFTA, Mexico will be enabled to follow, at an accelerated pace, the path which Canada took (namely, from having an inefficient and uncompetitive automotive sector prior to 1965, to having in 1992 an automotive sector which is wholly competitive in the American market context and capable, in the view of some assessments summarized by Johnson, of competing effectively with Mexico for a share of the largest automobile market in the world—that of the U.S). While, as Johnson points out, the predictions about the future of the North American automobile industry can only be made on the basis of assumptions, there are good reasons to believe that, eventually, all three countries' automotive industries will be better off as a result of NAFTA.

If there are reservations, it is about the anticipated impact on Canada because of the potential for Mexican production to displace production currently occurring in Canada and because of the difficulties Canadian parts manufacturers might face in competing with their counterparts in Texas and southern California. However, as Johnson points out, all of the potential difficulties that might be faced by the Canadian automotive sector will ensue whether Canada is part of NAFTA or not, arising as they do primarily as a consequence of the arrangements made between the United States and Mexico. By being part of NAFTA, Canada acquires the greater certainty and specificity of the regulations respecting the rules of origin, and acquires access to the Mexican market for its output. That market access will be significant to the extent that the trade agreement, together with a thoroughgoing domestic liberalization program, succeeds in boosting the level of Mexican incomes.

Textiles and apparel

One of the sectors which historical experience predicted would be negatively affected by increased trade access was the textile and apparel sector. Long the focus of protectionism on both sides of the Canada/U.S. border, these industries were subject to special treatment in the FTA and, as pointed out by Eric Barry and Elizabeth Siwicki from the Canadian Textiles Institute in their fascinating paper, were the subject of a special negotiating group for NAFTA.

The objective of the negotiators in the FTA had been to liberalize some trade between the parties within the region while still greatly restricting trade in textiles and apparel from countries outside the region. Particular details of the implementation of this objective, both in the FTA and now in NAFTA, are of sufficient complexity that a very significant fraction of the article is taken up by a lucid description of the provisions of the Agreement. No useful purpose could be served by an attempt to summarize here for introductory purposes what is already a concise and heroic effort at summary by the authors.

Fortunately, the most interesting aspect of the article is not the description of the provisions of the Agreement and how it compares with the Canada/U.S. Free Trade Agreement. Most interesting are the comments made by the authors about the impact that the Free Trade Agreement has already had with respect to trade in textiles and apparel and their prediction, on the basis of this experience, of the consequences of NAFTA.

Say the authors, "The reality of the FTA and the need to adapt acted as a psychological trigger and firms began to look beyond the domestic market. In 1990, with a recession in Canada and the U.S.; with textile duties down by only two-tenths; and with a high Canadian dollar; textile exports to the U.S. increased by 28 percent. In 1991, exports held that gain and increased by another 15 percent. In 1992 they increased by another 30 percent." The authors point out that this spectacular performance in the textile area has been mirrored to some degree in the apparel side as well. "[I]t was widely assumed in 1987 that the Canadian market would be flooded with U.S. garments. This has not happened. Canada had a positive balance of clothing trade with the U.S. before the FTA. Since the FTA, instead of disappearing, this positive balance has continued to grow at an increasing rate."

There has also been a robust U.S. reciprocity in these trade arrangements. American readers may appreciate the fact that, notwithstanding these trade developments, the U.S. continues to enjoy a $1 billion trade surplus in its textile trade with Canada.

The authors conclude by noting that the prospect of the Free Trade Agreement caused a boost in the Canada/U.S. textile trade even before it was signed. They report that similar activity is happening between Canada and Mexico as exports of textiles from Canada to Mexico have grown by 85% in the first half of 1992, while imports of textiles and clothing from Mexico have also begun to increase.

The agriculture sector

Agriculture is proving to be one of the most difficult areas in which to accomplish trade liberalization. As Thomas Grennes points out in his comprehensive review of the agriculture provisions of the Agreement, some considerable ground has been gained in the form of trade creation, with only a modest amount of trade diversion. In the agriculture area, the Agreement consists of two separate bilateral arrangements between the United States and Mexico and between Canada and Mexico. The U.S./Canada Free Trade Agreement provisions for agriculture remain in effect for those two countries. In consequence, Grennes' article is largely an assessment of the impact of NAFTA on agriculture in the United States and in Mexico. His thorough assessment includes an indication of the trade effects, with its indication of a modest diversion of orange juice production from Brazil to Mexico, for example; a half billion dollar increase in food exports from the United States to Mexico and a $166 million increase in exports from Mexico to the United States. Concerns that lower Mexican standards will reduce the quality of food in the United States are dismissed, both by the Agreement and Grennes, in that the phyto sanitary standards currently in existence will be retained under the new agreement, with no reduction in U.S. standards.

Grennes expresses some concern about the fact that NAFTA does not explicitly provide for an accession clause; however, trade negotiators indicated during the course of negotiating the Agreement that their objective was to produce a general agreement that would set out the desirable principles of a liberalizing trade framework. Such a framework would be of such generality that any country which wished to do so would then be in a position to affirm the general principles while reserving on some particular points. The signatories of NAFTA have attached restrictions or exceptions to the general agreement for each of Canada, the United States, or Mexico, where that was felt to be necessary. The Agreement can, therefore, be expanded more easily than even an accession clause would have permitted, as it provides the opportunity for explicit, different timing, for example, of the decay of existing protection and other specifications in modification of the general principles that are contained in the NAFTA framework.

Grennes does lay to rest some concerns that have been expressed about the employment impact of the Agreement in Mexico. NAFTA opens up trade in corn, which is an essential Mexican product at the moment, employing large numbers of people. Grennes' observation is that the structure of employment in the *ejidos* will be affected by the fact that Mexican law regarding them has been modified, tending to lead to concentration of these lands back into economically and efficiently sized farms—a process that would have occurred with or without the North American Free Trade Agreement. There will be dislocation and rising unemployment due to the changes in domestic Mexican agriculture policy but these are not primarily related to NAFTA.

All in all, Grennes' assessment of the agricultural features of the Agreement are quite positive, although, he is sorry that the period of removal of trade barriers is going to be extended for fifteen years, thus reducing the present value of the changes which are being made, for all parties concerned. In his view, the liberalization could be done more rapidly to the benefit of all parties.

Financial Services

Somewhat greater enthusiasm is expressed by John Chant, in his assessment of the financial sector provisions of NAFTA. Chant notes first that the chapter respecting the financial sector could not simply be an extension of the FTA provisions because of the differences in the approach to financial regulation pursued in the three countries. Canada and Mexico pursue a system ruled by law, while the U.S. has a system ruled by specific and changeable regulations. Chant also points out that any such national agreement between the three countries would be only part of the story, in any event, because of the right of provincial and state governments to engage in their own regulation of financial institutions.

Respecting the diversity both of the signing parties and of any prospective future signatories, the Agreement is structured according to the most general principles, permitting a liberalized trade in financial services, with appropriate provisions for the right of establishment and national treatment. It also makes provisions for reservations to these principles by each of the signatories. The reservations consist both of those taken on behalf of the national government and those which may subsequently be registered by lower levels of government. Canada registered only one reservation, whereas the U.S. presented 18 and Mexico 26.

Chant concludes that all of the parties got some of what they wanted out of the negotiation but that Canada was, perhaps, the most successful, particularly in light of the fact that NAFTA extends to the financial sector the provisions for dispute settlement mechanisms which were not available under the FTA. In fact, financial sector disputes and issues have the benefit of a separate disputes resolution process with the ability to intercept difficulties before they become a significant trade irritant.

Perhaps the most encouraging aspect of the Agreement is the fact that it takes a liberalizing attitude toward the application of law with regard to the issue of national treatment. One of the things that investors most fear from expanding a service network into a foreign country is that they will be treated differently from resident nationals in the application of the law. It is typical in trade agreements that *de jure* national treatment is provided, ensuring that foreign institutions receive equal treatment under the law. However, Chant notes, "Nothing in *de jure* national treatment guarantees that foreign institutions will not be harmed by seemingly equal legal treatment that effectively limits them because of their different circumstances." NAFTA takes a more comprehensive attitude towards national treatment and requires competitive national treatment, i.e. "that the differential impact of the law on domestic and foreign institutions does not place foreign institutions at a disadvantage in their ability to compete."

In summary, Chant concludes that "The NAFTA financial sector provisions were much more than a reworking of the FTA provisions to include a third country . . . NAFTA was crafted around principles expressing the requirements for freedom of trade in financial services . . . permits countries to accept the agreement at different stages of financial development and work toward the eventual opening of their domestic financial markets to international competition. As a multilateral agreement, the NAFTA financial sector provisions offer potential benefits to countries other than Canada, Mexico and the U.S. by providing a framework in which a variety of financial sector needs can be met if these countries choose to join an expanded NAFTA."

Energy

The energy arrangements in the Agreement are analyzed by G.C. Watkins, immediate Past President of the International Association for Energy Economics and a person with a unique grasp of the complexities of North American energy trade. Watkins' assessment of the energy provisions of NAFTA is mixed. On the one hand, he regards it as an asymmetrical deal in which Canada and the United States have carried forward their commitment in the 1988 Free Trade Agreement and, indeed, embellished it to provide greater freedoms, while Mexico, reflecting the provisions of its Constitution, has declined to participate in this reciprocal liberalization process. On the other hand, Watkins does not regard this as an entirely bleak result since there is considerable liberalization as to sourcing of suppliers in the energy sector and some liberalization in the market for petro-chemicals, which liberalizations he believes will ultimately act as a lever to pry open the Mexican energy market.

One of the asymmetries in the Agreement relates to the so-called proportionality clause. This clause, a remnant of the Free Trade Agreement between Canada and the United States, provides that in the event that the Government of Canada should impose a restriction on the export of energy for reasons of conservation, supply shortages or price stabilization, the share of the total supply available for export purchase may not fall below the average level in the previous 36 months. This specific provision does not apply to Mexico, although a general prohibition of restrictions on trade in energy and in basic petro-chemicals which is contained in the General Agreement on Tariffs and Trade, of which all three countries are signatories, would presumably apply to Mexico.

On the other hand, Canada has been given the protection, denied to Mexico, of the right to export energy into the U.S. market, and is subject only to national security restrictions of a very tightly circumscribed nature. Canadians lost access to the U.S. energy market, in part, during the 1950s and 1960s under regulations passed in the guise of pursuing U.S. national security interests. This history is a matter of some future concern to the development of energy supplies in Canada, which are aimed at the U.S. market. Failing to agree to the proportionality clause meant that Mexico is not eligible for a tighter national security criterion, as specified in Article 607.

While Watkins believes there is considerable unfinished business in the energy sector in North America, he does conclude that the Agreement "confirms and modestly strengthens the energy provisions prevailing under the FTA between Canada and the U.S. This is not enough to generate euphoria, but a sense of quiet satisfaction would be justified."

Section III—Framework Issues

Rules of Origin

NAFTA is an arrangement whereby the participating countries agree to give preferential treatment to those inside the pact. The question naturally arises as to how countries can trade freely among themselves without, in the process, opening their borders to products from everywhere in the world at those same, preferential tariffs? Evidently, Mexico would be a very attractive venue through which to export the products of the Pacific Rim into North America if Mexico were a route around the tariffs imposed by Canada and the United States. Similarly, Canada, for example, would be an excellent way for British Commonwealth countries to seek access to the American market, bypassing American tariffs protecting the U.S. textile industry.

Of course, while consumers and, arguably, everybody in all three countries could be better off if a universal free trade regime could be adopted, the reality is that tariffs express the current state of political support for liberalizing trade arrangements, and it is *not* the intent of the original trade agreement to abolish all such trade barriers. Accordingly, there must be a way, within the Agreement, to ensure that products which pass duty free or without other difficulty between the consenting parties in the trade agreement are actually products of those countries and not interloping products from other areas. The rules of origin (where was the product produced) and regional value content (production value added in the North American region) requirements are the way in which this is achieved.

In his very complete discussion of this topic, Professor Peter Morici, of the Canada/U.S. Centre of the University of Maine, notes that, given the pressures under which they found themselves, the negotiators did very well to limit the extent to which these Rules of Origin and content requirements have been used to impose further protectionism. In particular, Morici notes that the Rules of Origin provided for in NAFTA are less onerous than had been sought by industrial pressure groups and represent a kind of compromise between Canadian (and Mexican) liberalizing interests and U.S. protectionists. The rules regarding regional value content are generally superior to those contained in the Canada-U.S. Free Trade Agreement and are less likely to promote the kinds of difficulties that resulted in, for example, the Honda Automobile case under the old rules.

One derogation from the provisions of the FTA has happened in the area of determining the value of parts in the automotive industry. Under the provisions of the FTA, negotiators had agreed to replace the 1965 Canada-U.S. Auto Pact rules of tracing with a roll-up rule (which basically provided that the value of a given part would be treated as having completely originated in North America, if it was at least 50% produced there), but tracing has once again reappeared in NAFTA.[2]

While Morici congratulates the negotiators for having avoided, in these protectionist times, a more draconian regime, he also makes a number of suggestions about how they may, over time, modify the rules to further increase their efficiency from the economic point of view.

Disputes settlement

Trade agreements represent a partial surrendering of the power to impede international trade. They do not eliminate such power, however, and protectionists still have access to a variety of means, both political and procedural, to harass foreign producers who are successful in penetrating domestic markets. As noted, it does not matter that these incursions are generally in the interest of consumers in the importing country. Local producers lose out when consumers chose the foreign-produced item, and the losers will use whatever laws there are to attempt to harass their competitor. The result is that a dispute will often arise as the foreign competitor rightly surmises that the domestic producer is misusing trade law to get the upper hand in what should be an economic contest for the sympathy of the domestic consumer.

In his concise yet comprehensive treatment, Gilbert Winham of Dalhousie University surveys the provisions that have been included in NAFTA for dealing with this sort of problem. As he notes, the FTA made explicit and, in some kinds of disputes, unique and innovative arrangements for the bi-national review of such actions. In the case of general disputes, the provisions followed the example set down in the GATT and were not particularly successful. NAFTA makes new and better

---

2 So, for example, an engine having a value of $1,000—$501 of which had been spent in North America—would be a $1000 value contribution toward North American sourcing; whereas, a $1,000 engine of which $499 had been spent in North America, would not qualify at all. So the value was either rolled up to the total cost of the component, in this case $1000, or rolled down to zero, depending on whether the 50% requirement had been met or not. Under the new rules, as in the 1965 Autopact, tracing of all components will be utilized so that the same engine would qualify for $499 or $501 worth of the total, with no rolling up or rolling down.

arrangements for the resolution of these disputes, attempting to push the problems down to working groups and technical committees while they are still small and manageable.

In the case of anti-dumping and countervail actions, Winham notes that unprecedented arrangements were included in the FTA for the review, by bi-national, objective panels, of decisions taken by domestic agencies. Although under attack from U.S. sources from the beginning of the negotiations, these bi-national disputes panels are included as a permanent feature of NAFTA (they had been included in the FTA as a temporary expedient with a maximum life of seven years).

Winham, who has been selected as a member of three of the thirty disputes panels that have been struck under the FTA, also sees great benefit to all three parties from the extension of the disputes mechanism to include Mexico. Now a proven process of disputes resolution, the provisions of Chapter Nineteen of NAFTA will provide transparency and certainty where this has been lacking. It will also be an instrument for change in the Mexican legal framework regarding countervail and anti-dumping legislation and procedure since, as with Canada and the U.S., this aspect of Mexican law will now be subject to scrutiny by the international panels. Winham infers that the existence of the NAFTA disputes settlement provisions will aid domestic Mexican reformers to accomplish their goal of making the Mexican legal process more transparent and comparable in certainty to the Canadian and American systems.

Investment provisions

Arguably the most important aspects of any trade agreement are its provisions respecting investment. Foreign direct investment is an increasingly common route by which foreign competitors enter a domestic market. The security of their investment and the knowledge that they will be treated fairly or at least the same as domestic investors are key elements in the decision to flow capital into a particular country.

Alan Rugman and Michael Gestrin provide a thorough examination of the way in which NAFTA treats investment and insist that, in this respect, the agreement is much more than the FTA plus Mexico. The FTA is, however, the precursor and it contained four basic elements: national treatment (as noted above); reservation of certain sectors (culture in Canada, transportation in the U.S.); the retention of a review mechanism (the U.S. Exon-Florio measure and Investment Canada); and the prohibition of "performance requirements" such as export requirements.

According to the authors there are five areas where the investment chapter in NAFTA has been changed: the definition of investment (broadened); the security of investment (international arbitration and full and fair compensation in the event of expropriation); the application of the "most favoured nation" principle to investments (investors to be treated no less favourably than those of any other investor nation); the replacement of "grandfathering" with explicit lists of restrictions (makes NAFTA more transparent than the FTA) and changes to the rules regarding performance requirements (two more restrictions regarding technology and exclusive supplier arrangements have been added).

The authors judge that on the whole the new provisions in NAFTA will encourage intra-regional investment flows and indeed even improve flows from the rest of the world into the region. In that sense, NAFTA improves on the FTA. However, there are some remaining difficulties that require future attention and other provisions that contain a potential threat to investment liberalization. There are two areas of particular concern. The anti-trust exemption which U.S. high-tech firms have been given in order to form consortia has not been extended to Mexican and Canadian firms. The second area for concern is the U.S. Exon-Florio provision and the associated Committee on Foreign Investments in the United States. The newness of this provision means that there is little experience to guide investors on how it may be used. The Canadian experience with the Foreign Investment Review Agency in an earlier, more primitive era, suggests that such agencies can pose significant impediments to the free flow of investment.

Environmental considerations

The impact of trade liberalization on the environment has emerged as one of the major impacts in the debate surrounding NAFTA. Indeed, indications are that President Clinton will seek stronger environmental provisions in the Agreement as a condition of his support. Mexican reluctance to accept stronger environmental protection provisions, perhaps including mandatory harmonization of environmental legislation and enforcement within the free trade area, might well jeopardize NAFTA. Hence, the relationship between trade liberalization and the environment is of critical importance to any overall assessment of the Agreement.

In his chapter, Professor Steven Globerman sets out the major theoretical relationships between trade liberalization and the environment and reviews the available empirical evidence on these relationships. There are two relationships identified as being especially important. One is the link between economic growth and environmental pollution. A second is the link between differences in environmental standards and the relocation of businesses. Environmentalists argue that economic growth will lead to increased pollution and that countries with weaker environmental laws and enforcement will draw investment away from countries with stronger laws and enforcement.

With respect to the first relationship, the evidence is, at best, ambivalent. Specifically, it demonstrates that for particular forms of pollution, higher incomes associated with economic growth will lead to reductions in emissions. In other cases, it will lead to increased emissions. Certainly, there is no support for an unequivocal view that higher income levels result in environmental degradation. If anything, the reverse is true.

With respect to the second relationship, the available evidence is quite persuasive in demonstrating that differences in environmental laws and regulations (as actually enforced) have little impact on the location decisions of businesses. The apparent exceptions to this conclusion, a few resource based industries, have actually relocated from the U.S. and Canada for reasons other than environmental costs.

Implementation of the current NAFTA promises certain additional indirect environmental benefits. To the extent that the Agreement leads to some dispersion of economic activity away from the U.S.-Mexican border, it will alleviate congestion problems in that region. Moreover, the sense of cooperation engendered by the Agreement stands to promote cooperation on trans-border environmental problems.

Conclusion

The cumulative impression from this careful assessment of the North American Free Trade Agreement is that it is a worthwhile contribution to the liberalization of trading arrangements in North America. The gains from this particular extension of the previously negotiated arrangement between Canada and the United States are more immediately available to Mexico and the United States, but Canada will benefit as well. The technical aspects of the agreement are an improvement on the provisions of the Canada-U.S. deal and are innovative in many areas including the articles affecting environmental protection, financial services, investment, energy and the settlement of disputes. The formulation of the agreement as a statement of general principles from which the signatories dissent by appended restrictions means that it will be relatively easy to add other countries in the hemisphere—an objective that is increasingly widely shared.

The agreement offers economic development opportunities and immediate gains in welfare. It is most important, however, for the great hope it offers for the future social and economic well-being of the hemisphere.

Steven Globerman and
Michael Walker

About the authors

Eric Barry

ERIC BARRY IS PRESIDENT of the Canadian Textiles Institute—the national trade association of the Canadian textile manufacturing industry—and has been actively involved as an industry advisor in a number of trade negotiations including the Multifibre Arrangement, the Canada-U.S. Free Trade Agreement, the Uruguay Round of Multilateral Trade Negotiations, and the North American Free Trade Agreement. From 1986 to 1988 Mr. Barry was a member of the Textiles, Footwear and Leather Sectoral Advisory Group on International Trade (SAGIT), its chairman from 1988 to 1991, and is now chairman of the Textiles, Fur and Leather SAGIT. Since 1988, he has been a member of the International Trade Advisory Committee (ITAC).

He received his B.A. from Sir George Williams University, Montreal. From 1977 to 1983, Eric Barry was a member of the Standards Council of Canada. He is the author of more than 100 articles in business publications in Canada, the U.S., and Europe.

John Chant

JOHN CHANT IS PROFESSOR and Chair of Economics at Simon Fraser University where he specializes in monetary economics. He has served as research director of the Financial Group at the Economic Council of Canada, producing the study *Efficiency and Regulation* which served as background for the 1980 Bank Act. He is author of several books including *The Economics of the Canadian Financial System: Theory, Policy and Institutions*, *The Allocative Effects of Inflation*, and *The Market for Financial Services*. An expert on the regulation of financial institutions in Canada, Dr. Chant has served as a consultant to the Bank of Canada, the World Bank, the Royal Commission on the Economic Union and Development Prospects of Canada and other government departments and agencies.

Michael Gestrin

MICHAEL GESTRIN IS A POLICY ANALYST and lecturer in international business at the University of Toronto. His recent research has included studies of European and American corporate response to administered protectionism. Mr. Gestrin has an M.A. in economics from the University of Toronto and has travelled and worked extensively in Europe and Asia.

Steven Globerman

STEVEN GLOBERMAN HOLDS A PH.D. in economics and is currently professor of economics at Simon Fraser University and Adjunct Scholar at The Fraser Institute. He has served on the Faculty of Commerce and Business Administration at the University of British Columbia, the Faculty of Administrative Studies at York University, and the Faculty of Business Administration at Simon Fraser University. He has consulted for government agencies and private sector organizations and has published over 50 journal articles and 15 books and monographs on various aspects of economics and public policy.

Thomas Grennes

THOMAS GRENNES IS PROFESSOR of economics at North Carolina State University, Raleigh, and research fellow at the Independent Institute in Oakland, California. He undertook graduate work in economics at the University of Chicago, and he is the author of the books *The Economics of World Grain Trade* (with P. Johnson and M. Thursby), and *International Economics*, and is the editor of *International Financial Markets and Agri-*

cultural Trade. A contributor to many scholarly volumes, his many articles and reviews have appeared in the *American Journal of Agricultural Economics, Journal of World Trade Law, World Economy, Journal of International Money and Finance, Quarterly Journal of International Agriculture*, and other journals.

Jon Johnson

JON R. JOHNSON IS A PARTNER in the Toronto law firm of Goodman & Goodman (internationally Goodman Freeman Phillips & Vineberg). He graduated from the University of Toronto Law School in 1968 and was admitted to the Bar of the Province of Ontario in 1970. In 1980, Mr. Johnson received his LLM in Business Law from Osgoode Hall Law School.

As a legal advisor in Canada's Trade Negotiation Office, he participated in the Canada-U.S. Free Trade Agreement with respect to automotive provisions. Mr. Johnson has advised External Affairs Canada in connection with various FTA Rules of Origin issues, and currently advises External Affairs Canada respecting the NAFTA Rules of Origin and related issues. He is the co-author of *The Free Trade Agreement: A Comprehensive Guide* (Canada Law Book, 1988). His recent papers include "The Effect of the Canada-U.S Free Trade Agreement on the Auto Pact," being published in Maureen Appel Molot, ed., *Driving Continentally: Will the NAFTA Fix Honda?* The Canada-United States Free Trade Newsletter, vol. 3, no. 2, Summer 1992, and "The NAFTA Rules of Origin—A New Approach?" in *The Canadian Law Newsletter*, October, 1992.

Peter Morici

PETER MORICI IS A PROFESSOR of Economics and Director of the Canadian-American Center at the University of Maine. Prior to joining the University in 1988, he served as Vice President of the National Planning Association where he is now an adjunct Senior Fellow. He is the author of eight books and many journal articles on trade policy, North American integration, and Canadian-American relations. His recent efforts include *Trade Talks with Mexico: A Time for Realism* (Washington, D.C.:

National Planning Association, 1991) and *Making Free Trade Work: The Canada-U.S. Agreement* (New York: Council on Foreign Relations, 1990).

Rogelio Ramirez De la O

Rogelio Ramirez De la O holds a Ph.D. in economics from Cambridge University (Fitzwilliam College) and a B.A. in economics from the National Autonomous University of Mexico. His specialization and doctoral dissertation on foreign direct investment in Mexico was published in 1983 in a less technical form, entitled, "From Improvisation to Failure—The Policy of Foreign Investment in Mexico." He has published numerous other works on international investment, foreign trade, and in recent years, Mexican economic policy.

He is the sole partner and president of Ecanal, S.A. (Economic Analysis for Company Planning), a firm whose periodic analysis of the Mexican economy and government policy is directed at major corporate clients, including some of the largest multinational firms. Ecanal has been publishing the monthly *Economic Report on Mexico* and the quarterly *Special Report on Mexico* since it was founded in 1977 by the British economist, the late Dr. Rodvers Opie.

Before joining Ecanal, Dr. Ramirez worked for two years at the United Nations Centre for Transnational Corporations in New York, where he researched the influence of transnational corporations on the balance of payments and on intra-firm international trade.

He is a member of the American Economic Association and the Royal Economic Society, advisor to top management of several multinational firms, and provost of the University of the Americas.

Alan Rugman

ALAN M. RUGMAN IS PROFESSOR OF INTERNATIONAL BUSINESS at the University of Toronto. Previously, he has held tenured appointments at Dalhousie University and the University of Winnipeg. He has also been a visiting professor at Columbia Business School, London Business School, and Harvard University.

His 16 books include: *Multinationals in Canada* (1980), *Inside the Multinationals* (1981), *Business Strategies and Free Trade* (ed. 1988), *Inter-*

national Business in Canada (ed. 1989), *Multinationals and Canada-United States Free Trade* (1990).

Dr. Rugman was a member of Canada's International Trade Advisory Committee from 1986-88 while the Canada-U.S Free Trade Agreement was being negotiated. Since then he has served on the sectoral trade advisory committee for forest products.

As a leading authority in international business, Dr. Rugman served as Vice President of the Academy of International Business in 1989-90 and was elected a Fellow of the Academy in 1991. He has lectured widely across North America, in Western Europe and in East Asia.

Elizabeth Siwicki

ELIZABETH SIWICKI IS VICE PRESIDENT, trade policy, at the Canadian Textiles Institute, the national trade association representing Canadian textile manufacturers. As part of her work with CTI, Ms. Siwicki has been actively involved in a variety of trade policy related activities including the development of industry positions and advice to government officials on the Multifibre Arrangement, the Canada-U.S. Free Trade Agreement, the Uruguay Round of Multilateral Trade Negotiations, and the North American Free Trade Agreement. She is executive assistant to the chairman of the Textiles, Fur and Leather SAGIT.

Elizabeth Siwicki has a B.A. in Communications from Concordia University, Montreal, and an M.B.A. from McGill University, Montreal.

Michael A. Walker

Michael A. Walker is Executive Director of The Fraser Institute. Born in Newfoundland in 1945, he received his B.A. (summa) at St. Francis Xavier University in 1966 and his Ph.D. in economics at the University of Western Ontario in 1969. From 1969 to 1973 he worked in various research capacities at the Bank of Canada, Ottawa, and when he left in 1973 was Research Officer in charge of the Special Studies and Monetary Policy Group in the Department of Banking. Immediately prior to joining The Fraser Institute, Dr. Walker was Econometric Model Consultant to the Federal Department of Finance, Ottawa. Dr. Walker has also taught Monetary Economics and Statistics at the University of Western Ontario and Carleton University.

Dr. Walker writes regularly for daily newspapers and financial periodicals. His articles have also appeared in technical journals, including the *Canadian Journal of Economics, Canadian Public Policy, Canadian Taxation* and the *Canadian Tax Journal.* He has been a columnist in *The Province,* the Toronto *Sun, The Ottawa Citizen, The Financial Post,* the Sterling newspaper chain, and community newspapers across Canada.

He is an author, editor, and contributor to more than twenty books on economic matters, some of which include *Balancing the Budget; Flat-Rate Tax Proposals; Reaction: The National Energy Program; Rent Control: A Popular Paradox; Unions and the Public Interest; Discrimination, Affirmative Action and Equal Opportunity; Privatization: Theory and Practice; Trade Unions and Society; Privatization: Tactics and Techniques;* and *Freedom, Democracy and Economic Welfare.*

Dr. Walker is a member of the Mont Pèlerin Society, the Canadian and American Economic Associations, and the International Association of Energy Economists.

G. Campbell Watkins

PRESIDENT OF THE CALGARY-BASED economic consulting firm DataMetrics Limited, Campbell Watkins is also Adjunct Professor of Economics at the University of Calgary. His involvement in economic research and policy spans a range of positions including Chief Economist at the Oil and Gas Conservation Board (1965-1969), Associate Economist at the Royal Bank of Canada (1970-1971), Director of Economic Studies at the Gas Arctic Group (1971-1072), and Petroleum Advisor to the Tanzanian Minister of Energy (1987). Dr. Watkins is Past President of the Economics Society of Alberta, Immediate Past President of the International Association for Energy Economics, fellow of the Royal Statistical Society, and member of the American Statistical Association. Dr. Watkins was a contributor to four earlier Fraser Institute books: *Oil in the Seventies* (1977); *Reaction: The National Energy Program* (1981); *Petro Markets: Probing the Economics of Continental Energy* (1989); and *Breaking the Shackles: Deregulating Canadian Industry* (1991).

Leonard Waverman

Dr. Waverman is a professor in the Department of Economics, University of Toronto, and director of the University's Centre for International Studies. He received his B.Com. and M.A. from the University of Toronto (1964 and 1965) and his Ph.D. from M.I.T. in 1969. He has been a visiting scholar at the University of Essex, Stanford University, and the Sloan School at M.I.T.

Dr. Waverman specializes in industrial organization, and anti-trust, energy, and telecommunications economics. He has authored numerous scholarly works, was a board member of the Ontario Energy Board, and currently is a board member of the Ontario Telephone Service Commission. He has consulted widely in both Canada and the United States.

He is the editor of the *Energy Journal* and has been associate editor of the *Canadian Journal of Economics*. He has also served on the Executive Committee of the European Association for Research in Industrial Economics.

Sidney Weintraub

SIDNEY WEINTRAUB IS DEAN RUSK PROFESSOR of International Affairs at the Lyndon B. Johnson School of Public Affairs, the University of Texas at Austin, and distinguished visiting scholar at the Center for Strategic and International Studies in Washington, D.C. He has written extensively about North American economic and political issues. His most recent books on this theme are *A Marriage of Convenience: Relations Between Mexico and the United States* (1990); and co-editor of *U.S.-Mexican Industrial Integration: The Road to Free Trade* (1991).

Gilbert Winham

GILBERT R. WINHAM IS THE ERIC DENNIS MEMORIAL PROFESSOR of Government and Political Science at Dalhousie University. He received a Diploma in International Law from the University of Manchester in 1965 and a Ph.D. from the University of North Carolina at Chapel Hill in 1968. He is a member of the federal government's International Trade Advisory Committee (ITAC) and chaired a task force of that body on GATT

Institutional Reform. Professor Winham has served on three FTA Dispute Settlement panels and was a Research Co-ordinator for International Political Economy for the Macdonald Royal Commission. In 1990-91 Professor Winham served as the Claude T. Bissell Professor of Canadian-American Relations at the University of Toronto. He conducts training simulations of trade negotiations for developing country trade officers at the GATT on a semi-annual basis. Professor Winham has authored articles and books on international trade policy and negotiations, including *International Trade and the Tokyo Round Negotiation*, 1986; *Trading with Canada: The Canada-US Free Trade Agreement*, 1988; and *The Evolution of International Trade Agreements*, University of Toronto Press, 1992.

The North American Free Trade Agreement as Negotiated: A U.S. Perspective

Sidney Weintraub

Introduction

THE NORTH AMERICAN FREE TRADE AGREEMENT (NAFTA) as negotiated is a massive document of thousands of pages. Much of the verbiage deals with exceptions to free trade. In some sectors, such as textiles and apparel and agriculture, complex and lengthy legal contortions were needed to move from protection on a global scale to less onerous restrictions applicable to trade in North America.

Consequently, the agreement is not an easy read. NAFTA is sure to keep many lawyers, economists, and public servants gainfully occupied for years making interpretations that will have modest social welfare benefits. Fortunately, the complexities will diminish over time. North America will have something approaching free trade in goods, including agricultural commodities, after a transition period of 10 years, but up to 15 years in some sectors and, in a few cases, even longer. The agreement could have been "clean" and relatively brief—certainly shorter than it is—if it contained fewer exceptions to free trade and freedom of cross-border investment. Yet, despite the derogations, the agreement does move toward greater freedom in economic relations among the three countries.

The discussion that follows looks at the agreement from a U.S. perspective. First, the structure of the agreement is examined. This is followed by an analysis of what is omitted and what is most contentious. The two final sections will contain this observer's analysis of the likely consequences of the agreement on the U.S. economy and the nature of the debate that is unfolding over approval of the agreement by the U.S. Congress. There is a brief concluding comment.

Structure of the Agreement

The agreement has a preamble and 22 chapters.[1] The phasing of tariff reductions is set forth in a separate, lengthy document.

The chapters have their own annexes to deal with particularly contentious themes or where the text needs clarification or elaboration. Thus, there are detailed annexes on the automotive sector and textiles and apparel in chapter 3 (national treatment and market access); separate annexes in chapter 10 (government procurement) clarify the extent of obligations undertaken, such as listing the government entities for which procurement obligations are liberalized; and in chapter 12 (cross-border trade in services), annexes set forth the extent to which professionals and providers of land transportation can operate in countries other than their own. Chapter 7 on agriculture has two subchapters, on market access and on sanitary and phytosanitary measures.

---

1 These are objectives, general definitions, national treatment and market access, rules of origin, customs procedures, energy, agriculture, emergency action, standards-related measures, government procurement, investment, cross-border trade in services, telecommunications, financial services, competition policy monopolies and state enterprises, temporary entry for business people, intellectual property, publication notification and administration of laws, review and dispute settlement in antidumping and countervailing duty matters, institutional arrangements and dispute settlement procedures, exceptions, and final provisions.

In addition to annexes to the specific chapters, there is an extensive section of reservations by each country to the obligations stated in the text of the agreement for chapters 11 (investment), 12 (cross-border trade in services), and 14 (financial services). These are primarily what are called "transitional exceptions." For example, Mexico's gradual opening of its financial services market (including banking, insurance, and investment services) to foreign investment is set forth in this part of the agreement. By contrast, the nonapplicability to Mexico of provisions on foreign investment in oil and natural gas and for sharing supplies of these products with the other two countries during periods of shortage is written into the agreement itself (in chapter 6, energy). The nonapplicability in this case is intended to be durable. Canada's exclusion of cultural industries from the provisions of NAFTA is written right into chapter 21 (exceptions) as an annex. This, too, is not intended to be a transitional exception.

The use of separate annexes for transitional exceptions should clarify the negotiating context for countries which later seek accession to NAFTA. If transitional issues can be dealt with outside the core text of the agreement, this is intended to make clear that accession negotiations should deal only with the transitional provisions. Nevertheless, Mexico was able to negotiate permanent derogations from the text of the Canada-U.S. free trade agreement (FTA), which was the model used in the NAFTA negotiations. The oil exclusion noted above is a particularly significant example of this. There is no way to guarantee that other acceding countries will be unable to do the same in the future.

Mexico entered more exceptions and reservations, both in sheer numbers and in significance, than the other two countries combined. The most important exception is in the energy chapter. Indeed, the first sentence of this chapter reads as follows: "The Parties confirm their full respect for their Constitutions." (Article 601(1)). This makes clear that the Mexican state reserves for itself exploration and exploitation of crude oil and natural gas, and various activities that flow from this, including refining and foreign trade in these products. The Mexican reservations that are intended to be transitory, as in automotive trade and investment and in the provision of financial and other services, are best seen as Mexico's way of gradually opening itself to free trade.[2] Mexico's tariff reduction schedule is slower than for the other two countries. These differences in trade and investment opening reflect Mexico's less-developed status coupled with its more closed economy as the transition gets under way. For the most part, all three countries will be at equal levels in trade liberalization at the end of the transition period, or generally after 10 years.

The text of the agreement incorporates provisions of the General Agreement on Tariffs and Trade (GATT) throughout. The three countries, all of which are contracting parties to the GATT, resolve in the preamble to build on their respective rights and obligations in the GATT. This is done again in chapter 1 (objectives), in chapter 3 (trade in goods) under which various GATT articles are incorporated into NAFTA, chapter 6 (energy and basic petrochemicals), and elsewhere. The intent is to emphasize that NAFTA is a supplement, not a replacement, to the rights and obligations of the three countries in the GATT. However, article 103 states that in the event of an inconsistency between NAFTA and other agreements, the provisions of NAFTA shall prevail, unless otherwise specified. Various international environmental agreements are also incorporated into the NAFTA and, in these cases, NAFTA is subordinated in the event of an inconsistency.

As long and as detailed as it is, the text of the agreement is not the final word on the structure of the arrangement. There are provisions in almost every chapter for the formation of committees or working groups for further work on aspects of the agreement. There is thus a committee for consultation and problem solving for trade in goods, on worn clothing, trade in agriculture, sanitary and phytosanitary measures, standards, small business, financial services, and private commercial disputes. Working groups are to be created on rules of origin, agricultural subsidies, and for temporary entry for business persons. These committees and working groups are merely those listed in chap-

---

2 Reading through these Mexican reservations, one gets a sense of how Mexican nationalism developed. For example, in the reservations under chapter 12 (cross-border trade in services), one learns that only Mexicans "by birth" may serve as ship captains, pilots, ship masters, machinists, mechanics, etc.

ter 20 (institutional arrangements and dispute settlement procedures). Other groups, less formal in structure, are called for throughout the agreement.

An agreement as comprehensive in subject matter as NAFTA requires continual consultation to work out the problems that will inevitably arise. Some of these problems will deal with policy; a free trade commission made up of cabinet level representatives or their designees is established for this purpose. Others will deal with implementation matters. Rosters of experts will have to be put together under the dispute-settlement provisions of the agreement. Like the Canada-U.S. FTA, NAFTA has a variety of dispute-settlement provisions. Chapter 19 authorizes the replacement of judicial review of antidumping and countervailing duty determinations by binational panels, similar to what now exists in chapter 19 of the Canada-U.S. FTA. Chapter 20 of NAFTA authorizes the establishment of arbitration panels to make recommendations on disputes not resolved through the good offices, conciliation, or mediation of the commission. The agreement calls on the commission to establish an advisory committee on private commercial disputes. Chapter 11 establishes a procedure for settlement of cross-border investment disputes. Disputes arising under the chapter on financial services will have their own settlement procedures.

The purpose of the agreement is to facilitate increased interaction among traders and investors in the three countries. In addition, the framework of the agreement requires much consultation among government officials, in many cases assisted by private business people and technicians, to clarify ambiguities that will arise. If the agreement succeeds in its primary purpose, to facilitate trade and production in North America, this will inevitably lead to the deepening of interchange among nationals in all three countries.

The agreement, if approved by the three legislatures, will enter into force on January 1, 1994. Any party can withdraw six months after providing written notice of its intention to do so. The accession clause leaves open membership to any other country, regardless of location, subject to a prior negotiation and the necessary approval procedures in the existing member countries.

The agreement does not cover all the themes that have arisen in the debate on free trade. The Mexican authorities, when they took their initiative for free trade with the United States, wished to include provisions on migration. Other than for chapter 16 (temporary entry for business people), this theme is not included.

U.S. and Canadian labour unions and legislators sympathetic to their position wanted inclusion of workplace standards. This theme is not included in the agreement, although two side arrangements were concluded between Mexico and the United States to deal with this issue. The first is a memorandum of understanding on labour cooperation, essentially a procedure for the exchange of information, and the second an agreement which establishes a consultative commission on such issues as labour laws, workplace conditions, and labour standards applicable to migrant workers.[3]

Environmentalists in all three countries made a successful effort to include provisions on this theme in the agreement as well as in parallel understandings. Other than passing references to environmental issues in article XX of the GATT, this is the first major trade agreement that deals consciously and comprehensively with this theme.[4] As such, NAFTA may well be a precursor for inclusion of such provisions in other agreements, including the GATT itself in future rounds of trade negotiations.

Trade agreements in the past generally dealt exclusively with trade issues. The Treaty of Rome establishing the European Economic Community was much more comprehensive, but this was seen from the outset as setting in motion a political process in Western Europe. The Canada-U.S. FTA, by contrast, was seen as a trade agreement without

---

3 The text of this agreement is included in a "Report of the Administration on the North American Free Trade Agreement and Actions Taken in Fulfilment of the May 1, 1991 Commitments," dated September 18, 1992. This document accompanied the submission of the text of the NAFTA to the Congress by the Bush administration and was designed to demonstrate that the commitments made by President Bush at the time fast track was extended were met.

4 Article XX(b) of the GATT permits contracting parties to take measures "necessary to protect human, animal or plant life or health"; article XX(g) permits such measures "relating to conservation of exhaustible natural resources if such measures are made effective in conjunction with restrictions on domestic production or consumption."

the deep political content of the Treaty of Rome. The free trade rather than the customs-union option was chosen deliberately for this reason. Nevertheless, the Canada-U.S. FTA dealt not only with trade, but also with related issues. The NAFTA is even more comprehensive in its inclusion of environmental and intellectual property issues. The NAFTA covers agricultural trade more fully than did the Canada-U.S. FTA. One can quarrel with omissions from the NAFTA, but it is not possible to argue that this is a narrow trade agreement.

Omissions from the Agreement

Labour unions in the United States argue that the biggest omission is the failure to deal with Mexico's enforcement of its safety and sanitary standards. This issue will be discussed later in the section on the debate in the United States on whether and with what conditions to approve the agreement.

Energy

Mexico's exceptions in chapter 6 (energy and basic petrochemicals) are a major omission. Since the expropriation in 1938 of foreign oil properties and the formation of Petróleos Mexicanos (Pemex), the Mexican state has had exclusive control over what in the agreement are called "strategic activities and investment" in the oil and natural gas sector.[5] Those familiar with Mexican history are aware of the sensitivity of this issue. The expropriation of the foreign oil properties is seen even today as a second declaration of independence. Mexico, in the last few years, has been willing to alter other parts of its constitution, for example to modify the *ejido* system of land tenure, itself a highly emotional issue,

5 In annex 602.3, this reservation of activities to the Mexican State lists the following: "(a) exploration and exploitation of crude oil and natural gas; refining or processing of crude oil and natural gas; and production of artificial gas, basic petrochemicals and their feedstocks; and pipelines; and (b) foreign trade; transportation, storage and distribution, up to and including first hand sales of the following goods: crude oil; natural and artificial gas; goods covered by this Chapter obtained from the refining or processing of crude oil and natural gas; and basic petrochemicals."

and to permit restoration to private buyers of the commercial banks nationalized in 1982; but state control of the oil industry was considered sacrosanct. Or, at least it was by the government and the Mexican negotiators. In the end, this position was accepted. The inability to alter the Mexican position on petroleum risk contracts was a major disappointment to U.S. negotiators.

The issue is not trivial. U.S. imports of crude oil from Mexico were US$4.3 billion in 1991, about 14 percent of all imports from Mexico.[6] The level of trade is less germane than the security of supply from a neighbour with whom a free trade agreement is being contemplated. Little investment has been made in recent years in oil and natural gas exploration and exploitation in Mexico because of the lack of resources during the difficult economic stretch in the 1980s. The main request of the U.S. negotiators, therefore, was to find some way to permit foreign investment in exploration and exploitation. This is possible in other countries in which the state controls this resource. Mexico was prepared to offer service contracts, which it has always been willing to do. It was not prepared to offer contracts under which the investor would take the risk but also share in the benefits that might accrue. Mexico argued that a risk contract implies some share of ownership of the profits and would thus violate the constitution. The most the Mexican negotiators would concede was a provision that reads: "The Parties shall allow state enterprises to negotiate performance clauses in their service contracts." It remains to be seen what this will mean in practice.

In times of supply restriction, Article 605 stipulates that any party to the agreement cannot reduce the proportion of total exports of energy or basic petrochemical products to the other parties. This is based on the proportion during the previous 36-month period for which data are available. Any restriction must not disrupt normal channels of supply of importing countries. The same article prohibits raising export prices for these products higher than domestic prices. Mexico exempted itself from this article. It applies, therefore, only in oil and natural gas trade between Canada and the United States.

---

6 U.S. Department of Commerce, International Trade Administration, *U.S. Foreign Trade Highlights 1991*, (Washington, D.C., 1992) p. 129.

Investment

One of the main reasons why Mexico took the initiative for free trade with the United States was to attract foreign investment. Indeed, much investment has been flowing into Mexico in recent years. Foreign investment, direct and portfolio, increased from US$3.5 billion in 1989, to US$4.6 billion in 1990, and then to US$12.3 billion in 1991. Of this, more than a third, or US$4.8 billion, was direct investment in 1991.[7] Mexico was attractive to foreign investors because of a combination of its own, open economic policy, plus the attraction of the large North American market for its industrial output.

Under these circumstances, one would have expected Mexico to eliminate its restrictions on foreign direct investment. This was mostly done, but not fully. Mexico retains a screening process for acquisitions of more than 49 percent of ownership of an enterprise controlled by Mexican nationals, with a modest threshold of US$25 million at first but rising to US$150 million after 10 years. After that, the threshold will be adjusted for growth in Mexican gross domestic product "but in no case will the threshold to be applied exceed that of Canada."[8] By agreeing to a screening and threshold for U.S. foreign direct investment in the Canada-U.S. FTA, the United States set itself up for similar asymmetrical treatment by Mexico. Giving up a clean agreement on foreign investment was a concession to the Mexicans that U.S. negotiators would have preferred not to make.

In the investment chapter, the three parties agree to eliminate performance requirements. These refer to mandatory export levels, achievement of a given level of domestic content, forcing investors to purchase local goods and services, relating the level of permitted imports to the value of exports achieved, or relating domestic sales that are permitted to export accomplishments. However, Mexico will eliminate these performance requirements only gradually. It will take 10 years for

---

7 Banco de México, *Indicadores Económicos*. This is a publication for which new, updated loose leaf sheets are published monthly. The data above come from the May 1992 sheets, p. IV-2.

8 NAFTA agreement, Reservations, Annex I, Schedule of Mexico, pp. I-M-6 and 7.

full elimination of performance requirements in the automotive sector. Once again, Mexico took its cue from the example in the Canada-U.S. auto agreement. These are not crucial omissions or limitations because they disappear over a reasonable transition period.

Agriculture

The provisions on trade in agriculture set up, in effect, two separate bilateral agreements for the United States, one with Mexico and the other with Canada. The rules affecting tariffs and nontariff barriers in U.S.-Canada trade in agricultural products are generally those contained in the existing FTA between the two countries. There are trilateral provisions on domestic support and export subsidy issues; a working group on agricultural subsidies will be established. A single agreement on agricultural trade in North America would have been preferable.

However, the agricultural understandings between Mexico and the United States are quite impressive, especially in light of the protectionism that has prevailed for decades in this sector. The main impediment to coming to closure in the Uruguay round in the GATT has been precisely the unwillingness of many countries—the European Community (France) and Japan in particular—to fully address issues of agricultural protection. Mexico and the United States accomplished much more in freeing bilateral agricultural trade than almost all observers had expected.

Under the agricultural chapter (chapter 7), Mexico and the United States agree to convert all nontariff barriers in their agricultural trade to tariff-rate quotas as opposed to ordinary quotas. These tariff quotas call for zero tariffs within the quota limits with over-quota amounts subject to regular tariffs. These over-quota tariffs will be set at a rate deemed to be equivalent to the protection offered by the current quota limitations and then decline to zero, generally over a 10-year period. The phase-out period for tariffs will be 15 years for some sensitive products—corn and dry beans for Mexico, orange juice and sugar for the United States. The 15-year phaseout for these four products represents significant concessions on both sides. These products have long protective histories and the concessions as negotiated will face stiff internal opposition in the two countries.

While this discussion examines the agreement from the vantage of the United States, a word is useful on the commitment undertaken by Mexico. Corn and beans are the main staples in the Mexican diet, as sugar and frozen orange juice are not for the United States. Mexico's agricultural policy has long been based on supporting the production of these two products, subsidizing urban consumers of these products, and limiting imports to the extent possible. Mexico is still about one-third rural and by far the largest cohort of growers and labourers for any product are engaged in corn production in rainfed areas of Mexico. The owners of *minifundio* and the daily labourers involved in corn production number from three to four million people. Mexico is thus taking a gamble on agricultural policy far more audacious than anything being undertaken by Canada or the United States, and certainly more bold than anything contemplated in other industrial countries.

Mexico's domestic program during the 15-year transition period to free trade in corn calls for assistance to establish rural-based industries and to facilitate a gradual migration out of the villages where the bulk of this population lives. Some concern has been raised that this liberalization will lead to mass emigration not just to Mexican cities, but to the United States. Hinojosa and Robinson estimate that the elimination of protection for corn will lead to the emigration of 800,000 Mexicans to the United States.[9] Even if they are correct, their analysis omits the fact that the population involved is probably the poorest in Mexico: people with low incomes, inadequate diets, little health care, and few educational opportunities. The Mexican authorities concluded that a restructuring of corn policy was needed—free trade or no free trade—and NAFTA offered the opportunity to accomplish this.

One final comment on agriculture is warranted, this time dealing with U.S. sensitivities. U.S. sugar policy has long been highly protectionist. Sugar growers and their supporters have been able to maintain U.S. prices well above world prices and in the process distribute the cost to foreign countries, such as the Dominican Republic, the Philippines,

---

9 Raul Hinojosa-Ojeda and Sherman Robinson, "Alternative Scenarios of U.S.-Mexican Integration: A Computable General Equilibrium Approach," working paper 609, Department of Agricultural and Resource Economics, University of California, April 1991.

and Australia—all U.S. allies. The agreement also liberalizes the U.S. sugar import program. The formula is complex; however, at the end of a 15-year transition period, restrictions on sugar trade between Mexico and the United States will be eliminated.[10] This, of course, will provide no benefit to other countries that export sugar to the United States.

Principal U.S. Sensitivities

The most contentious aspect of NAFTA for the United States is not what is in the agreement itself, but the very fact of having free trade with a developing country whose wages are so much lower—about 14 percent of the U.S. level for production workers in manufacturing in 1991.[11] This competitive concern is at the heart of the debate in the United States on approval of the agreement.

It is precisely this fear of low-wage competition that makes three aspects of the agreement highly contentious. These are the provisions on trade in the automotive industry, textiles and apparel, and fresh fruits and vegetables. The first two of these, automotive and textiles and apparel, are covered primarily in separate annexes to chapter 3 (national treatment and market access). Automotive trade between Canada and the United States will continue to be guided mostly by the terms of the 1965 auto pact, as subsequently amended.

The U.S. auto industry has been severely buffeted in recent years. Profitability, market share, and employment have all gone down. It is only in recent years that U.S. producers have begun to correct their inadequacies, but these changes will require further lowering of employment levels. This was precisely the basis for a strike by a local of the United Auto Workers (UAW) at a General Motors tool and die plant in Lordstown, Ohio, in late August and early September 1992. GM had announced plans to close this plant, eliminating 240 jobs. The strike was

---

10 There is a modest exception to this statement in that imports of Mexican sugar for U.S. sugar re-export programs will remain subject to U.S. most-favoured-nation tariff rates.

11 The percentage figure is from the U.S. Bureau of Labour Statistics. It is calculated on the basis of the market exchange relationship between the U.S. dollar and the Mexican peso.

intended to be a protest not only about closure of the Lordstown operation, but against GM's announced intention to trim a further 74,000 jobs from its payroll. The nine-day strike was settled after causing much disruption to GM production at other plants that depended on the output from Lordstown, but the deeper issue remains.[12]

Problems in the auto industry are related much more to competition with Japanese and European producers—many of whom have established U.S. production facilities—than with Mexico. But growth in the Mexican industry has not been negligible. Complete motor vehicles and parts are now the most important U.S. imports from Mexico. Taken together, their value was higher than crude oil imports in 1991. Motor vehicle parts are the most important imports from maquiladora plants in Mexico.[13] The U.S. labour unions believe that the maquiladora plants, because they are based in large part on cheap Mexican labour, deprive U.S. workers of jobs. A common critical metaphor for NAFTA used by U.S. labour unions is that it will lead to the maquiladorization of Mexico—that is, make Mexico a haven for low-wage jobs and require the Mexican authorities to keep wages low in order to attract this kind of foreign investment. There is no convincing evidence that the Mexican authorities are deliberately seeking to keep wages down. Indeed, real wages have been rising in the past two to three years after declining for most of the 1980s along with the general economic decline in Mexico, but the charge has wide currency nevertheless.

The automotive provisions in the agreement as they relate to Mexico have four interconnected elements: reduction in import barriers; liberalization of investment laws and regulations; the elimination of performance requirements by Mexico; and rules of origin. The first three can be summarized rapidly.

U.S. tariffs on passenger cars will be eliminated immediately upon entry into force of the agreement (these duties are now only 2.5 percent

---

12 *New York Times*, September 6, 1992, p. 1, has a discussion of the strike.

13 These imports are based on U.S inputs sent outside the United States and, under U.S. harmonized tariff schedule subheadings 9802.00.60 and 9802.00.80, pay the duty on the value added outside the United States when they re-enter the country.

ad valorem); the tariff on light trucks will be reduced immediately to 10 percent (the most-favoured-nation, or MFN, rate is 25 percent), and then phased out over five years; U.S. tariffs on other vehicles will be phased out over 10 years. Mexican automotive tariffs are higher than those in the United States. Mexico will reduce its tariff on passenger automobiles by 50 percent immediately (the current MFN rate is 15 percent) and phase out the remaining tariff over 10 years; the tariff on light trucks will be reduced by 50 percent immediately and be phased out over five years; and the tariffs on all other vehicles will be phased out over 10 years. All three countries will eliminate duties on parts in three stages: some immediately; others over five years; and a small proportion over 10 years. The agreement calls for Mexico to gradually phase out its restrictions on the import of used vehicles. The full elimination of prohibitions for used cars of all ages will not occur until January 1, 2019.

The investment provisions in this sector are governed generally by the investment provisions in chapter 11 of the agreement. There are two important exceptions. Foreign investors are now limited to a maximum of 40 percent equity in auto parts production, although exceptions are possible. Under the agreement, this will rise to 100 percent immediately for what are called "national suppliers" in Mexico's auto decree (that is, those firms that meet particular levels of national value added in their production) and to 49 percent for other auto parts producers. The latter will rise to 100 percent after five years.

Mexico's performance requirements will be reduced gradually, as noted earlier. The automotive provisions of the agreement call for Mexico's national value-added requirements for auto manufacturers to decline gradually to 29 percent by the year 2003, and trade balance requirements will be eased over the same period. The agreement calls for a review of the status of the North American automotive sector no later than December 31, 2003.

Finally, perhaps the most contentious issue in the automotive negotiations was setting the rules of origin—how to calculate them and what percentage should apply. A free trade agreement permits each member country to maintain its own tariffs against nonmember countries. Consequently, to avoid the problem of transshipment of imported items from the low tariff to the high tariff member of an FTA, a rule of origin is needed to determine what constitutes a national or regional product eligible for duty-free treatment. However, this technical matter can be transformed into a protectionist one by increasing the level of regional content required for an item to receive preferential treatment. This protectionist aspect took its most severe form in the NAFTA in two sectors, automotive and textiles and apparel.

The rules of origin for automotive goods are complex. (They are set forth in chapter 4, rules of origin.) Simplifying for the purpose of this discussion, the regional value content that makes a vehicle eligible for free trade under NAFTA will rise in two steps to 62.5 percent after the year 2002 for passenger automobiles and light trucks and engines and transmissions for such vehicles, and to 60 percent for other vehicles and parts. This is under the net-cost formula for calculating regional value.[14] To avoid disagreements of the type that arose in calculating the regional value content of Hondas shipped from Canada to the United States, the elements that go into the calculation are spelled out more precisely than was the case in the Canada-U.S. FTA. In addition, the three countries have said they will trace the value of automotive parts imports from outside the NAFTA region to improve on the accuracy of the calculation.

The purpose of the high regional value content is to prevent automotive producers other than those now producing in the three countries from taking advantage of preferential provisions of the NAFTA by merely establishing assembly plants in one of the three countries—particularly Mexico—and then enjoying duty-free treatment in the entire North American market. The rules of origin make it necessary to carry out much of the production of parts in the three countries to enjoy duty-free treatment for their vehicles.

The rule of origin in the Canada-U.S. FTA is 50 percent. However, the nature of the calculation is different from NAFTA and there was no deep tracing provision. Thus, a precise comparison cannot be made between the Canada-U.S. FTA 50 percent rule and the NAFTA 62.5 percent provision. It is by no means clear, either, how well deep tracing will work or how much it will cost. The big three U.S. auto producers

---

14 The agreement provides two methods for calculation of regional value, a net cost method and transaction value.

had fought hard for a content provision of 65 percent for passenger cars. The Canadian negotiators forced the compromise to 62.5 percent.

It is by no means evident, either, how NAFTA will affect the automotive industries in the three countries. Mexico, over the transition period, will have to discard many of the elements that helped it develop its industry—high protection, forcing foreign producers to balance auto sector imports with exports, and insisting on minimum levels of Mexican content. However, Mexico will still retain many competitive advantages, such as lower wages combined in some plants with levels of productivity comparable to plants in Canada and the United States. The Canadian weakness is its parts sector. The U.S. disadvantage is the incompleteness of its restructuring in this industry, especially for General Motors, coupled with higher wages. The auto producers believe that they need the Mexican production—or if not Mexico, some other low-wage location—for those operations with a high labour content if they are to remain competitive with Japanese and European production. The UAW, by contrast, sees this as a low-wage strategy that will inevitably deprive its members of jobs.

Some analysts of the automotive industry believe that North American production and sales integration will be a net gain for the U.S. and Canadian industries.[15] The thrust of the argument is that the Mexican market will itself grow and that a division of production will occur under which cheaper, entry-level cars and trucks will be produced in Mexico using parts from the maquiladoras in northern Mexico, while larger cars and trucks will be produced in Canada and the United States. This scenario requires changing the U.S. corporate fuel economy (CAFE) regulations to count small autos produced in Mexico by U.S companies as domestic U.S. products. This change is included in the text of the agreement.

The second sector of great contention in the United States is textiles and apparel. This is really two separate industries, the mill sector producing textiles and the apparel sector. These have long been protected industries in the United States and other industrial countries, as

---

15 James P. Womack, Daniel T. Jones, and Daniel Roos, *The Machine that Changed the World: The Story of Lean Production* (New York: Harper Perennial paperback, 1991, from original Macmillan edition, 1990), pp. 264-267.

witness the durability of the import quota structure of the multifiber arrangement (MFA) and its predecessors.

The sensitivity of opening the U.S. market for textiles and apparel rests on several foundations. The two industries together have 29,000 plants spread throughout every state in the union, ship about $64 billion each in value (1990 data), and together employ almost 1.4 million people (1990).[16] Yet this is a case in which the Mexican industries are as deeply concerned, perhaps more so, than their U.S. counterparts. The cost of mill production in Mexico is considerably higher than in the United States because of inferior inputs, outdated technology, and capacity underutilization.[17] Because of its labour-intensive nature, Mexico has a cost advantage in apparel production, but the industry is nevertheless in a precarious condition. This is an industry in which workers in both countries share similar concerns.

The provisions of NAFTA in this combined textile and apparel sector take precedence over those of the MFA. The NAFTA language is extremely detailed and complex for textiles and apparel, in part because the agreement must deal with liberalization, item by item, using the starting point of the MFA. Complexity of protection has given way to complexity of liberalization, mainly because it is staged and deals with a variety of tariff and nontariff barriers on hundreds of individual items. In addition, the rules of origin are, if anything, more burdensome (more protectionist) than in the automotive sector. Three aspects of the agreement will be noted here: tariff and quota reduction; safeguards, because these are important in an industry with so many workers; and rules of origin. What follows is a simplified description of the agreements in these three areas.

Tariffs are to be phased out by all three countries over a maximum period of 10 years for products that meet the rules of origin. The United

---

16 Gary Clyde Hufbauer and Jeffrey J. Schott, *North American Free Trade: Issues and Recommendations* (Washington, D.C.: Institute for International Economics, 1992), pp. 264-266.

17 Ovidio Botella C., Enrique García C., and José Giral B., "Textiles: Mexican Perspective," in Sidney Weintraub, Luis Rubio F., and Alan D. Jones, eds., *U.S.-Mexican Industrial Integration: The Road to Free Trade* (Boulder, Colorado: Westview Press, 1991), pp. 193-220.

States will immediately remove import quotas on those textile and apparel products produced in Mexico that meet the rules of origin and will gradually phase out quotas, generally over 10 years, on the products that do not meet those rules.

The safeguard provisions have their own complex rules. For goods meeting the rules of origin, safeguard measures must take tariff form. The language as to when a safeguard can be invoked is the usual artful language for these emergency actions.[18] Under these circumstances, for goods meeting the origin criteria, emergency action can consist of suspending further tariff reduction or increasing the rate of duty to the MFN rate in existence at the time or to the rate when NAFTA went into effect, whichever is lower. This action normally can last for no more than three years and may be taken only once during the transition period. When the rule of origin is not met, then emergency action can take quota form, again normally to last for up to three years. There are other specific limits on the quota action that may be taken.

Finally, the rule of origin is based on the principle of yarn forward. A product must be made of NAFTA cloth, and of textiles made of NAFTA yarn. There are exceptions for certain fabrics in short supply in North America, such as silk and linen. Other exceptions permit tariff rate quotas (that is, preferential treatment up to a given quota level) for yarns, fabrics, and apparel that do not meet the rules of origin. The tariff quotas for Canadian products in the Canada-U.S. FTA have been increased. The whole structure of textile and apparel rules of origin will be reviewed no later than January 1, 1998.

This is one sector (or two, if the two industries are treated separately) in which significant trade effects may occur. If the MFA is retained, one should expect diversion of production, and hence exports to the United States and Canada, from other suppliers to Mexico.

---

18 If the product "is being imported into the territory of another Party in such increased quantities, in absolute terms or relative to the domestic market for that good, and under such conditions as to cause serious damage, or actual threat thereof, to a domestic industry producing a like or directly competitive good, the importing party may, to the extent necessary to remedy the damage or actual threat thereof...", which is then followed by the allowable steps. Annex 300-B, Textiles and Apparel Goods, Section 4(1).

Hufbauer and Schott anticipate that U.S. exports will increase in unfinished goods and that Mexico will increase its exports of finished products. This, they believe, will come from the diversion of investment to Mexico to exploit its advantage if the MFA remains in place. They speculate that Mexican exports of textiles and apparel to the United States may reach US$3 to US$5 billion in 10 years, an increase of US$2 to US$4 billion.[19] The U.S. International Trade Commission also expected Mexican exports of textiles and apparel to the United States to increase. While the ITC did not provide precise estimates, its tone is less pessimistic from the U.S. trade balance view than that of Hufbauer and Schott.[20]

Import liberalization in the agricultural sector was most sensitive for Mexico for its staple crops, corn and beans. Canada's special safeguard measures as set forth in chapter 7 (agriculture) are for fresh cut flowers, tomatoes, onions, cucumbers, broccoli, cauliflower, and frozen strawberries. U.S. sensitivities in this sector are similar to Canada's. Special tariff classifications were established in the U.S. harmonized schedule for tomatoes, onions, eggplants, chili peppers, squash, and fresh watermelons to differentiate between those periods when these products come to market from U.S. production and when imports from Mexico are more welcome.

The fresh fruit and vegetable growers in the United States, mostly in California, Florida, and Texas, stand to lose from NAFTA. Thus, a tradeoff exists within the U.S. agricultural sector. The gains should go primarily to grain and soybean producers and the losses are more likely for fresh fruit and vegetable growers. How this gets resolved must still play itself out.

While this discussion has concentrated on a few areas of particular sensitivity, trade liberalization is always contentious in the United States, as it is elsewhere. It pits the general public, which should be a force for import liberalization but is a dispersed group, against special

---

19 Hufbauer and Schott, p. 278.

20 U.S. International Trade Commission, *The Likely Impact on the United States of a Free Trade Agreement with Mexico*, USITC publication 2353 (Washington, D.C.: USITC, 1991), pp. 4-38 to 4-41.

interests which are more focused in their desire for protection. This is the scenario as the U.S. Congress opens deliberations on approval or rejection of NAFTA. The U.S. debate, as it unfolds, will deal with many more commodities than have been listed here as being particularly sensitive to import competition.

Impact on the U.S. Economy

There is no single answer to the question of how NAFTA will affect the U.S. economy. If there is a consensus among economists, particularly those who have subjected it to quantitative analysis, it is that the short-term effect will be small but positive, and that the long-term impact will depend much on the dynamic effect in Mexico.[21] This conclusion is reflected in a recent book reporting on a conference at the Brookings Institution. The direct effects are expected to be small because U.S. import duties are already low and nontariff barriers will be phased out gradually. Because the United States supplies some 70 percent of Mexico's imports, sustained economic growth there should lead to a bilateral U.S. trade surplus, heavily concentrated in capital goods, extending over several decades.[22] This scenario of greater growth in U.S. exports than imports, is, as the participants at the Brookings conference note, "... strikingly at odds with much of the public debate that foresees large-scale relocations of production facilities."[23] Even if there is a modest increase in U.S. economic growth and gross employment from NAFTA, there will almost surely be intersectoral shifts and thus dislocations in particular industries and communities. The studies of the effects of NAFTA on the U.S. economy have taken a variety of forms.

---

21 The quantitative analyses of NAFTA were done before the proposed text was released. However, there is little in the text that would affect the projected outcome of these quantitative studies from what was anticipated earlier.

22 Barry P. Bosworth, Robert Z. Lawrence, and Nora Lustig, "Introduction," in Lustig, Bosworth, and Lawrence, eds., *North American Free Trade: Assessing the Impact*, (Washington, D.C.: Brookings Institution, 1992), pp. 2-3.

23 *Ibid*, p. 2.

Those that have the greatest credibility, at least to economists, are computable general equilibrium (CGE) models, mostly static, but a few incorporate dynamic aspects. The CGE models are mostly the work of academic economists.[24] The CGE models cannot be used as predictions because the conclusions vary with the nature of the assumptions—whether the projections are based on constant or increasing returns to scale, the nature of product differentiation incorporated in the modeling, and the extent of investment flows that are posited. But they do give an indication of the direction of changes that can be expected from NAFTA.

Drusilla Brown has provided an overview of a number of the leading CGE models, including an evaluation of the role of different modeling assumptions.[25] Her conclusion is that the models clearly indicate that NAFTA will increase welfare in North America, including in the United States, but most particularly in Mexico. The gains are modest, less than 1 percent of GNP, when differentiated products and constant returns to scale are assumed. The welfare gains are higher, about 2 to 4 percent of GNP for Mexico, when products are assumed to be homogeneous across producers, incorporate increasing returns to scale, or both. Adding capital flows increases the welfare gains to Mexico to 4 to 7 percent, and then even in the range of 10 percent when productivity growth is endogenized.

Weintraub examined three types of models: overall CGE models, sectoral models, and those that use other quantitative techniques or are essentially descriptive.[26] The static CGE model of Brown, Deardorff, and

---

24 Twelve CGE models are contained in U.S. International Trade Commission, *Economy-Wide Modeling of the Economic Implications of a FTA with Mexico and a NAFTA with Canada and Mexico*, USITC publication 2508 (Washington, D.C.: USITC, 1992).

25 Drusilla K. Brown, "The Impact of a North American Free Trade Area: Applied General Equilibrium Models," in Lustig, Bosworth, and Lawrence, eds., *North American Free Trade*, pp. 26-68.

26 Sidney Weintraub, "Modeling the Industrial Effects of NAFTA," in Lustig, Bosworth, and Lawrence, pp. 109-133.

Stern showed positive wage and growth effects in all three countries and a need for only modest intersectoral factor reallocations.[27] The dynamic models showed larger welfare gains for all three countries.[28] Perhaps the most widely cited U.S. study of the effects of NAFTA is that of Hufbauer and Schott, presumably because it is presented in language comprehensible to noneconomists. This is not a CGE model, but bases its projections on historical experiences of other countries that have taken the kind of trade liberalizing measures in which Mexico is engaged. Their model shows higher growth in mutual exports between Mexico and the United States and in employment in the two countries than do the static CGE models.

A paper by Faux and Lee comes to a conclusion diametrically different from the CGE and the Hufbauer-Schott models discussed above.[29] This paper anticipates substantial job losses—the authors cite studies that project losses of between 290,000 and 490,000 U.S. jobs over 10 years—as a result of diversion of investment from the United States to Mexico. In addition, the paper concludes that wages for unskilled U.S. workers are apt to decline. This paper is labelled a "briefing paper." It draws on other studies and newspaper articles for its major conclusions.[30] Its conclusions, in my view, are not well substantiated, but its

---

27 Drusilla K. Brown, Alan V. Deardorff, and Robert M. Stern, "A North American Free Trade Agreement: Analytical Issues and a Computational Assessment," paper presented at a conference on North American free trade sponsored by the Fraser Institute, the Center for Strategic and International Studies, the University of Toronto Centre for International Studies, and the Stanford University Americas Program, Washington, D.C., June 27-28, 1991.

28 The two that were examined were Timothy J. Kehoe, "Modeling the Dynamic Impact of North American Free Trade," working paper 491, Federal Reserve Bank of Minneapolis, March 1992; and Leslie Young and José Romero, "A Dynamic Dual Model of the Free Trade Agreement," University of Texas at Austin and El Colegio de México, 1991.

29 Jeff Faux and Thea Lee, "The Effect of George Bush's NAFTA on American Workers: Ladder Up or Ladder Down," Washington, D.C.: Economic Policy Institute, 1992.

30 The most important of these other studies are Edward E. Leamer, "Wage Effects of a U.S.-Mexican Free Trade Agreement," NBER working paper

figures on U.S. employment losses are widely cited by opponents of NAFTA.

The Office of Technology Assessment (OTA) in a recent study came to what can best be described as ambiguous conclusions—that open trade could increase living standards in both Mexico and the United States, but only if there are significant other changes in U.S. and Mexican policies.[31] The main policy prescription concerns the need to improve worker skills in the United States. The study also makes recommendations for a comprehensive worker adjustment program, and suggests further negotiations to establish a number of North American commissions on the environment, and labour and social welfare. The central conclusion of the study is that ". . . whether a NAFTA works for or against either country will depend on how integration is managed."[32] What is then described in the study, however, is only marginally about how NAFTA is managed, but mostly about how the U.S. economy is managed. The recommendations are mostly consistent with those of the Democratic majority in the Congress.

My own view is similar to that of the majority of mainstream economists. This is that the United States will benefit economically from NAFTA, modestly at first and then more substantially over time as Mexico's economy grows, but that compensation is required for those people who will suffer from the adjustments that will take place in the U.S. economy. These adjustments are required, with or without NAFTA. There can be little long-term benefit for the U.S. economy if noncompetitive sectors are protected. A high-wage future requires activities which embody much research, innovation, and technological advance. These activities require a skilled workforce and not one that

---

3991, Cambridge, Mass.: National Bureau of Economic Research, February 1992; and Timothy Koechlin, Mehrene Larudee, Samuel Bowles, and Gerald Epstein, "Effect of the North American Free Trade Agreement on Investment, Employment and Wages in Mexico and the U.S.," mimeograph, February 1992.

31 U.S. Congress, Office of Technology Assessment, *U.S.-Mexico Trade? Pulling Together or Pulling Apart?* ITE-545 (Washington, D.C.: U.S. Government Printing Office, October 1992).

32 *Ibid*, p. 4.

seeks to compete with Mexico on the basis of which country pays lower wages. Necessary requirements for a high-wage future are much more investment in education and training, more emphasis on research, and the willingness to adjust to the changing global situation. The countries with which the United States must compete if it wishes to remain an advanced economy are Germany, others in Western Europe, and Japan, and not developing countries like Mexico. All these points are made in the OTA study, although that study talks about management of NAFTA while my judgments deal with the management of the U.S. economy.

The argument in favour of NAFTA is that North America is a natural market for the United States. In 1991, 28 percent of U.S. exports went to Canada and Mexico. The two countries are already the first and third trading partners of the United States. For them, the dominant market is the United States; Canadian and Mexican business people are only now beginning to know each other. When the Mexican economy declined during the 1980s, so too did Mexican imports. In 1986, U.S. exports to Mexico were only US$12 billion. The Mexican economy started to recover that year and by 1991 U.S. exports to Mexico had climbed to US$33 billion. In 1992, they are running closer to US$40 billion; Mexico is beginning to compete with Japan as the second largest U.S. export market. The principal determinant of Mexico's import level is its income growth. And the principal source of Mexico's imports is the United States.

It is clear from scanning the themes dealt with in NAFTA that it is much more than a trade agreement. U.S. trade with the other two countries both follows and stimulates investment in them. Much of the trade that takes place is based on coproduction arrangements. Many of the engines produced in Mexico end up in cars assembled in the United States. The parts and accessories shipped from the United States to Mexico often end up in cars assembled in Mexico or are further manufactured in maquiladora for re-export back to the United States.[33] More than half of Mexico's manufactured exports to the United States are now intrafirm. The same is true for Canada's manufactured exports to the

---

33 U.S. imports of internal combustion engines from Mexico were almost US$700 million in 1991. U.S. motor vehicle parts and accessories shipped to Mexico in 1991 were valued at US$3.2 billion.

United States. As trade in industrial inputs as opposed to finished products increases, the need for low trade barriers becomes imperative if North American producers are to remain competitive.

This, as much as absolute levels of trade, explains the support of multinational producers for free trade in North America. The ability to choose manufacturing location on efficiency grounds—on relative factor endowments—without regard to import barriers should enhance competitiveness of North American producers.

The Free Trade Debate in the United States

President Bush submitted the legal text of NAFTA to the Congress on September 18, 1992. The fast-track legislation gives Congress 90 calendar days to examine the agreement before the President can sign it, which he did in December. While congressional hearings began even before the text was formally submitted, they dealt largely with a few issues. These are the adequacy of the environmental provisions in NAFTA and concern over the lack of attention in the agreement to workplace health and safety standards in Mexico. A third labour-related issue is the degree to which the U.S. administration will provide financial support and retraining for workers who lose jobs as a consequence of increased imports from Mexico stemming from NAFTA. This is not an issue appropriate for inclusion in an international agreement, but rather one for the administration to work out with the Congress.

The implementing legislation, which constitutes the true vote on NAFTA, will not take place until the new U.S. Congress meets in 1993. It is thus relevant that Bill Clinton has stated that he supports NAFTA but will not sign implementing legislation "until we have reached additional agreements to protect America's vital interests. But I believe we can address these issues without renegotiating the basic agreement."[34] The main issues he and congressional Democrats have stated must be addressed are those listed above: the environment, work standards, and retraining and adjustment assistance. While these three

34 Remarks by Governor Bill Clinton, North Carolina State University, Raleigh, October 4, 1992.

issues are at the center of the public debate, there is another level of debate, less public but more informed, about the details of the NAFTA dealing with specific concessions. The two levels come together in that many congressional opponents of NAFTA are quite prepared to stress Mexico's lack of enforcement of workplace standards or environmental laws when their real concern is competition with an industry in their districts, whether automobiles and parts, textiles and apparel, fresh fruits and vegetables, or whatever. The micro-level debate will become more public when the implementing legislation is taken up and the special protectionist interests are out in full force.

Environment

The nature of the debate taking place can be sketched in here.[35] The environmental issue burst forth when President Bush informed the Congress of his intention to negotiate a free trade agreement with Mexico. In order for him to enter into these negotiations, he required extension of fast-track authority under which these discussions are conducted. One of the conditions the Congress imposed was to include environmental issues in the agreement. After some initial resistance on the grounds that this was a trade and not an environmental agreement, President Bush consented and promised that environmental issues would either be made part of the agreement or be dealt with on a parallel track. The U.S. administration did both.

In chapter 1 (objectives), NAFTA accords priority to three international environmental agreements to which the United States is a party: the convention on international trade in endangered species of wild fauna and flora, 1973; the Montreal protocol on substances that deplete the ozone layer, 1987 and amended 1990; and the Basel convention on the control of transboundary movements of hazardous wastes and their disposal, 1989, on its entry into force for the three countries. If this last

---

35 Some of the details of the environmental and labour standards debate as they affect NAFTA can be found in the collection of three essays in "The Social Charter Implications of the NAFTA," *Canada-U.S. Outlook,* vol. 3, no. 3 (August 1992). *Canada-U.S. Outlook* is a quarterly publication of the National Planning Association, Washington, D.C.

does not enter into force, NAFTA accords priority to two bilateral agreements: that between Canada and the United States concerning the transboundary movement of hazardous waste, signed at Ottawa in 1986; and the agreement between Mexico and the United States on cooperation for the protection and improvement of the environment in the border area, signed at La Paz, Baja California Sur, 1983. In addition, Mexico and the United States agreed in the spring of 1992 to a cooperative plan for improving the environment at their border. This was part of the parallel track.

The concern expressed in the debate on the NAFTA has been less on Mexico's legal structure for protection of the environment, although it is weak and poorly funded, than on misgivings over Mexico's willingness and ability to enforce its laws and regulations. The opposite side of this argument is that NAFTA is the best assurance the environmentalists can now have about Mexico's commitment to improving its environment. Recent increases in Mexican budgets for environmental infrastructure and enforcement of laws and regulations would almost certainly not have come about if NAFTA had not provided the impetus.

NAFTA has other provisions designed to assure those in the United States concerned about the environment. Each country is empowered to choose the level of protection of human, animal, and plant life or environmental protection that it deems appropriate. Each country can adopt standards and sanitary and phytosanitary measures that it chooses, including those more stringent than international standards. Each country agrees not to lower its health, safety, or environmental standards to attract investment. This is not fully enforceable if there is bad faith on the part of any country; but it would be even less enforceable—the provision might not even exist—in the absence of NAFTA. The factual issues in disputes concerning environmental standards can be submitted for resolution in the NAFTA framework and the burden of proof is on the complaining country.

The Clinton speech supporting NAFTA proposed the establishment of an environmental protection commission with substantial powers and resources to, as he put it, prevent and clean up water pollution, encourage the enforcement of each country's own environmental laws, and provide a forum to hear complaints. This commission would presumably be trilateral. The OTA study had a similar recommendation for the establishment of a bilateral U.S.-Mexico environment protection commission.

The proposal has aroused Mexican concern. The official in charge of the environmental arm of Mexico's Secretariat of Social Development (Sedesol in its Spanish acronym) has stated that Mexico will not accept a supranational authority.[36] Presumably, neither will Canada. And probably neither will the United States.

Workplace conditions

Workplace sanitary and safety issues raise a different set of problems, although U.S. labour unions and some environmental groups made common cause in opposing the grant of authority to the president to negotiate NAFTA. Basic worker rights as defined in U.S. legislation include the right of association, the right to organize and bargain collectively, prohibition of any form of forced or compulsory labour, a minimum age for employment of children, and acceptable conditions of employment with respect to minimum wages, hours of work, and occupational safety and health. These issues are not included in the text of NAFTA. Parallel negotiations are taking place on them.

The debate in the NAFTA centres, once again, not on Mexico's laws and regulations, but on their enforcement. Mexico does not have and cannot afford an army of inspectors to assure compliance with workplace safety and health conditions, as the United States does—or tries to do, not always successfully. The minimum age for employment in Mexico is 14, but young people aged 14 to 16 may not work more than six hours a day or in hazardous occupations. The maximum work week for persons other than minors is 48 hours, although many contracts call for fewer hours. Mexico does have a system of minimum wages, but they are low. Overtime work calls for double the hourly salary.

The most sensitive issue for U.S. workers in competing activities is the fear that low Mexican wages will give Mexican products a competitive edge and force down U.S. wages in these activities. This is hard to deal with head-on in an agreement. Organized labour therefore opposes

---

36 Sergio Reyes Lujan, as quoted in the *U.S.-Mexico Free Trade Reporter*, October 19, 1992.

NAFTA. But if there is an agreement, worker rights is an appropriate subject for discussion. By being on a parallel track and not part of NAFTA itself, violation of worker rights is not subject to the dispute settlement mechanism. This may prompt a drive to incorporate these rights into the agreement, either directly or by reference to the parallel track understanding.

Here again, Clinton—and the OTA—proposed establishment of a commission for worker standards and safety which would have extensive powers to educate, train, develop minimum standards, and settle disputes. A U.S.-Mexico consultative commission on labour matters has, in fact, been established pursuant to a side agreement completed at about the same time that the NAFTA negotiations were concluded. Will a consultative commission as opposed to one with extensive powers satisfy the U.S. Congress? Would Mexico or Canada be prepared to enter into a commission that has supranational power over labour standards? Would the United States? Stand by for the answer in 1993.

Retraining and adjustment assistance

President Bush stated when he obtained congressional approval to negotiate free trade with Mexico that worker adjustment assistance would be provided. Then, in August 1992, President Bush proposed a worker adjustment initiative to be funded at $10 billion over five years. Of the $2 billion each year, the president proposed that $335 million be reserved specifically for NAFTA-related dislocations, and an equal additional amount be available for this purpose if the Secretary of Labour so decided.

This, in the end, may be the most divisive issue of the congressional debate because it requires the appropriation of substantial funds from a tight budget. President Bush never said what would have to give way to make room in the budget for his proposal. The contentious aspects of this issue will be: retraining for what; for how long should financial benefits be provided to affected workers; how to fund the costs. A related theme that will need resolution is the criteria that will be used to determine if a worker is entitled to retraining and financial assistance. Labour union leaders would like this to be an entitlement, not a discretionary program, but this will be a hard sell at a time when other entitlement programs are mushrooming and consuming large parts of the U.S. budget.

This is a debate whose resolution must take place at home, in the United States, and not within the structure of NAFTA. Yet its resolution will be essential for congressional enactment of the implementing legislation. My judgment is that this will be the most difficult issue to resolve for NAFTA to come into existence.

Concluding Comment

Despite its comprehensive nature, U.S. negotiators did not obtain all they sought. This is most evident in the energy field with respect to foreign risk contracts in petroleum exploration, but is true also in other areas. The United States would have preferred symmetry in all three countries on dealing with foreign investment, but both Canada and Mexico reserve the right to screen acquisitions of domestic companies. The big three auto producers would have preferred a rule of origin of 65 percent for passenger cars rather than the 62.5 percent figure in the agreement. All these differences will come out in the debate on implementing legislation.

Beyond that, the United States made concessions that will be opposed by interests that now enjoy protection. Fresh fruit and vegetable growers in California, Florida, and Texas will certainly object to the concessions on these products. U.S. sugar producers will object to the eventual loss of protection should Mexico augment its sugar production. U.S. truckers and teamsters will undoubtedly express concern over lower-paid Mexican drivers having the right, after a transitional period, to make deliveries in the interior of the United States.

The combination of these micro-level objections with the broader issue of free trade with a low-wage, developing country whose past record on enforcement of its own laws on working conditions and the environment makes it impossible to say with certainty whether NAFTA will be approved in the United States. Economists generally favour low international trade barriers. It is thus no accident that most economists who have studied NAFTA have come out in its favour. Producers and workers are not necessarily impressed with the arguments of economists. Their interests are more immediate. Their positions are determined by how they believe NAFTA will affect their well-being.

Legislators, who must ultimately say yea or nay on NAFTA, are clearly influenced by all these pressures.

The Canada-U.S. FTA was a relatively simple matter for most U.S. legislators. Canada is a more familiar place to them than Mexico. It is a developed country with roughly comparable levels of wages, working conditions, and social structure. Mexico's relatively low wage level has stimulated much protectionist concern in the United States. Beyond that, the debate in the United States has made it clear that there is much distrust that Mexico will enforce its own laws and regulations on working conditions and environmental issues and, *a fortiori,* live up to the letter and spirit of its undertakings in NAFTA.

Yet I find it unfortunate that the debate has taken this mistrustful tone. I hope that by the time the U.S. Congress must act, it will do so on the basis of what is agreed in the text and in parallel undertakings—which is substantial—and not on what their stereotypes about Mexico might be.

The NAFTA Agreement: A Canadian Perspective

Leonard Waverman
Centre for International Studies, University of Toronto

Introduction

THE NAFTA ANNOUNCED ON August 12, 1992 offers advantages and challenges for Canada. Critics will note the small current trade between Canada and Mexico, Mexico's low labour costs, Mexican competition with Canadian goods in U.S. markets and the supposed failure of the existing FTA as reasons for Canada to spurn the agreement.

In my opinion, to reject NAFTA could be a fundamental long-term error for Canada. My thoughts are based on the following three propositions:

1. The Mexican challenge to Canadian exports to the U.S. would be greater without Canadian participation in NAFTA (the so-called hub-and-spoke model [see Lipsey, Wonnacott]).

2. NAFTA offers a number of significant improvements over the FTA from the Canadian perspective (though it still contains several serious defects).
3. The Americas are changing, Canada's best interests are in working towards a new order in the Americas from North to South.

Canada cannot "escape" Mexican growth and competition by staying out of NAFTA. Whatever the marginal changes induced in Mexico due to NAFTA, these will surely arise because of the large size of the U.S. market. If NAFTA is required to induce Mexican entrepreneurs to invest more at the margin in Mexico, that investment will be almost the same with or without adding Canada to the agreement. *Thus by staying out of NAFTA Canada will not affect Mexican growth and exports*. Canadian tariffs are already low against Mexico. Even with only a U.S.-Mexico FTA, Mexican producers would become more significant competitors in Canadian markets because improved access to the U.S. market will improve Mexican efficiency through economies of scale, increased production runs, and so forth. Whatever new Mexican competition Canadians will face in U.S. markets will exist even if Canada does not take part in NAFTA. Competition in U.S. markets does not depend on which trade agreements Canadians decide to join.

A U.S.-Mexican free trade agreement, therefore, leads to a certain amount of "pain" for Canada. However, being outside the agreement will lead to fewer "gains" for Canada. Mexican tariffs are triple the Canadian average and imports to many Mexican sectors face formidable barriers. Therefore, preferential access to the Mexican market will be valuable, and NAFTA, by lowering Mexican trade and investment barriers for the U.S. and Canada, will lead to preferential advantages for these two nations or in the parlance of trade economists, "trade diversion" against Asia and Europe.

A major reticence voiced in Canada against joining NAFTA is the feeling that the Canada-U.S. Free Trade Agreement (FTA) has been the major cause of the large number of job losses, especially those in the manufacturing sector, which have occurred since 1989.

I surveyed five recent analyses of the impacts of the FTA on industrial output and employment in Canada. Three of these five studies show the FTA as a potential source for a small but significant number of job losses—45,000 to 53,000 out of the 365,000 manufacturing jobs lost in Canada since January 1, 1989. No one disputes the fact that Canada faces severe problems including high unemployment (and to this point few innovative policies have been put forward), but violent disagreement exists over the source of the problems and of the job losses. These studies all suggest that the major blame is not the FTA but elsewhere. For example, Rodrique Tremblay points to the 55 percent increase in Canadian manufacturing costs relative to the U.S. since 1986 as the major culprit. Adding Mexico to the Free Trade Agreement will add marginally to adjustment pressures but Mexico, as stressed above, will be a more fit competitor (and a richer nation) even without Canada in the Agreement. What is essential economically and politically in Canada, is to alter domestic policies including new transition programs to assist in retraining those who are caught by the new global pressures.

Finally, enormous changes are traversing Latin America. Countries which for generations have looked inward, basing economic policies on state enterprises, protection and import substitution, are opening up and making far reaching basic changes in the structure of their markets. Latin America is integrating into North America. The new vision of the Americas necessitates a reexamination of Canadian strategies and a shift towards the huge market and opportunities of the South.

Mexico and Canada in U.S. Markets

In 1991, Canada exported $96 billion (U.S.) worth of goods and services to the U.S., while Mexico exported $29 billion to the U.S. How will NAFTA affect Canadian sales in U.S. markets? Charts 1a and 1b detail the distribution of Canadian goods exports to the U.S. from 1990 through the first half of 1992. Chart 2 provides basic information on the sectoral distribution of Canadian and Mexican exports to the U.S. in 1990.

Products of the transportation sector make up 35 percent of Canadian goods exports to the U.S. However, these export figures exaggerate the importance of the transport sector since many of the components contained in cars assembled in Canada and shipped to the U.S. are of U.S. origin. The automotive sector accounts for nearly 13 percent of Canadian manufacturing, and overall manufacturing employment in Canada is 15 percent of total Canadian employment. Thus, while automotive exports are important, the direct employment in that sector

Chart 1a

Canadian Goods Exports to the U.S., 1990

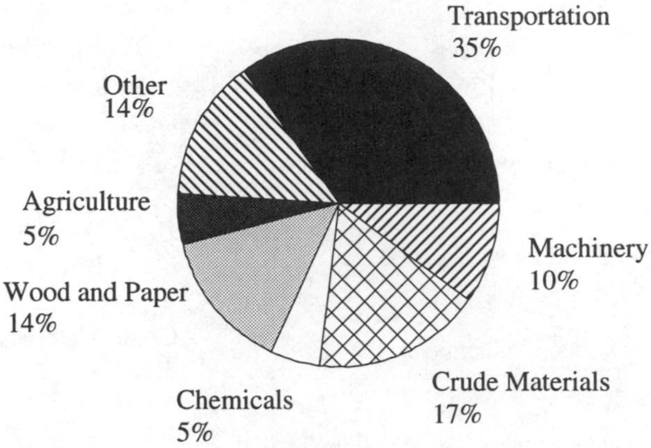

Total value of exports: $105,090,317,000.

Canadian Goods Exports to the U.S., 1991

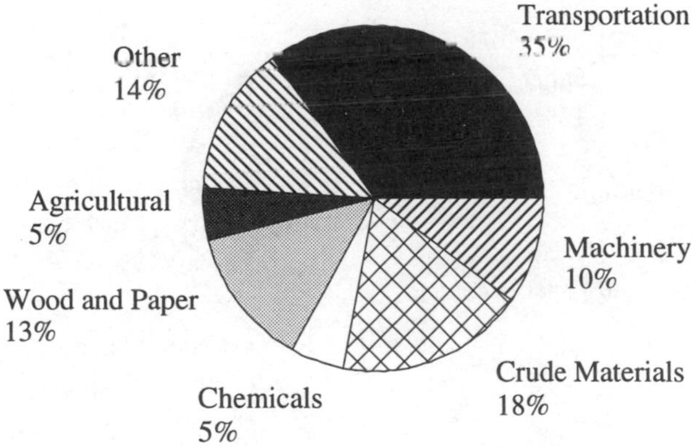

Total value of exports: $103,448,744,000.
Percentage change from 1990: -1.6%.

Source: Statistics Canada, Merchandise Trade Statistics.

Chart 1b

Canadian Goods Exports to the U.S.:
First Quarter of 1991

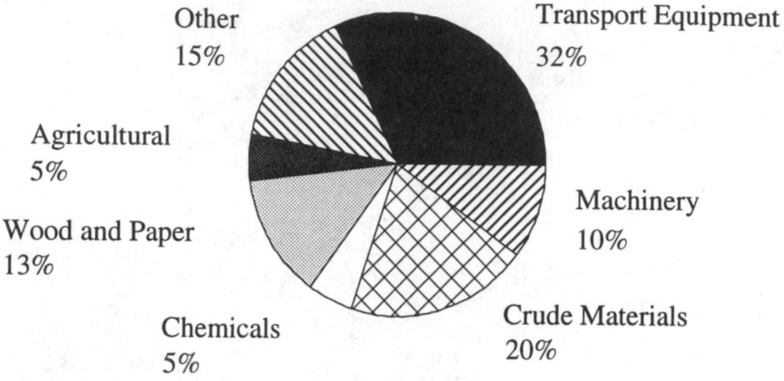

Total value of exports: $33,756,788,000.

Canadian Goods Exports to the U.S.:
First Quarter of 1992

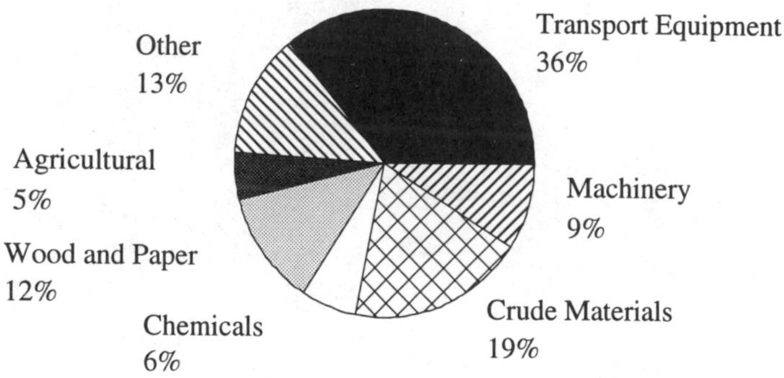

Total value of exports: $37,436,288,000.
Percentage increase from 1991: 10.9%.

Source: Statistics Canada, Merchandise Trade Statistics.

Chart 2

Goods Exports to the United States, 1990

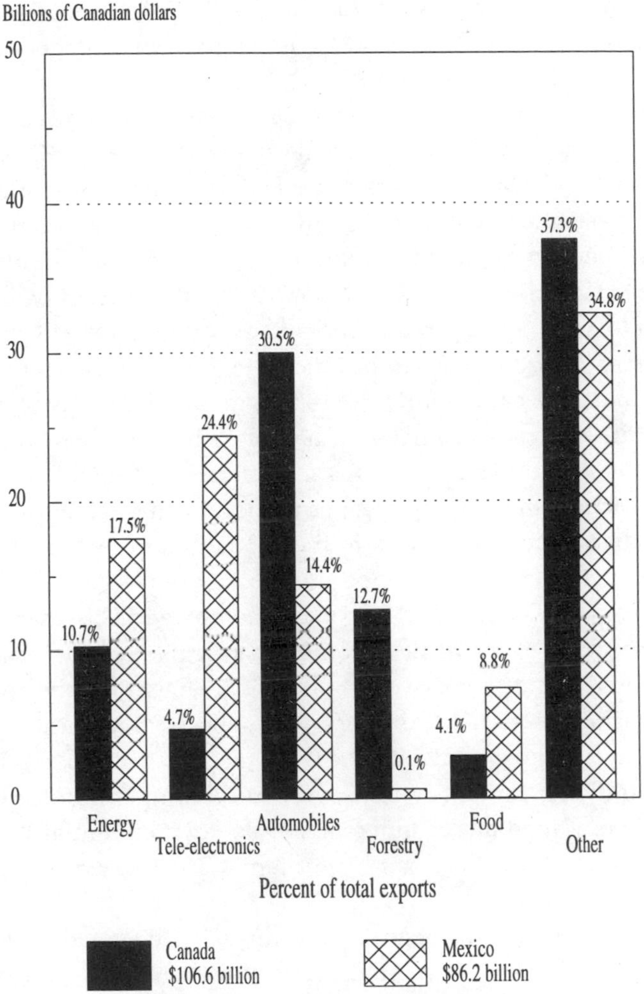

Source: Statistics Canada, Dec. 1991, Summary of Canadian International Trade, "Canada's and Mexico's Trade Position in the United States (U.S.) Market," Catalogue 65-001 (published March, 1992).

accounts for some 2 percent of the Canadian labour force. Twenty-two percent of the products of the Canadian manufacturing sector are exported, 80 percent of these to the U.S. Thus, some 3.5 percent to 4.0 percent of the Canadian labour force is directly employed in exports to the U.S. Adding indirect effects (the steel in the cars etc.) and services would expand this figure two- to three-fold. Still, Canada is primarily a service economy with 72 percent of its employees engaged in the provision of services.

The distribution of Canadian and Mexican exports to the U.S. is quite different (see Chart 2). Automobile products represent 30 percent of Canadian exports but only 14.4 percent of Mexican exports; tele-electronics products represent 24.4 percent of Mexican exports to the U.S. but only 4.7 percent of Canadian exports. Forestry product exports are important to Canada (over $12 billion in 1990 and nearly 13 percent of all exports to the U.S.) but an unimportant export item for Mexico.

Within each of these broad product categories the distribution of Canadian and Mexican exports to the U.S. market varies as well. For example, finished vehicles make up half of each of the two countries exports to the U.S., but Mexico ships small cars and Canada large cars and vans. Mexico ships many engines to the U.S. market and Canada few; Canadian exports of trucks to the U.S. are large while Mexican exports of trucks to the U.S. are not.

It is clear that Canada and Mexico do compete in U.S. markets to some degree. However, Mexican competition will surely be greater if Canada is not part of a Mexico-U.S. trade agreement for the reasons given in the introduction. Mexico, or any country for that matter, is free to sign any trade agreement with the U.S. that makes its citizens better off. These trade agreements will provide more competition for Canadian exporters. Canadians cannot retain *negotiated* preferential access to U.S. markets. The only recipe for longer-term Canadian export success is Canadian excellence.

Were the U.S. to sign separate agreements with Canada, Mexico, and other countries in Latin America or elsewhere, it would be the "hub" in a hub-and-spoke system (see Lipsey, Wonnacott). As the hub, the U.S. would be the only country in this system with duty-free access to all markets. Canada, for example, would have duty-free access only to the U.S. market but not to Mexico or the other countries in the system.

As a result of this asymmetric market access, the U.S. would be the natural investment location for any company wanting duty-free access to all countries. Canada and other "spoke" countries would lose out in the long run.

The Experience of the FTA

The Canada-U.S. Free Trade Agreement came into force on January 1 1989. The Canadian and U.S. economies (along with Europe, Japan etc.) have been mired in deep recession since 1990. Some observers blame the FTA for the majority, if not all, the Canadian job losses. The Canadian population at large appears to share this perception. There have been all too few serious unbiased analyses of the effects of the FTA, partly because serious economic analysis requires a number of years of data in order to disentangle the various factors which impact on the economy. The several such studies undertaken differ in their results but none blame the FTA for a major share of the enormous job losses which have occurred since 1990.

A 1991 study by Peter Pauly, for example, finds slight favourable impacts of the FTA. A 1992 study by Rodrique Tremblay attributes three quarters of all manufacturing job losses in the 1986-91 period to two causes—the substantial 55 percent increase in costs relative to U.S. and the recession. In 1992 Aileen Thompson analyzed how the stock market reacted to announcements of FTA events (such as the signing of the Agreement). She finds that significant positive effects occurred for two industries and negative (but statistically insignificant) effects for seven industries. Schwanen's 1992 study finds positive elements of the FTA's impact by investigating the changes in Canadian exports and imports since 1989 identifying those goods and services which were affected the most by tariff reductions in the FTA agreement. Gaston and Trefler, in a preliminary 1992 study using an econometric model of labour supply and demand in Canada (which includes the effects of trade liberalization), find employment losses from the FTA.

Pauly (1991) utilized a linked set of macro-econometric models to isolate the impacts on Canada (and the U.S.) of the FTA. In order to ask econometric models to sort out the variety of impacts on GNP, employment etc., Pauly had to pose a counter-factual path for macroeconomic events in the absence of the FTA. Pauly suggests that these results, obtained in 1991, "must be interpreted with extreme caution" and "provide as good an impression of the macroeconomic effects of the FTA as one is likely to get at this stage."

What counter-factual world has Pauly posed? Pauly assumes what economic theory states—that in the absence of the FTA a) exports and imports from the U.S. would have been lower (Schwanen proves this to be true), b) Canadian productivity would have been lower (there is no corroborating evidence of this), and c) investment in Canada would have been lower (the Government of Canada suggests that this is true). The results of imposing this alternative path and comparing it to the actual path of the Canadian economy are as follows:

1. Actual GNP in 1991 is 0.4 percent above what would have occurred without the FTA
2. Without the FTA, unemployment would have been a little higher
3. Inflation has been reduced (by two-tenths of 1 percent) because of the FTA
4. Imports, exports and business investment would have been slightly lower without the FTA.

Rodrique Tremblay examines the impacts of five effects on job losses in Canada in the 1986-91 period:

1. the real appreciation of the Canadian dollar of 18.1 percent
2. the 10.8 percent lower productivity growth in Canada than in the U.S.
3. the 11.2 percent increase in manufacturing wages in Canada relative to the U.S.
4. the recession
5. the FTA

Tremblay estimates the effects of these factors on manufacturing job losses as follows:[1]

---

1 Tremblay utilizes a simple model of labour demand. See his Appendix B.

1.	The increase in Canadian relative costs (factors 1, 2 and 3 above)	-146,000
2.	Recession – Canada	-126,000
	– U.S.	-12,000
	Total	284,000
	Total manufacturing job losses 1986-1991	319,000
	Manufacturing job losses due to other factors	45,000

Thus, according to Tremblay, the major impact on job losses in Canada in the 1986-91 period was the 55.2 percent relative increase in real costs for Canadian manufacturers in the 1986-1991 period. The recession is the second most important factor. Third is the combination of all other forces (tax changes and free trade).

Thompson (1992) provides an alternative means of investigating the impacts of the FTA by studying the impacts of significant FTA events on the stock valuations of the TSE 300 and a broader index.[2] Did these "events" provide abnormal returns to stock market investors?—the agreement on the FTA, October 3, 1988; the gaining strength of the Liberal party in October 1988 and the vows to abrogate the FTA if elected; and the conservative government election on November 21, 1988. None of these events had statistically significant effects, although the second event was consistent with a negative expected impact of free trade while events one and three had positive expected impacts.

Thompson points out that these aggregate effects mask industrial distributions—the FTA creates winners and losers. Accordingly, industries were grouped according to whether the expected effects were negative, positive or indeterminant according to Litvak (1986) and the MacDonald Commission Report. Industry level effects (stock market prices) are significant for event one but not for events two or three (remember that the aggregate effect of event one was negative but not

---

2 The TSE/Western data file including all stocks on the TSE and some stocks on the MSE and VSE.

significantly so). The food and beverage, textile, apparel, furniture, printing, rubber and plastics, and footwear industries had stock market decreases in value when the FTA agreement was reached on October 3, 1988. Positive stock market effects occurred for lumber and wood and paper. Other industries had indeterminate effects. However, the only statistically significant effects were for lumber, wood, and paper (all positive), and electronics (negative effect but indeterminate, *a priori*); the sum of each of the negative and positive groups was tested and found to be statistically significant.[3] Thompson (1992) states:

> It is striking that all of the Canadian cumulative abnormal returns corresponding to industries for which the lobbying and MacDonald Commission information provide consistent predictions have the expected sign. In addition, although only a few of the cumulative abnormal returns are statistically significant, many of them are quite large. During the three trading days of event window four, the values of the paper and industrial machinery portfolios increased by over 4 percent net of market-wide effects, and the values of the lumber and wood products and primary metals portfolios increased by 3.7 percent and 2.4 percent net of market-wide effects. The rubber and plastics products and electronic and electric equipment portfolios experienced abnormal declines greater than 4 percent during these three days and the textile, apparel, furniture and printing portfolios each experienced abnormal declines of over 2.5 percent. (p. 9)

Schwanen (1992) examines how Canada's trade pattern has changed since the FTA began. Economic theory suggests that trade in commodities liberalized under the FTA should expand faster than trade in commodities not affected by the Agreement. The actual data bears this out. Table 1 has been produced from the data compiled by Schwanen 1992. For merchandise, there is a clear trichotomous relation-

---

3 Thompson also notes that the information contained in each so-called event was not totally new, thus the probabilities of the FTA did not go from zero to one each time new information arrived but changed existing positive probabilities say from .5 to .75. If one uses, as an example, a change in probabilities from .5 to .75, then, the stock market abnormal returns in the paper industry suggest gains from the FTA of 19 percent.

ship; goods liberalized in the FTA had rates of growth for U.S./Canada trade (exports and imports) substantially greater than for goods not so liberalized, and Canada/U.S. trade in goods not liberalized grew (or fell less) than trade between Canada and the rest of the world (except for some goods imports (2b and 2c)). Schwanen's work is not definitive

Table 1: Trade Patterns, 1989-91

	Changes in Category	Trade 1991 $B Amount	Net change 1989-91
1a)	Canada's merchandise exports to the U.S., liberalized	$41.1	+16.2%
1b)	Canada's merchandise exports to the U.S., not liberalized	23.4	-2.2%
1c)	Canada's merchandise export to ROW	34.0	-4.5%
1d)	Canada's service exports to the U.S., liberalized	3.2	13.5%
1e)	Canada' service exports to the U.S., not liberalized	1.9	12.3%
1f)	Canada's service exports to ROW	3.2	4.4%
2a)	Canada's merchandise imports from the U.S., liberalized	49.5	+14.0%
2b)	Canada's merchandise imports from the U.S., not liberalized	10.2	-8.2%
2c)	Canada's merchandise imports from ROW	34.6	+1.9%
2d)	Canada's service imports from the U.S., liberalized	5.6	12.5%
2e)	Canada's service imports from the U.S., not liberalized	3.2	23.6%
2f)	Canada's service imports from ROW	3.5	0.6%

Source: Calculations made on data contained in Schwanen, 1992.

however—cause and effect are inferred from these statistics. "The facts [these data] so far are more consistent with the optimistic scenario of free trade supporters than with the views of detractors" (Schwanen p. 13). However, would examining these same data for say 1980-1985 show the same patterns? Did the negotiators liberalize where trade was already growing rapidly? Without examining data for periods before the FTA, it is difficult to conclude from examining trade data for 1989-91 alone that the FTA *caused* trade expansion.

Gaston and Trefler in a preliminary 1992 analysis estimate the impacts that the tariff reductions in the FTA will have on Canadian employment and wages. The authors begin with an interesting survey of the existing literature, summarizing the expected impacts that protection and trade will have on employment and wages. The main conclusions of the survey are

- changes in exports have large and positive effects on employment
- changes in imports have large and negative effects on employment
- export oriented industries are associated with higher wages
- protected industries are associated with lower wages
- "in response to tariffs and imports, union workers make much greater wage adjustments than their non-union counterparts" (p. 8)
- employment is much more sensitive to imports than are wages
- "a worker who is forced to switch industries because of trade displacement faces a cut in wages with the loss of industry—and firm-specific human capital" (p. 15)
- "low-paid workers will be the group of workers that is most affected by trade liberalization" (p. 17)
- "in the long run, trade liberalization would induce a reallocation of workers out of low-paid manufacturing jobs and into high-paid manufacturing jobs which in turn would increase manufacturing wages" (p. 7)
- liberalization of trade forces adjustment of workers from protected, low-wage industries to higher wage jobs. This "will mostly benefit the low-skilled union members...the ones who find it most difficult to find a new job" (p. 20)

Gaston and Trefler then examine the potential impacts of the FTA on employment in Canada and the U.S. by estimating econometrically a model of labour supply and labour demand over the 1979-1991 period. The FTA is represented in the model only by its impact on tariffs. The effects of exchange rates, GNP changes and interest rate differentials are also incorporated as these clearly impact employment. Table 2 attached here (Table 5 in Gaston and Trefler, 1992) shows actual employment losses in the two countries between 1988 and 1991. There are two essential points to raise about this Table. First, note the magnitude of job losses in Canada relative to those in the U.S. In a number of industries Canadian job losses are three to five times as great as job losses in the U.S. Second, in only three industries were there job losses in Canada and job gains in the U.S.—food and beverages, metal mines and paper.

Gaston and Trefler note that the correlation between employment changes across the 22 industries for Canada and the U.S. over the 1988-91 period is .58—similar factors are affecting employment in both countries.[4] Even after accounting for the host of independent influences—tariffs, imports, exports, domestic GNP, exchange rate and the interest spread—changes in Canadian employment on an industry by industry basis are still highly correlated with U.S. employment changes. The elasticity of employment changes in Canada with respect to employment changes in the U.S. is .865. A 10 percent increase (or decrease) in U.S. employment is associated with an 8.65 percent change in Canadian employment.[5]

Table 3 provides summary data on job losses from Gaston and Trefler in column one; the second and third columns are the rates of productivity advance in the sector in the 1980-85 period for Canada and the 1980-86 period for the U.S. taken from Denny *et al.* 1991. I have calculated the correlation between changes in total factor productivity (TFP) across these industries to be 0.29 (a 10 percent increase in TFP in

---

4 Gaston and Trefler conclude that these high correlations suggest job flight to the U.S. This is incorrect; in my view correlation is not causation.

5 There is no effect of changes in Canadian employment rates on U.S. employment rates.

Table 2: Employment and Wage Growth, 1988-1991

SIC Industry		Canada				United States			
		$\Delta l_j/l_j$	$\Delta w_j/w_j$	Δt_j	$\Delta m_j/m_j$	$\Delta l_j/l_j$	$\Delta w_j/w_j$	Δt_j	$\Delta m_j/m_j$
31	Manuf: leather	-17.8	-0.1	-2.9	-15.8	-6.4	-0.3	-2.1	-20.4
24	Manuf: wood products	-12.6	4.1	-0.3	-5.3	-3.9	-2.1	0.1	-7.7
22	Manuf: textiles	-12.4	-0.1	-1.0	2.4	-3.4	-0.8	-1.5	8.2
25	Manuf: furniture	-12.2	-0.4	-2.2	-9.5	-3.7	-1.4	-1.1	2.0
23	Manuf: clothing	-11.8	0.2	-1.7	16.5	-2.2	-1.4	-2.4	-6.7
34	Manuf: metal fabricating	-10.7	0.2	-0.8	-8.4	-2.3	-1.9	-0.6	-8.0
35	Manuf: machinery	-10.5	-0.2	-1.0	-24.6	-2.1	-1.6	-0.5	0.2
32	Manuf: non-metal minerals	-9.0	-0.5	-0.5	-10.8	-3.4	-2.3	-0.2	-7.1
36	Manuf: electrical	-8.4	0.2	-0.9	2.8	-3.6	-1.7	-0.8	16.4
39	Manuf: instruments & misc.	-7.4	1.3	-0.7	-37.8	-2.3	-1.4	-0.9	3.6
33	Manuf: primary metals	-6.5	-0.6	-0.4	-3.1	-2.8	-1.7	0.0	-8.3
20	Manuf: food & beverages	-5.2	-0.7	-0.4	9.4	1.5	-2.1	0.1	4.3
37	Manuf: transport	-4.6	-1.1	-0.3	-11.7	-3.6	-1.1	-0.3	-4.2
10	Mining: metal mines	-4.5	0.7	0.0	4.2	5.8	-1.3	0.0	-13.5
27	Manuf: printing	-4.5	-1.2	-0.3	5.6	-0.8	-1.8	0.0	-13.3
30	Manuf: rubber & plastic	-4.2	0.2	-0.9	1.1	-0.8	-1.6	0.6	1.5
21	Manuf: tobacco	-3.6	1.6	-1.6	4.4	-4.6	0.0	-2.6	25.0
26	Manuf: paper	-3.3	-0.4	-0.8	6.5	0.2	-2.0	-0.1	-4.3
28	Manuf: chemicals	-1.9	-0.2	-1.0	5.5	-0.7	-1.3	-0.3	-2.3
14	Mining: non-metals	-1.3	-0.8	-0.1	-7.5	-0.6	-1.5	0.0	1.8
29	Manuf: petro & coal	0.3	-1.6	-0.1	-15.2	-0.6	-0.4	-0.1	4.5
11	Mining: mineral fuels	0.5	1.0	0.0	-15.2	-0.8	-1.0	0.0	6.7

Notes: j indexes industries, l_j is employment, w_j is earnings, t_j is the tariff rate, and m_j is bilateral imports between Canada and the U.S. Figures are year-to-year percentage changes averaged over 1988-89, 1989-90, and 1990-91. For tariffs, figures are year-to-year changes averaged over the same years.

Source: Gaston and Trefler, 1992, table 5.

Table 3: Canada—Changes in Employment, 1988-1991; Productivity Growth, 1980-85

SIC Industry		Canada Employment Changes	Canada Productivity Growth 1980-85	U.S. Productivity Growth 1980-86	Canada-U.S. Relative Efficiency 1983-85*
31	Manuf: leather	-17.8	0.88	-0.10	n.a.
24	Manuf: wood products	-12.6	n.a.	n.a.	n.a.
22	Manuf: textiles	-12.4	0.65	0.53	0.817
25	Manuf: furniture	-12.2	0.54	-0.23	0.886
23	Manuf: clothing	-11.8	0.65	-0.20	n.a.
34	Manuf: metal fabricating	-10.7	0.55	0.11	0.786
35	Manuf: machinery	-10.5	-0.94	3.10	n.a.
32	Manuf: non-metal minerals	-9.0	-0.09	0.06	n.a.
36	Manuf: electrical	-8.4	3.25	1.86	0.930
39	Manuf: instruments & misc.	-7.4	-0.14	-0.06	n.a.
33	Manuf: primary metals	-6.5	1.11	0.00	1.081
20	Manuf: food & beverages	-5.2	0.01	1.03	0.937
37	Manuf: transport	-4.6	0.59	0.18	0.948
10	Mining: metal mines	-4.5	n.a.	n.a.	n.a.
27	Manuf: printing	-4.5	0.29	-0.56	n.a.
30	Manuf: rubber & plastic	-4.2	0.94	1.48	n.a.
21	Manuf: tobacco	-3.6	-1.42	-2.97	0.930
26	Manuf: paper	-3.3	-0.48	1.45	1.030
28	Manuf: chemicals	-1.9	0.41	0.53	0.846
14	Mining: non-metals	-1.3	n.a.	0.06	n.a.
29	Manuf: petro & coal	0.3	0.09	-0.25	0.939
11	Mining: mineral fuels	0.5	n.a.	n.a.	n.a.

*Canada/U.S. A number below 1.0 means that the Canadian industry is less efficient than its U.S. counterpart.

Sources: Column (1) Gaston and Trefler 1992; Columns (2)-(5) Denny *et al.* 1991.

the U.S. (or Canada) is associated with a 2.9 percent increase in TFP in the other country). Thus both employment and productivity changes in Canada are significantly correlated with those in the U.S. Similar forces are at work. One might suppose that employment losses were concentrated in the industries where productivity growth was the lowest. This is not evident in Table 3. Productivity growth over the 1980-85 period however might not say a lot about relative efficiency and costs. Column 5 in Table 3 provides estimates of the relative level of absolute efficiency for these industries as between Canada and the U.S. The correlation between the relative efficiency of Canadian industries (relative to the U.S.) and job losses in Canada is .43 for the eleven industries for which data exist. There is then evidence that lower total factor productivity in Canada does cost jobs.

Several other issues suggest that the correlations between job losses in Canada and the FTA may be misleading.[6] First, the high level of aggregation in Gaston and Trefler masks opposing effects. The job losses in Canadian mining and job gains in that aggregate sector in the U.S. are in different actual industries. Second, note that trade between the two countries has fallen in a number of industries. This occurred in leather, wood products, non-metallic mines, primary metals and transport equipment. It is hard to argue that the FTA decreased employment in both countries by decreasing trade. Third, there are an important number of industries where tariff changes are close to zero—wood products (Canadian employment loss 12.6 percent); non-metallic minerals (employment loss 9 percent); primary metals (employment loss 6.5 percent); food and beverages (employment loss 5.2 percent); metal mines (employment loss 4.5 percent); printing (employment loss 4.5 percent); mining non-metals (employment loss 1.3 percent); manufacturing petroleum and coal (employment gain 0.3 percent), and mining-mineral fuels (employment gain 0.5 percent). To relate employment losses to tariff reductions, given this range of job losses across industries

---

6 It is important to point out that the Gaston and Trefler work is a preliminary analysis, and one which ignores the impacts of a number of other crucial factors on employment. Primarily, global forces which are creating structural change in a number of countries are ignored.

with little tariff reductions, shows that significant other factors are at work.

Gaston and Trefler compute the marginal effects of tariff reductions on employment and wage levels in Canada, given import levels, trade changes and the effects of the recession. They find a negative effect on employment in Canada of the tariff reductions in the FTA. Why do they find this when the literature surveyed shows net gains from trade liberalization? The answer is twofold. First, Canadian tariffs are higher than U.S. tariffs so that U.S. import penetration into Canada generated by the FTA is greater than increased Canadian import penetration into the U.S. Second, they cannot model the benefits of more assured access.

The FTA also affected exports and imports as Schwanen (1992) and Pauly (1991) demonstrate. Thus, a more accurate measure of the short-run impact of the FTA would incorporate these effects as well. I estimate, from the Gaston and Trefler model, that the effect of the phase out of tariffs between Canada and the U.S. in the 1989-1992 period was a reduction in Canadian employment of some 42,000-63,000 employees (or 53,000 for an average estimate).[7] I think this exaggerates job losses because of the omissions in the model.

While there have been, in my view, more dislocations to this point than economists predicted, it is short sighted, I think, to concentrate on the FTA as the source of Canada's economic problems. Four of the five

---

7 Estimated as follows (using coefficients from Gaston and Trefler, Table 7): Canadian tariffs on U.S. goods averaged 3.2 percent in 1989; I assume the tariffs have fallen by one third in the three years. The impact of a 1 percent reduction in Canadian tariffs is estimated to be an employment loss of .748 x 1.0 percent or .75 percent. U.S. tariffs averaged 2 percent in 1989. A .66 percent fall in U.S. tariffs increased Canadian employment by .142 x .66 or 0.09 percent. Assume that Schwanen is correct and the FTA caused export and import changes. Canadian exports to the U.S. rose 9.3 percent in the three years 1989-91. This increased Canadian employment by .37 percent (0.04 x 9.3 percent); the impact of imports has a marginally positive impact on Canadian employment, 0.05 percent (.005 x 10.5 percent). The aggregate impact is a fall in employment of 0.42 percent. Employment in 1988 averaged 10.1 million (Statistics Canada—72.002, this is a consistent base with the Gaston-Trefler study which excludes agriculture, professionals, etc.); 0.42 percent of this is 42,400. Using short-run elasticities estimated over 1988-91, employment loss would be .62 percent or 62,600.

studies I examine here do show some job losses. However, unemployment in Canada since 1989 has risen by 880,000, 365,000 of this in the manufacturing sector (see Tremblay, 1992, p. 18-19). Job losses attributable to this point to the FTA might account for 15 percent of Canadian manufacturing job losses since 1989.[8] Many respected researchers have been warning for years of the loss of Canadian competitiveness (see Daly or Porter for two examples). Dismembering the FTA will not improve Canadian productivity, reduce costs or improve access to the U.S. and other markets. The majority of current Canadian problems require real and serious solutions to fundamental issues of education, training, labour markets, entrepreneurship, etc. Canadian firms are adjusting to the realities of a North American economic space (see Blank and Waverman, 1992). Forcing the costs of adjustment once again, this time to a market of 26 million Canadians at the northern edge of the Western Hemisphere as the whole Hemisphere (a market of 445 million people) is beginning to form would be, in my opinion, unwise

In the remainder of the paper, I highlight some of the key changes in the NAFTA agreement which are an improvement over the FTA.

Autos

In another chapter in this book, Jon Johnson provides an important substantive analysis of the changes in NAFTA for the auto sector. Clearly the important issue in the auto sector is the rules of origin.[9]

I will not repeat Johnson's analysis. The bottom line is that the 50 percent rule-of-origin in the FTA becomes 62.5 percent for passenger cars and engines in 2002, rising from 56 percent in 1998. These increased domestic content provisions are a trade-off for improved definitions.

Therefore, simply for Canada-U.S. trade, what effects do the new rules have? Under the FTA rules as they were being interpreted, uncertainty was raised for producers as to whether particular direct costs

---

8 This does not mean that in the longer term there will not be job gains because of the FTA. Restructuring takes time, especially in today's unfortunate economic climate.

9 See the paper by Peter Morici elsewhere in this volume for details on the rules of origin.

would be challenged. NAFTA reduces that uncertainty. However, there is now a "certain" higher rule-of-origin and a regional value content for three countries (RVC) instead of the either "in or out" rules before for two countries (a part was either a qualified import—thus duty free—or not). An exact comparison could only be done by a company or a government official. Johnson argues (and I concur) that the effective content requirement likely has been raised after incorporating the changes in calculations.

Will an increase (assume hypothetically by 15 percent or 7 percentage points) in required content hurt Canadian producers? That is, are auto producers in Canada importing some 40 to 45 percent of net cost from outside the U.S., Canada and Mexico? Chrysler utilizes a number of Asian-sourced parts, as does Ford to a lesser degree. Both of these companies use Asian-made capital goods as well. If one considered the capital equipment used by some Big Three auto plants as foreign, these plants might not meet the new content rules. However, all capital equipment is considered as originating, no matter the origin.[10] Only the imports of original equipment parts count against RVC. RVC can be averaged over a model line (say Honda Civic) in a class (minis, subcompacts, compacts, midsize, large) in one plant; over a class in a plant, or over a model line (Article 403.4). Thus, larger producers with more models in a plant or a greater number of plants have more room to average. Asian producers tend to have fewer plants and fewer models and more parts imports. Who then is the rule aimed at?

An important issue is why 62.5 percent. Some have suggested that this was an average between the 60 percent desired by Canada and the 65 percent wanted by the U.S. (see the *Globe and Mail*, August 15, 1992, p. B2). I am unimpressed by this rationalization. After all, why is 62.5 percent more desirable than 60 percent? Is this just a shift at the margin for more local North American produced parts? One suggestion (*Globe and Mail*, August 15, 1992, p. B2) is that "achieving more than 60 percent North American content requires significant investments in power train manufacturing—the engines and transmissions that rank high in value

10 Capital equipment is classified as "indirect material" in NAFTA (Article 415). Article 408 states "An indirect material shall be considered to be an originating material without regard to where it is produced."

in any car." This point must be carefully considered since autos are products which cannot have RVC continually changed at the margin; at some point (but is it 62.5 percent?) a big lump of net costs must be added—say an engine. Thus, 62.5 percent or 65 percent RVC may be equivalent to 80 percent RVC if the component made RVC by the change in rules is 15 percent to 20 percent of the costs of a car.

It is evident that Mexico's present Auto Decrees limit imports of parts and vehicles and promote exports. These decrees must be phased out by January 1, 2004 (see Johnson's chapter).

Adding Mexico complicates the calculations in two ways. First, Mexico is part of RVC, therefore out-sourcing to Mexico assists Canadian assemblers allowing them lower costs but retaining RVC. Second, Mexico becomes an alternative to Canada to earn RVC. Which effect will win out in the long-run? Recent research by Markusen *et al.* suggests that the elimination of Mexican controls will favour Canada in the long run. This study suggests that the NAFTA rules will lead to an increase in employment in parts and engine production in Canada offsetting a loss of Canadian employment in assembly. This study's conclusions rest on a number of key assumptions and the gains to Canada may be exaggerated. It is however important to emphasize that the interrelationships of the domestic content provisions are complex and it is not evident to a number of researchers that Mexico will become the preferred site for all forms of automotive manufacturing.

Textiles and Apparel

Trade in textiles and apparel (T&A) is not "free" in most developed countries. The U.S. and a number of other importers and exporters utilize the multi-fibre agreement to govern trade in T&A through a series of product and country specific quotas and tariffs.

There have been a number of complaints that the changes in NAFTA will lead to serious harm for the Canadian apparel industry (see articles in *Le Devoir*, August 13 and 14, 1992). This is likely exaggerated.[11] Canadian apparel manufacturers have been able to practice trade diversion to a substantial degree in the U.S. since 1989. Canada's share of the

---

11 See the paper by Barry and Siwicki elsewhere in this book.

U.S. woolen suit market has gone from 1 percent in 1989 to nearly 7 percent today because only Canadian producers' exports can use third country fabrics and enter U.S. markets duty free—a saving of some 40 percent over exporters from outside North America (see Smith, 1992). It is true that the "fibre forward" rule and low growth rates for quotas in men's woolen suits are not to Canada's benefit. Textiles (where NAFTA gives significant increased quotas to Canadian producers) and apparel are clearly sectors where, with managed trade and under-managed trade, big wins and big losses can occur.

Energy and Petrochemicals

The Mexican constitution makes energy and basic energy products the prerogative of the state. Foreign investment is not allowed. However, the definition of what constitutes a "basic" product has changed over time and shifts markedly in NAFTA.[12] Mexico retains control for domestic investors (the state, largely) over crude oil, natural gas and five petrochemical products (butane, ethane, heptane, hexane and pentane). Foreign investment in other areas (such as ammonia and methane) are allowed. The government procurement section does open up the potential for Canadian and U.S. firms bidding on energy developments. Article 605 of NAFTA repeats Article 904 of FTA preventing government restrictions from reducing the proportion of energy exports below a 36 month moving average. However, Annex 605 states that this Article shall not apply as between the other parties and Mexico.

Canadians have paid too little attention to energy and petrochemicals assuming that the Mexican government's control over PEMEX would eliminate increased competition. This majority view may be in error. Crucial for oil supplies are new developments, reserve additions and replacements. The finding costs for oil and natural gas are likely significantly lower in Mexico than in the U.S. or Canada. Thus NAFTA, by increasing confidence in the Mexican economy, by opening up the Mexican government procurement market, and by explicitly allowing Canadian and U.S. firms to be used for exploration and development in

---

12 Energy provisions are dealt with in the paper by Campbell Watkins in this volume.

Mexico, will lead to more emphasis on finding Mexican oil and gas. While this may lead to lower finds in Canada in the short to medium term, Canadian expertise could play an important role in the expansion of the Mexican energy sector.

Services

NAFTA applies the general principles of National Treatment and MFN to the service sector but without a great liberalization of cross-border trade. In addition, most existing impediments to trade are grandfathered. Thus most air services, most maritime services, basic telecommunications, and social services, are exempt. Road transport in Mexico is liberalized, as it needs to be for Mexican competitiveness.

Financial services[13] are liberalized, allowing financial institutions established in the U.S. or Canada[14] to expand in Mexico under a set of safeguard mechanisms limiting total market share and individual firm size until the year 2000. After 2000 there are no limits on Canadian and U.S. presence but non-Mexican bank acquisitions may be subject to a 4 percent cap.[15] The Agreement allows people in one country to purchase financial services located in another country, within limits. National Treatment means that any new service which domestic firms are allowed to offer can be offered by firms from the other countries. Article 1409, however, allows the continuation of certain existing non-conforming measures at the federal or state/provincial levels. A Financial Services Committee is established to supervise the implementation of this section of the Agreement, to examine technical issues, and to participate in dispute resolution.

---

13 Financial services are discussed in the paper by John Chant.

14 These need not be Canadian or U.S. majority owned, simply corporations duly registered (i.e. meeting the tests of Canada and of the U.S.).

15 Aggregate limits may be put in place between 2000 and 2004 for a duration of three years if foreign financial affiliates reach 25 percent of the commercial banking sector or 30 percent of the securities industries (measured by aggregate capital) (See Annex VIIIB).

Agriculture

Two bilateral agreements are proposed: U.S.-Mexico, and Canada-Mexico, within an overall trilateral framework which establishes tariff reductions and overall "rules of the game." Canada and Mexico will eliminate all tariffs or NTBs except in the dairy, poultry, egg and sugar sectors. In these other sectors, Mexico replaces its quotas with "tariff rate quotas," tariffs which yield the same imports as the quotas, or with ordinary tariffs. These tariffs fall to zero over a ten-year period (except for corn and dried beans which have fifteen years). Opening up Mexican field grains and cattle markets to Canadian exporters is a plus, as is the opportunity for Canadians to have Mexican vegetables and fruits at times when the Canadian climate is not conducive to production.

The ability of Canadians to take advantage of agricultural markets in Mexico depends on a host of other factors. Transport links are crucial. Since transport is largely exempt from NAFTA, will rail and truck links allow Canadian grain and cattle to move expeditiously to Mexico? How will trade credits and export financing react? Trade in goods and services are interlinked and it will be necessary for Canadian services to facilitate increased trade in agriculture (and the other liberalized goods).

Antidump and Countervail Procedures

A serious omission from NAFTA is the absence of a significant new impediment to the use of antidump and countervail procedures against free trade partners. The FTA made the same error. Adding Mexico clearly complicates Canada-U.S. agreement on a subsidies code. In this area, it is suggested that we are waiting for Godot, spelled G-A-T-T. However, within the EC, firms cannot accuse foreign firms of pricing below cost using costing formulae that no domestic competitor has to meet. This is the reality of antidump law. In the private-interests driven and micro-trade policy domain of the U.S. International Trade Commission, antidump is at best harassment and at worst offensive protectionism. NAFTA does little that is new to remove these protectionist elements. While Dispute Resolution is an important counter to pure protectionism (see Horlick 1991),[16] the ultimate aim must be to have National Treatment for predation rules under Competition Policy in NAFTA, as a replacement for the current domestic procedures. Trade cases levied against Canada by U.S. producers since 1989 account for a small percentage of actual Canadian exports. However, the threat of trade actions must inhibit pricing decisions in other industries, thus protecting U.S. firms. Some investment decisions would also be affected by these very public trade disputes. U.S. unilateralism is a reality but further steps must be taken to reduce protectionism within the free trade area.

Conclusion

NAFTA reduces trade barriers against Mexican goods in U.S. and Canadian markets. For most manufactured products, these barriers were already low. Thus, the new competition that Mexico will offer Canadian and U.S. producers will come largely from increased future production in Mexico that results from NAFTA. By staying out of NAFTA, Canada will not affect to any significant degree increased Mexican penetration of Canadian markets. To prevent this penetration, Canada would have to raise its barriers against Mexico, but GATT prevents this, in large measure. In addition, NAFTA is superior to the FTA in a number of ways.

NAFTA offers Canadian investors and exporters privileged access to the Mexican market. Privileged access to a large and growing market is an asset for Canada. Another issue is the increased competition that Canada will have with Mexico for the U.S. market. Is this detrimental and would staying out of NAFTA have been beneficial for Canada? In fact, Canada cannot prevent Mexico from succeeding in the U.S. market (although the U.S. could do so by increasing barriers to Mexican goods). So, staying out of NAFTA yields no positive effects for Canada.

Thus, my message is fairly simple. Mexico will succeed or not whether Canada is in NAFTA or not. We cannot affect Mexican growth by ignoring Mexico. Since the rise of Mexico as a competitive player, like the rise of Korea or Taiwan, is outside Canadian influence, the key

---

16 Also see the Gilbert Winham paper in this volume.

to Canadian success is to concentrate on internal matters—job training, the extent of intra-provincial barriers, venture capital, the building of the "Canadian diamond" (see Porter, 1992), the set of interrelated goods and services production which leads to enhanced productivity, exports and higher incomes. Canada is facing new challenges; Mexico is but one of these. However, greater competition from Mexico will be felt by low-skilled employees, Canadians already hurt by increased global competition. Innovative transition and retraining programs are needed.

Bibliography

Blank, Steven and Leonard Waverman, 1992, "The Changing Infrastructure of North America and Its impact on Canada's Relations with North America: A Concept Paper," North-South Center, University of Miami.

Denny, Michael, J. Bernstein, M. Fuss, S. Nakamura, and L. Waverman, 1991, "Productivity in Manufacturing Industries—Canada, Japan and the United States, 1953-1986: Was the 'Productivity Slowdown' Reversed?" *CJE* 1991.

Gaston, Noel and Daniel Trefler, 1992, "The Labour Market Consequences of the Canada-U.S. Free Trade Agreement: A Preliminary Assessment," October, University of Toronto, mimeo.

Horlick, Gary, and F. Amanda DeBusk, 1992, "The Functioning of the FTA Dispute Resolution Panels," in Waverman (ed.): *Negotiating and Implementing a North American Free Trade Agreement*, Fraser Institute/Centre for International Studies.

Lipsey, Richard G., 1990, "Canada at the U.S.-Mexico Free Trade Dance: Wallflower or Partner?" *Commentary*, No. 20, August: C.D. Howe Institute.

Litvak, Isaiah A., 1986, "Freer Trade with the U.S.: The Conflicting Views of Canadian Business," *Business Quarterly*, Spring.

Pauly, Peter, 1991, "Macroeconomic Effects of the Canada-U.S. Free Trade Agreement," paper in the Studies on the Economic Future of North America series, Fraser Institute/Centre for International Studies.

Porter, Michael, *Canada at the Crossroads*, BCNI and Minister of Supply and Services, 1991.

Schwanen, Daniel, 1992, "Were the Optimists Wrong on Free Trade? A Canadian Perspective," *Commentary*, No. 37, October: C.D. Howe Institute.

Trembley, Rodrique, 1992, "L'Émergence d'un Bloc Économique et Commercial Nord-Américain: la Compétitivité de l'Économie

Canadienne et la Politique du Taux de Change," Université de Montréal, Départment de Sciences Économiques, Cahier 9212.

Thompson, Aileen J., 1992, "The Canada-United States Free Trade Agreement and Stock Prices," mimeo, October 10.

Wonnacott, Ron, 1990, "U.S. Hub-and-Spoke Bilaterals and the Multilateral Trading System," *Commentary*, No. 23, October: C.D. Howe Institute.

The North American Free Trade Agreement from a Mexican Perspective

Rogelio Ramirez De la O
Ecanal, Mexico

IN THIS PAPER I DISCUSS the main features of the North American Free Trade Agreement (NAFTA) from the perspective of what I understand Mexican objectives and policy to be. The first part discusses the background of the agreement and Mexico's objectives at the launch of trade negotiations. The second part is a brief description of NAFTA's features and a discussion of controversial issues and of the effects I anticipate the agreement will have in Mexico. Finally, this chapter considers the themes for public debate over NAFTA in coming years.

Background and Mexico's Objectives

A free trade agreement between Mexico and its North American partners became necessary on two grounds:

1. First, as a result of the experience of economic stabilization between 1983 and 1985, it became clear to the government that long-term investment in Mexico could materialize only if the macroeconomic framework and economic policy were on a solid footing. Given the abrupt policy shifts of the 1970s and early 1980s, a stable economic regime, i.e., one that could transcend changes in government, became a prerequisite for investment and growth.

   After initial efforts to liberalize its trade sector, Mexico joined the General Agreement on Tariffs and Trade (GATT) in 1986. This was regarded as an attempt to make trade liberalization both progressive and permanent, but adherence to the multilateral trading system failed to spark new long-term investment in Mexico, as this system is limited in coverage of agriculture and services and does not address the specific issues of Mexico-U.S. bilateral trade. Furthermore, GATT membership could eliminate neither peak import tariffs in Mexico's main U.S. market, nor protectionist measures against Mexican exports. The importance of trade with the U.S. led Mexico in 1985 to sign an understanding with that country on subsidies and countervailing duties, in which Mexico obtained the benefit of the "proof of injury" requirement for U.S. producers seeking to threaten Mexican exports by protectionist pressure. In 1987, after joining GATT, Mexico signed a Framework Agreement on trade and investment with the U.S. Even these agreements, however, did not bring about a generalized liberalization motivating long-term investment in Mexico. Negotiations for a comprehensive free trade agreement with North America began in 1990, focusing largely on its potential to spur investment.

2. Secondly, a relatively new feature in the world economy is that economic blocks can reduce the participation of third countries in the expansion of regional trade. In addition, German reunifi-

cation was seen as causing a massive transfer of resources from western into eastern Europe and provoking global capital scarcity. Formal trade links with North America were thought to partially alleviate the negative effects on Mexico by enhancing its potential as a recipient of foreign investment resulting from resource reallocation, once access to our main export market (the U.S.) was assured.

Apart from these motivations, Mexico wanted an agreement to accelerate economic recovery, as the prolonged restructuring of the economy was seen to be taking considerable time to deliver tangible progress to the majority of Mexicans. The effects of stabilization policies could be softened by economic growth, based on a greater injection of foreign resources to finance imports while maintaining foreign debt service. To prevent domestic capital from flowing abroad and to eventually attract foreign capital, the government had to re-focus its strategy not only on maintaining export growth, but on reducing inflation.

In December 1987, a new policy to fight inflation set nominal targets for the peso/dollar exchange rate. The policy was successful, but at the cost of a substantial appreciation of the real exchange rate: accumulated inflation in the four years to December 1991 was 180.2 percent, while the nominal peso/dollar rate rose by only 38.0 percent. To maintain exports under this regime called for increased efficiency and more investment. Investors demanded macroeconomic stability and permanence in the economic policy regime, and business opinion linked this with the free trade agreement.

Despite greater industrial efficiency and productivity, the combination of the strong exchange rate and higher investment caused trade and current-account deficits on the balance of payments. The current surplus of $3.8 billion in 1987 became a deficit of -$13.3 billion in 1991, expected to reach -$21 billion or -6.5 percent of GDP in 1992. As this deficit expanded, new uncertainties emerged over Mexico's capacity to attract enough foreign capital to finance it.

Such circumstances made the trade agreement more desirable, as it was perceived to ensure a steady flow of foreign finance, in addition to providing more certainty for long-term investment by ensuring market access for Mexican exports. The latter had recorded high growth in past years and faced low average tariffs in the U.S. and Canada. Even so, there were high tariffs on some products while others remained threatened by sporadic protectionist measures, examples of which are the embargo on exports of tuna, countervailing duties applied to cement exports and a prohibition on exports of fresh avocado.

Mexico's Negotiating Position

In 1985, Mexico began to liberalize trade, eliminating nearly all import licenses and reducing import tariffs. Imports of goods rose from 9.5 percent of GDP in 1985 to 12.5 percent in 1989, and an estimated 15.3 percent this year. The liberalization drive, which permitted increased exports, was clear to all despite the fact that an undervalued peso in 1985-86 could have acted as a halt on imports. The peso devaluation itself of 50 percent in 1985-86 was forced by a dramatic reduction in oil prices followed by massive capital outflows, rather than contrived as a protectionist device. Moreover, the strong under-valuation of the currency in real terms was short-lived as high domestic inflation soon dissipated any competitive advantage afforded by the devaluation.

Since liberalization was already extensive by 1991, NAFTA's average tariff phase-out period of 10 years is certainly longer than is needed by most industries. Long before the agreement was negotiated, Mexican industry had shown the effects of trade liberalization through losses in output and employment. Table 1 illustrates this for different manufacturing industries.

The high increase in output of the in-bond (maquiladora) industry, by contrast with other activities, illustrates the positive effects of trade liberalization when investment is mobile. This industry had been promoted by the Mexican government since the mid-1960s, partly to compensate for the termination of guest work programs in the U.S., but its growth in the 1980s was spectacular owing to the abundance of labour and relatively low wages.

Interestingly enough, the table suggests output per worker has increased little compared to the rest of industry. This is because such plants use highly efficient processes, transplanted to Mexico by mainly multinational firms, whose productivity is higher than in Mexican industry. Another reason is that capital investment in these plants is relatively low, as only labour-intensive processes are transferred to

Table 1: Growth in Manufacturing Output and Employment (1985 = 100)

	1985	1987	1990	1991	Annual Rate of Growth '87-'91	Jan-Jun '91-'92 (% Increase)
Manufacturing Output						
Total	100.0	96.7	120.7	124.9	6.6	1.8
Food, beverages	100.0	98.9	126.0	128.8	6.8	0.4
Textiles	100.0	90.7	99.7	95.7	1.4	0.7
Wood	100.0	103.0	87.9	86.4	-4.3	-5.3
Paper	100.0	117.9	122.8	121.4	0.7	-7.0
Chemicals	100.0	103.4	145.6	149.9	9.7	2.9
Non-metallic minerals	100.0	98.6	104.8	106.0	1.8	6.9
Basic metals	100.0	103.8	117.2	114.1	2.4	-7.4
Metallic products, machinery	100.0	88.7	130.2	149.8	14.0	6.7
Other	100.0	103.9	97.1	95.8	-2.0	8.7
"Maquiladora"	100.0	218.3	350.0	341.1	11.8	13.0

Table 1: Continued

	1985	1987	1990	1991	Annual Rate of Growth '87-'91	Jan-Jun '91-'92 (% Increase)
Manufacturing employment						
Total	100.0	97.2	100.0	98.4	0.3	-3.1
Food, beverages	100.0	102.7	108.0	108.7	1.4	-0.1
Textiles	100.0	97.1	90.5	85.8	-3.0	-4.5
Wood	100.0	98.8	91.0	89.9	-2.3	-3.3
Paper	100.0	101.0	101.1	99.7	-0.3	-3.8
Chemicals	100.0	101.8	104.9	103.1	0.3	-3.3
Non-metallic minerals	100.0	99.6	102.5	98.4	-0.3	1.0
Basic metals	100.0	80.1	75.7	70.6	-3.1	-10.1
Metallic products, machinery	100.0	95.1	103.5	103.9	2.2	-3.2
Other	100.0	89.3	102.4	103.9	3.9	-2.0
"Maquiladora"	100.0	145.5	215.5	223.2	11.3	10.8

Table 1: Continued

	1985	1987	1990	1991	Annual Rate of Growth '87-'91	Jan-Jun '91-'92 (% Increase)
Output/employment						
Total	100.0	99.5	120.7	126.9	6.3	5.1
Food, beverages	100.0	96.3	116.7	118.5	5.3	0.5
Textiles	100.0	93.4	110.2	111.6	4.6	5.4
Wood	100.0	104.2	96.6	96.1	-2.0	-2.1
Paper	100.0	116.7	121.4	121.8	1.1	-3.3
Chemicals	100.0	101.6	138.8	145.4	9.4	6.4
Non-metallic minerals	100.0	99.0	102.2	107.8	2.2	8.0
Basic metals	100.0	129.5	154.7	161.6	5.7	3.0
Metallic products, machinery	100.0	93.2	125.8	144.2	11.5	10.2
Other	100.0	116.4	94.8	92.2	-5.7	10.9
"Maquiladora"	100.0	150.0	162.4	152.8	0.5	21.5

Source: Institute of Information and Statistics.

Mexico, which precludes the jumps in productivity arising from greater capital investment.

NAFTA is bound to expand the in-bond "maquiladora" industry, as the agreement will allow it to sell its products in Mexico, enabling it to raise capital investment and undertake vertical integration, with the result that productivity and wages will most likely rise. In fact, given that there is ample experience of operations in this industry and that labour on the northern border area is relatively well trained, some firms are likely to prefer expanding investment in such plants as a way of increasing output, rather than setting up new plants in a different area. In-bond plants of non-North-American origin that source materials from Asia or Europe, however, will face the barriers of relatively high regional value content requirements.

Mexicans understood from the outset that NAFTA would have to include substantive measures to liberalize investment. This was consistent with the government's policy to attract more foreign investment, despite the fact that the 1973 Foreign Investment Law limited foreign equity to a maximum of 49 percent, subject to exceptional, case-by-case rulings of the National Foreign Investment Commission (NFIC).

In 1984, the government of President de la Madrid issued guidelines on foreign investment that defined areas where majority foreign ownership would be acceptable, but this was not an automatic rule, nor was the law changed. In 1989, the government issued the first Regulations to the 1973 law. These allowed majority foreign investment in specific areas with an automatic rule, but only if six criteria were met, among them an investment ceiling of $100 million, full compensation of imports by exports, location outside the main urban areas and technology "suitable" for Mexico. In the absence of these characteristics, the 49 percent limitation and special rulings by the NFIC apply. The implementation of NAFTA will bring further changes in this legislation to allow majority foreign investment without any need for specific approval.

By contrast with trade liberalization, where Mexico made substantial progress before NAFTA negotiations were initiated, services, and particularly public utilities, remained closed to any form of foreign participation. In fact, many public utilities were nationalized and hence closed to foreign interests. Resistance to opening such sectors, however, is variable: telephones and banks were smoothly reprivatized by President Salinas' administration, even though the Constitution reserved bank ownership exclusively for the government. By contrast, electricity, the railways and petroleum probably represent higher political stakes, although grassroots desire to keep such industries under national control is far less strong than the intellectual elite in Mexico has for many years argued.

Another reason the government has been reluctant to open up services to international competition is the strength of its alliance with private Mexican business, which has resulted in the protection of many economic activities from foreign competition. This explains why Mexican business is a powerful advocate of limiting the role of foreign investment.

A third, more incidental reason for reserving services to Mexican nationals, is that in the recent reprivatization of commercial banks, airlines and the telephone company, there was an understanding, sometimes explicit, that the government would keep foreign competition away.

The Mexican government was on early alert to refuse any negotiation of foreign investment in the oil industry, including exploration and production, refining, basic petrochemicals, and distribution of oil, gas, and gasoline. It also refused to guarantee a given level of oil supplies to North America or to reduce exports and domestic sales of crude in equal proportions in case of an emergency.

Main Features of the Agreement and Their Likely Effects on Mexico

The most important sections of the agreement refer to (1) trade of goods, (2) services, (3) investment rules, and (4) general standards. References to these sections are made only to highlight issues that deserve discussion because of their controversial nature or policy implications.

Trade of Goods

Tariffs and non-tariff barriers on trade of goods will be gradually eliminated under four schedules. In the immediate tariff phase-out, Mexico eliminated tariffs on 43 percent of its imports from the United

States and 41 percent from Canada, while the U.S. opened 84 percent and Canada 79 percent to imports from Mexico.

In the five-year schedule, Mexico included 18 percent of U.S. exports and 19 percent of Canadian, while the U.S. and Canada included 8 percent. In the ten-year schedule, Mexico should open up 38 percent of its imports, while the U.S. and Canada should open up 7 percent and 12 percent respectively, an accumulated 99 percent for all parties. In 15 years, all countries will open up the final 1 percent to their partners' exports.

This liberalization deserves important qualifications. As is shown in Table 2, much of the immediate phase-out of trade barriers against Mexican products excluded those in which Mexico is more competitive, such as tuna, shrimp, roses, live plants, glass tableware, steel pipes, ceramic and refractory bricks, and diesel engines. Canada, in addition, maintained safeguards against fresh fruits and vegetables and cut flowers. The elimination of tariffs on most products of interest to Mexico takes place over 5, 10 and 15 years.

However, fortunately, tariffs in Canada and the U.S. are at present not high enough to make a substantial difference, but the schedules also reflect the pace at which non-tariff barriers will be reduced, particularly in heavily restricted sectors such as agriculture and textiles.

Agriculture

The most important aspect of NAFTA regarding agriculture is the conversion, albeit too gradual, of non-tariff barriers into tariffs and tariff-rate quotas (TRQs).[1]

For a start, one half of U.S. farm exports to Mexico will enter with zero tariff the first day of the agreement, but a longer transition will apply to more sensitive products which, ironically, are those of greatest interest to all three countries: sugar, fresh fruit and vegetables for Mexico, and grains for the U.S. and Canada.

---

1 TRQs are discussed in detail in the chapter by Thomas Grennes in this volume.

Table 2: Sample of Export Products of Interest to Mexico Tariff Phase-out Schedule

Description	Immediate elimination of tariffs	Elimination of tariffs in 5 years	Elimination of tariffs in 10 years	Elimination of tariffs in 15 years
Fresh fruits				
Avocados			USA	
Grapefruit			USA	
Lemons, limes			USA	
Melons, watermelons			USA	Can
Oranges		USA		
Pawpaws ("Papaya")			USA	Can
Pears		Can		
Fresh vegetables				
Carrots	USA		Can	
Cauliflowers and broccoli		USA/Can		
Garlic	USA	Can*		
Lettuce, fresh or chilled		USA/Can		
Mushrooms		Can*	USA	
Onions, fresh or chilled	USA	Can*		
Peppers		Can*	USA	
Potatoes		USA/Can		
Tomatoes, fresh or chilled		USA*	Can*	

Table 2: Continued

Description	Immediate elimination of tariffs	Elimination of tariffs in 5 years	Elimination of tariffs in 10 years	Elimination of tariffs in 15 years
Other Food, Beverages				
Molluscs (nes)				USA/Can*
Scallops				USA/Can*
Shrimp				USA/Can*
Tuna fish				USA/Can
Live plants				USA/Can*
Roses				USA/Can*
Beer	USA/Can			
Rum	Can		USA	
Sugar	Special			
Tobacco		Can	USA	
Cotton textiles		USA/Can		
Fabrics		USA/Can		
Apparel		USA/Can		
Others				
Non-metallic minerals	USA/Can			
Float glass	USA/Can			
Glass mirrors	USA	Can		
Glass tableware	Can	Can	USA	USA/Can
Steel pipes for oil, gas			USA/Can	
Steel rods			USA/Can	
Flat, rod steel			USA/Can	

Table 2: Continued

Description	Immediate elimination of tariffs	Elimination of tariffs in 5 years	Elimination of tariffs in 10 years	Elimination of tariffs in 15 years
Ceramic bricks			USA	Can
Refractory bricks				USA/Can
Automobiles		USA/Can	USA/Can	
Diesel engines, parts				USA/Can
Autoparts		USA/Can		
Computers	USA/Can			
Parts	USA/Can			

Notes:
nes—not elsewhere specified
*Additional restriction

Source: NAFTA Tariff Phasing (Preliminary).

U.S. agricultural exports to Mexico will enter free from any import license or non-tariff barriers from the first day of the agreement, when such barriers will become TRQs or ordinary tariffs.

The negotiation of sugar was complex, since the U.S. was given a long, 15-year period to eliminate barriers on Mexican exports. The agreement allows a duty-free entry on a quota that rises from 25,000 metric tons (over three times the size of the present quota) to 150,000 metric tons between year 1 and year 7 after the agreement, and will disappear after 15 years. Nevertheless, the quota is conditional upon Mexico becoming a surplus producer, and its size will depend on the surplus, making exporters depend on Mexico's performance rather than on their own capacity to export. In addition, the quota is relatively small, if compared with that allocated to the Philippines or the Dominican Republic of over 400,000 tons.

Mexico obtained 15 years' protection for corn and beans, but it failed to obtain free access for fresh fruits, vegetables, and cut flowers, except to the U.S. during its unproductive seasons. It would be wrong, however, to consider this insufficient access as a trade-off for the long transition obtained in grains. Mexican producers of corn and beans do not represent commercial agriculture, but are subsistence peasant farmers for whom Mexico has no way of ensuring alternative occupations. By contrast, vegetable producers in North America represent business ventures unduly subsidised by the consumer. Another contrast worth considering is that corn and beans are the basic staples of Mexico, and are therefore much more important than fresh fruit and vegetables are for the U.S. and Canada.

Mexico signed two separate agreements on agriculture with the U.S. and Canada, which illustrates the difficulties for free trade in this area. The agreements contain an excessive number of qualifications and exceptions, but are still a great improvement over the present multilateral system. In fact, the conversion of non-tariff barriers into tariffs and TRQs is probably the model for the liberalization of European and Asian agricultural trade.

Automobiles

The only products eligible for free trade are those that meet a 62.5 percent rule of origin for passenger cars and light trucks, as well as engines and transmissions for such vehicles, and a 60 percent rule for other vehicles and auto parts based on a net cost formula.[2] This is a high rule that provides excessive protection for regional industry.

As was expected from this negotiation, the Mexican Automotive Industry Decree, which has evolved from numerous decrees since 1962 with the aim of developing a Mexican autoparts industry and eventually forcing firms to export, will be eliminated over 10 years. This is a very long and generous transition, which Mexican industry may not have to fully use. In addition, there is a reservation of market share for the Mexican autoparts industry for no less than 34 percent of total costs, and a limit of 49 percent on foreign investment in "national supplier" firms during the first five years.

---

2 See the chapters in this volume by Jon Johnson and Peter Morici for details about rules of origin and other changes affecting the auto sector.

The high rule of origin will be the greatest impediment to investment from third countries, which Mexico had hoped to attract. That is, importing the cabin and the transmission of a vehicle from Europe or Japan would often exceed 55 percent of the cost and thus disqualify the vehicle from free trade. The over-protective rules apply not only to cars, but also to engines and transmissions, while a 60 percent rule remains for all other parts. Producers from outside the region would therefore have to effect a substantial relocation of production in order to achieve the requisite regional content. Relocation on such a scale would be difficult for companies whose competitive strength is based on world sourcing programs, as in the case of world-class auto industry, and particularly when the Mexican market is not yet big enough to qualify.

Mercedes Benz, for example, last year announced investments in Mexico to assemble cars. Its plan is to produce only for the domestic Mexican market: 300 cars in 1993 and 500 in 1994. The limited scope and scale of this investment could have been expanded with a lower rule of origin. By contrast, the announced BMW investment in the U.S. is world-scale and oriented to capturing domestic demand in the world's largest single-country market.

Mexico will undoubtedly benefit from the investment made here by North American producers, but it will not necessarily become a global producer. The competitiveness of its industry will rather be determined by the competitiveness of North American producers.

But if the U.S. adopted a protectionist stance in pressing for a high rule of origin, so did Mexico in negotiating a period as long as 10 years for eliminating its auto-industry decree. This decree establishes national content requirements and export-performance to offset imports by car producers, regulations which were originally adopted under an import-substitution strategy, now long abandoned.

It was also wrong to maintain restrictions on foreign investment in autoparts for five years, during which time it should not exceed 49 percent of equity in "national supplier" firms, since, at the same time, a market share was being reserved for Mexican producers. Such a restriction is unwise because the autoparts industry badly needs new technology and capital in order to keep up with the expanding operations of car producers. International autopart firms will be discouraged from investing in this industry when they cannot control operations. As for the share of the market reserved for national suppliers, it seems unnecessary to add Mexican protection to the North American protection already granted by the high rules of origin and the 5- and 10-year tariff phase-outs. That is, the 60 percent rule on autoparts other than engines and transmissions is high enough, so that it is excessive to reserve market share as well.

Other Industries

In textiles, the transition period for eliminating most tariffs and non-tariff barriers was 10 years, but the tariff phase-out is almost irrelevant next to the complex system of rules of origin, quotas, TRQs, and different growth rates afforded to some quotas. A rule of origin called "yarn forward" will force producers to use North American yarns, while another, called "fibre forward," will force them to use materials made from North American fibres. In addition, there is a provision to review rules of origin before 1998 and to consult on the adoption of different rules and adjustments of TRQ levels.

This system of trade contains too high a degree of *ad hoc* management to be a good starting point for a competitive regional industry. Although Mexico is likely to attract North American investment to increase its exports and take advantage of production niches, it will still be operating under a heavily administered system whose rules could change.

The negotiation of the financial sector brings competitive pressures to bear on the newly reprivatized commercial banks, some of which will need time and resources before becoming modern and efficient concerns. In this case, however, it is clear that Mexico's interests lie not in protecting commercial banks, but in ensuring sound financing costs for industry. Banks in Mexico in general enjoy much higher spreads between funding and lending interest rates than is normal in western countries, to the disadvantage of Mexican borrowers.

Mexico will benefit from the access granted to foreign financial institutions firstly because they bring more competition which will exert downward pressure on interest-rate spreads, and secondly because of the more rapid modernization of finance for Mexican industry. It is, in fact, hard to see how an agreement with such important implications for Mexican industry could have been signed without opening the financial sector.

There is, however, a potential danger in the too rapid growth of credit to the economy, if this is pushed by competitive forces and the greater innovative capacity of foreign institutions, as it could fuel asset-price inflation and a consumer boom. This is a common experience in countries that liberalize their financial sector and is amply documented,[3] a situation which calls for strengthened regulations and cautious monetary policy.

Telecommunications

NAFTA failed to open up cross-investment opportunities in basic telecommunications; it only regulates access to public networks for those users who provide enhanced telecommunications services or intra-corporate communications. This partial opening is insignificant next to the restrictions maintained in the sector of basic telecommunications where considerable consumer gains were forgone, especially for Mexico, where the telephone system is expensive and inefficient.

The importance of a competitive telephone system for industry is paramount, as communications and data transmission between markets is ever more intense. Mexican exporters are at a disadvantage and will remain so until Teléfonos de México (Telmex), the sole private provider of such services, improves its technology and service. But under conditions of high growth in demand, substantial capital spending to be undertaken and the pressing need to control costs, there is every incentive to direct capital not to service improvement, but to new capacity, which raises cash flow and profits, while prices are also raised. Only competition can correct this situation, and for this reason it is a pity that NAFTA failed to open up this sector.

---

3 John Muellbauer and Anthony Murphy, "Is the UK Balance of Payments Sustainable?" *Economic Policy*, No. 11, Cambridge, October 1990; and Adrian Blundell-Wignall and Frank Browne, "Macroeconomic Consequences of Financial Liberalisation: A Summary Report," OECD Department of Economics and Statistics, Working Paper No. 98, Paris, February 1991.

An early opening would have provided relief to industry, since at present its costs are ominous, partly because of high rates, but mainly because of frequent transmission failures, which oblige users to make repeated calls. Since Telmex ignores most complaints from consumers, as is amply documented in the Mexican press, ironically this is a rare case where service failure boosts sales for the supplier.

Energy

NAFTA was not expected to open up the energy sector in Mexico, but this does not alter the fact that the oil industry badly needs a dramatic change that can only be facilitated by greater competition and freer international trade of products.

Mexico acquiesced only to opening the petrochemicals industry, whose "primary" sector has always been reserved to Pemex. NAFTA removed barriers to foreign investment in this industry, which the Government of Mexico was doing anyway, as it has insufficient resources to finance its development. Thus, Pemex will no longer produce petrochemicals; what passes for them, and are known as "basic" products, are in fact petroleum and gas by-products. Nonetheless, it remains to be seen whether this industry will attract foreign investment, since U.S. industry is highly efficient and integrated, has large surpluses, and can now export freely to Mexico. In addition, any large investment in Mexico requires an explicit commitment by Pemex to guarantee the delivery of the feedstock raw material, something which it has been systematically unable to do. It therefore appears that Mexico's opening of the petrochemicals industry came too late to be attractive to foreign capital.

The entire agenda of oil-industry modernization is left pending for the Mexican government to address at a later date. It would be in Mexico's interests to proceed with a radical transformation and the opening of exploration and production to private investment, including to foreigners, because higher growth under NAFTA will cause increased demand pressures and should be reflected in a growing trade deficit of oil and derivatives.

Services

The chapter on services is one of the richest sections of the agreement. It opened up various sectors of the Mexican economy, to the long-term advantage of the Mexican people. First of all comes transportation. In 6 years Mexico and its partners will grant each other access to cross-border trucking services, and in 7 years Mexico will allow 51 percent North American investment in bus and trucking companies providing international cargo services, taking this to 100 percent over 10 years.

The principle that applies to services is that of national treatment. There was also a commitment to grant most-favoured-nation treatment to NAFTA partners and to remove the legal residence obligation for those who provide services. There were also agreements on the criteria for professional competence in the three countries, and a mechanism for the mutual recognition of licenses and certifications.

Investment Rules

This section was also a breakthrough for Mexico's otherwise restrictive rules, in particular the 1973 Law to Promote National Investment and Regulate Foreign Investment. NAFTA also rules out "performance requirements" and requirements for minimum export or domestic content, domestic sourcing, or technology transfer.

NAFTA introduces three new elements that bring Mexican policies more into line with a global economy. These are: (1) a mandate to guarantee currency convertibility at market rates; (2) a prohibition on expropriating NAFTA investors except for a public purpose, on a non-discriminatory basis, and with compensation paid without delay and at fair market value with applicable interest; and (3) the option for the investor to resort to investor-state binding arbitration or the country's domestic courts in order to obtain monetary damages. The latter is also a substantial improvement, as it can save investors the complex network of Mexican litigation which is often extremely lengthy and costly. Rather than a concession to the U.S., this is an improvement on the present legal regime, where investors (both foreign and national) lack guarantees of appropriate arbitration, since the Mexican Judicial Power is not sufficiently independent from the Executive. An example of bad arbitration is the land expropriation carried out by President Echeverría in north-west Mexico in November 1976, compensation for which was still being paid in 1991. Another is the commercial bank nationalization by President López Portillo in November 1982, which first-instance courts considered a violation of the Constitution, until they were overruled by the Supreme Court in a controversial political decision.

Likely Effects of NAFTA on Mexico's Economy

The agreement will have two main economic effects on Mexico. One is on the macroeconomy, in particular higher growth potential and, *ceteris paribus*, a widening trade deficit. The other is on the restructuring of economic activity.

In the macroeconomy, the agreement produces its main effects via two mechanisms: (1) lifting the rate of investment as producers want to upgrade plant and equipment; and (2) increasing Mexican exports and incomes.

Given the effect on investment, NAFTA brings certain economic benefits to Mexico independently of the pace at which it facilitates access for Mexican exports; but the likely combination of the two effects should result in a higher rate of GDP growth than without NAFTA. That the increase in investment precedes the agreement is quite clear in Chart 1, where gross fixed investment per unit of manufacturing output and per worker is shown to rise steadily, despite tight monetary policy and high interest rates.

Table 3 comes from a revision of an estimate made two years ago to measure the impact of NAFTA on the macroeconomy.[4] In this update, a growing trade deficit is caused above all by high import growth, whose rate is assumed to be reasonably consistent with trends observed in recent years. For this reason, the deficit on current account should continue to deteriorate and bring pressure to bear on international reserves, even when high levels of foreign capital inflows are assumed. The important implication here is that the magnitude of such inflows

---

4 Rogelio Ramirez De la O, "A Mexican Vision of North American Economic Integration," in Steven Globerman, ed., *Continental Accord: North American Economic Integration*, Vancouver: The Fraser Institute, 1991.

Table 3: Macroeconomic Estimates for Mexico under NAFTA

	Historical		Estimate			
	1990	1991	1992	1993	1994	Assumption
GDP growth (%)	4.4	3.6	2.8	4.0	6.0	Steady growth
Gross fixed investment growth (%)	12.3	9.6	8.5	12.0	16.0	Higher growth
Manufacturing output growth (%)	5.1	3.9	2.0	4.5	6.5	Recovery
Imports of goods ($ Billion)	31.3	38.2	48.0	58.8	70.6	Moderate growth (23%)
Imports of services ($ Billion)	20.9	20.9	21.0	24.2	27.8	Moderate growth (15%)
Exports of goods ($Billion)	26.8	27.1	29.5	34.0	40.0	13% growth
Manufactures ($Billion)	14.0	16.0	17.6	21.1	25.3	20% growth
Exports of services ($Billion)	18.3	18.7	19.0	21.8	25.1	15% growth
Current account ($ Billion)	-7.1	-13.3	-20.5	-27.2	-33.3	—
Current account (% GDP)	-3.0	-4.7	-6.4	-7.3	-7.6	—
Capital account ($ Billion)	8.1	20.2	18.0	25.0	30.0	High capital inflows
Public borrowing ($ Billion)*	2.0	5.2	5.0	5.0	5.0	High capital inflows
Private capital ($ Billion)	6.1	15.0	13.0	20.0	25.0	High capital inflows
Resource gap ($ Billion)	0.0	0.0	-2.5	-2.2	-3.3	—
Change in reserves ($ Billion)**	2.2	7.8	0.0	0.0	0.0	—
Stock of reserves	9.7	17.5	15.0	12.8	9.5	Unfilled gap

*In 1990 and 1991, includes commercial bank liabilities.

**Includes a balance for errors and omissions, which are assumed to be zero in 1992-94.

Source: author's estimates.

excludes the possibility of the Mexican private sector playing the central role of financing development in the 1990s, as its foreign assets will be gradually depleted. Access must therefore be granted to foreign equity capital.

To put this estimate in perspective, Chart 2 shows a comparison of the forecast I made in 1990 with the actual deficit, which suggests that import growth has been systematically underestimated, partly owing to insufficient experience with the effects of trade liberalization. It must be borne in mind that such a forecast was then at the upper end of the range of deficit estimates. Government estimates at the end of each preceding year are shown as a reference.[5]

Thus, investment growth in Mexican industry follows a cycle of structural change, which is bound to continue with NAFTA's ratification and could accelerate when modernization reaches the large oil, electricity and infrastructure sectors. For this reason, the trade deficit will rise steadily, even if Mexican exports increase in response to the world economic recovery and to the recently created export capacity. In addition, particularly when NAFTA is ratified, rising incomes should cause import demand to rise, based on higher Mexican wages in the modern sector of the economy, combined with changing consumer habits.

Oil and electricity are expected to be back on the central stage of policy debates in Mexico. One reason for this is that their performance under the management and strategies of state-owned concerns, which have changed little since the 1970s, makes them anachronistic in a Mexican economy in rapid transformation. Politically, the Mexican government will find it increasingly difficult to justify the presence of such outdated institutions and monopolies in sectors that impinge so greatly on the productivity of Mexican industry as a whole.

Another reason is the mounting pressures on the current account of the balance of payments. The size of the trade deficit calls for additional oil exports, and in this respect closer trade relations with North America may represent a relief to Mexico rather than a pressure on its oil reserves,

---

5 See Juanita Darling, "Pact with U.S. Regarded as Boost to Mexican Wages," *Los Angeles Times*, January 9, 1991.

Chart 1

Trends in Investment and Productivity 1988-92

IQ 1988 = 100

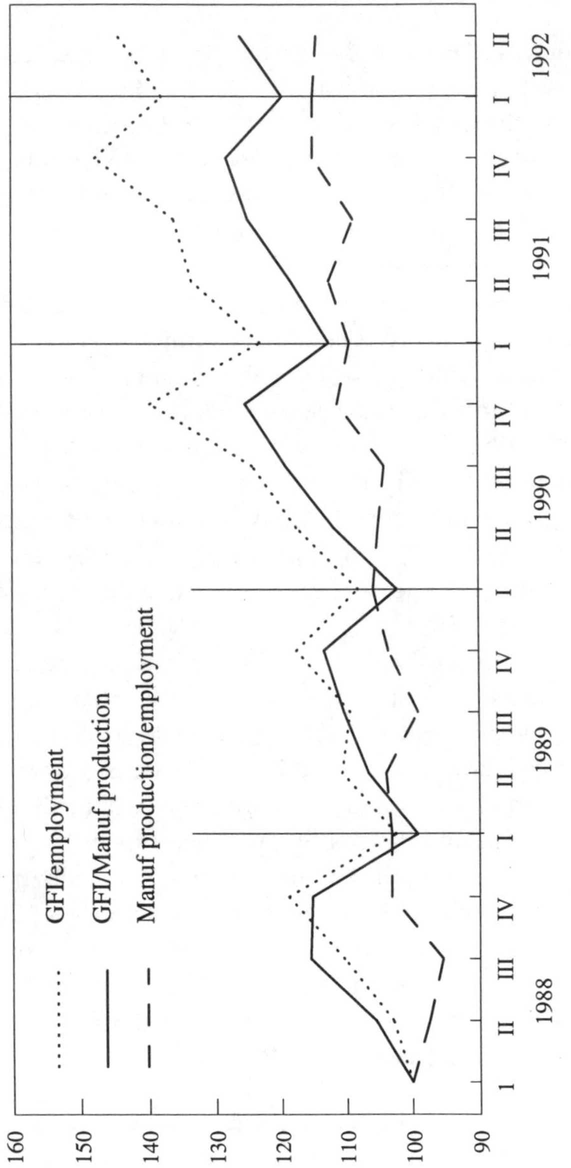

GFI = Gross Fixed Investment

Source: Bank of Mexico, Indicatores Económicos, various issues.

Chart 2

1990 Forecast and Actual Current Account

($ Billion)

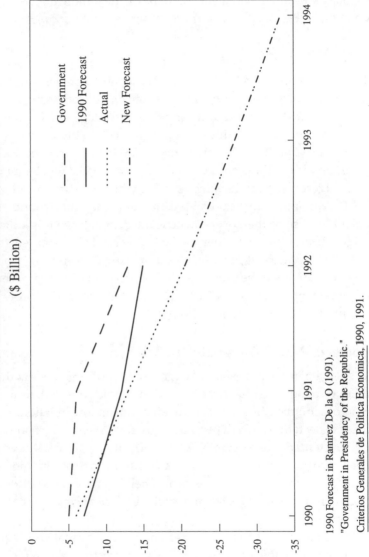

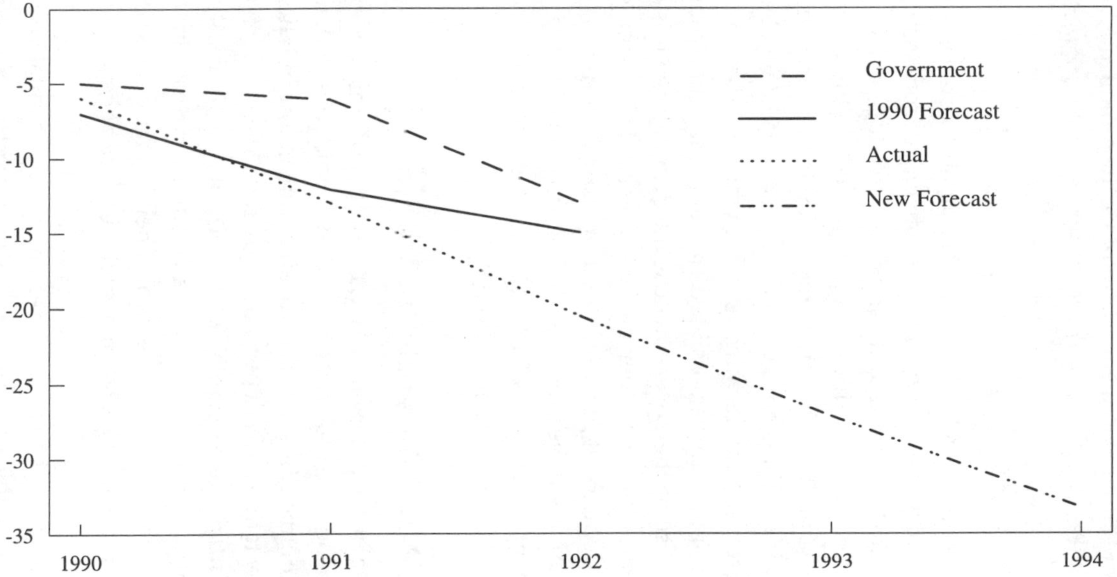

1990 Forecast in Ramirez De la O (1991).

"Government in Presidency of the Republic."

<u>Criterios Generales de Politica Economica,</u> 1990, 1991.

since increased oil output in the rest of the world may make it difficult to find markets. Apart from what Mexico could earn with additional crude exports and what it can save in refined products with higher capacity and better management, there are the capital inflows which the opening of the energy sector could generate.

Trade Diversion

Trade diversion effects from NAFTA against countries outside the region are potentially large, as can be concluded from our discussion of the auto industry, textiles and agriculture. In addition, Mexican public-sector purchases will afford a significant competitive edge to North American suppliers of capital goods for Pemex and the Electricity Commission (CFE), as one half of their procurement will be subject to a more rigorous and transparent system which will specifically protect NAFTA suppliers, to the possible disadvantage of third-country suppliers. Of course, if the government wanted to balance this situation, it might dictate that the other half be preferentially reserved for non-NAFTA suppliers. It is clear, therefore, that distortion and potential discrimination will be present until Mexico puts its entire government procurement under the same rules, so that no special protection is required for any specific supplier.

Focus of NAFTA Debates in Mexico

The debate in Mexico over NAFTA should be dominated by the fulfilment of people's expectations about well-paid jobs and an improved macroeconomic climate, reflected, above all, in low inflation. Fulfilling these expectations will depend on high investment, which in turn calls for substantial foreign capital inflows. Until now, inflows have mainly been repatriations made by Mexicans, but the increase in trade deficits will deplete their foreign assets, while their foreign debt is rising rapidly. Maintaining the inflow of capital will therefore depend increasingly on foreigners.

The central issue is that increasing foreign capital will require the elimination of the remaining investment restrictions, which would threaten the monopolistic and oligopolistic positions of large Mexican industrial groups. Demands for protection from increased foreign domination will be loud, and the government should resist them. The important point is that expanding Mexico's growth potential by allowing greater foreign investment would force a change in the historical alliance of post-revolutionary governments with private-sector groups. This is probably the justification for new anti-monopoly legislation which the Mexican government is preparing and which private groups have already started to oppose.

Opposition from local business to foreign investment liberalization has a long history in Mexico and is not based on "crowding-out" arguments, since the private sector does not have enough savings to finance the investment needed to lift the rate of growth of the economy. The opposition arises instead from the potential effect of foreign competition on the position of large Mexican groups, and thus on their prospective profits and accumulation. Their case for protection, however, has been considerably weakened, since continued economic growth calls for resources in excess of domestic savings and foreign private assets. In addition, North American economic and political interests will press hard for a meaningful opening of restricted areas, partly to reciprocate the much weaker investment restrictions in the U.S.

Another possible debate is over distribution, which is likely to deteriorate in Mexico before it improves, despite government programs to alleviate extreme poverty. One reason is that increased trade will provoke further adjustment in hurt industries, so that, while some sectors grow and employ more workers at higher wages, others will suffer and shed workers.

Another reason is that, in a regime of greater trade competition, income growth in Mexico will depend more than in the past on scarce factors which today are badly distributed: skills, access to good education and to state-of-the-art technology, and capital. Such growth would concentrate the gains from trade in fewer firms and social groups until economic expansion has been maintained for a long enough period to allow a widening of the employment base.

The debate over inequality, however, is not likely to last if the economy keeps expanding. In the longer run, income distribution should improve via the effects of trade on job creation and higher wages, but this will require that workers be trained to perform the high-productivity jobs that NAFTA will bring about, and that there be sufficient investment to create these jobs. Of course, these are not all the necessary conditions for improved income distribution, but the European experience of economic integration suggests that wages rise as productivity improves, and higher wages are a pre-condition of better income distribution. This topic, admittedly, deserves a separate discussion.

Concluding Note

Mexico benefits from this agreement because it is granted improved access to North American markets, even with the numerous qualifications for textiles, automobiles, and agriculture. But the main benefit lies in the fact that the agreement begins to scrap old industrial regulations and investment restrictions, which should help modernize the economy and give it an advantage over its Latin American partners. Unfortunately, the agreements on investment did not go far enough to plant a seed of change in the important energy sector, where bottlenecks to future growth are a result both of the character of the institutions in charge of such industries and of their regulatory and monopolistic framework. It is likely, however, that oil and electricity will return to the centre of the policy agenda soon, given their importance for the rest of the economy and for the capital account on the balance of payments.

The most important step ahead is for Mexico to make NAFTA meaningful and fully internationalize its economy by allowing foreigners to take a more important role in equity finance. In the absence of this participation, the high growth and capital formation expected from NAFTA will not have enough financial backing from capital markets.

NAFTA and the Trade in Automotive Goods

Jon R. Johnson
Goodman & Goodman[1]

CANADA, THE UNITED STATES, AND MEXICO have signed a North American Free Trade Agreement (NAFTA) with potentially major effects on the policy options open to the governments of each country. Reaching a common understanding for countries in such different circumstances was particularly difficult in the sensitive automotive sector.

The U.S. market for automotive goods is the largest of any country in the world. Historically, the U.S. market has been served by North American producers. However, in recent years, Japanese motor vehicle assemblers have made serious inroads into the market share of traditional U.S. producers. Concern with Japanese competition has driven U.S. policy with respect to its automotive sector with collateral effects on both Canada and Mexico. Certain elements in both the U.S. government and the U.S. automotive industry view Canada and Mexico as potential production platforms for Japanese and other third country

---

1 Internationally Goodman Freeman Phillips & Vineberg.

producers to penetrate the U.S. market with lightly processed goods on a preferential basis. Consequently, controlling access to the U.S. market was a priority for the U.S. negotiators.

The Canadian and Mexican negotiators had different concerns. The Canadian and Mexican governments are well aware that the U.S. automotive industry is large enough to satisfy the entire Canadian and Mexican demand for automotive products. The assembling industry in both Canada and Mexico is foreign owned. The major assemblers in Canada are the U.S. Big Three (General Motors, Ford and Chrysler), together with Honda and Toyota (Japanese), Hyundai (Korean) and CAMI (a General Motors—Suzuki joint venture). The major assemblers in Mexico are the Big Three, Nissan (Japanese) and Volkswagen (German). Proximity to the United States coupled with high levels of foreign ownership have resulted in neither Canada nor Mexico being willing to rely on market forces to assure an adequate level of domestic automotive assembling or parts production. Both have relied on government intervention to achieve that end. However, the forms of government intervention and the fundamental philosophies underlying them have been quite different. The Canadian government decided in the 1960s to permit Canada's automotive industry to be integrated with the U.S. industry, and directed its automotive policy towards ensuring that an adequate level of the integrated Canadian/U.S. industry remained in Canada. While Mexico has also been concerned that assembly and parts production take place in Mexico, the Mexican government has endeavoured to achieve this result through import substitution and export promotion. While the current Mexican regime is turning towards market solutions, the existing Mexican government automotive regulations are still incompatible with the full integration of Mexico's automotive industry into the North American one.

Canadian and Mexican automotive programs are so different that the Canadian and Mexican negotiators did not have a common cause against U.S. demands that the programs in each country be dismantled. The Canadian negotiators shared the objective of their U.S. counterparts that the Mexican market for automotive goods should be opened to much greater participation by both U.S. and Canadian producers. While the Mexican negotiators may have accepted the inevitability of the eventual dismantling of their policies, they had little sympathy with

Canada's position that Canadian automotive policies should be retained while Mexico's be scrapped.

The task of the NAFTA negotiators was to find a common ground among these conflicting concerns.

Canadian Automotive Policy and the Auto Pact

For the past thirty years, Canadian automotive policy has balanced integration of the Canadian and U.S. automotive industries with measures to ensure that an acceptable portion of the integrated industry remains in Canada. A productive Canadian automotive industry has been made possible through serving the larger U.S. market and continuing access to that market is a major Canadian policy objective. However, the by-product of integration is access by U.S. assemblers and parts producers to the Canadian market. Successive Canadian governments pursued a policy of making that access conditional on performance in Canada. The policy instruments used have been a relatively high tariff coupled with conditional duty remission.

Canada achieved both these policy objectives when it entered into the Auto Pact[2] with the United States. The Auto Pact, which came into effect in 1966, combined duty-free access to the U.S. market based on origin with conditional duty-free access to the Canadian market based upon assemblers in Canada meeting performance requirements.

For automotive goods entering the United States, the Auto Pact is a sectoral free trade agreement with the sole criterion for duty-free entry into the United States being the origin of the goods. The focus on the Canadian side of the Auto Pact is not origin but the performance in Canada by the importing assembler. The Auto Pact itself applied only to assemblers producing vehicles in Canada during the Auto Pact base year (August 1, 1963 to July 31, 1964). Those assemblers were the Big Three and Volvo, which had established an assembly operation in Nova Scotia. Following the Auto Pact coming into effect, the Canadian gov-

---

2 The full name of the Auto Pact is the *Agreement Concerning Automotive Products between the Government of Canada and the Government of the United States.*

ernment began conferring "Auto Pact status" by company specific duty remission orders on assemblers that met performance criteria similar to those contained in the Auto Pact.

To be eligible to import automotive goods duty free under the Auto Pact, the importer must be a vehicle assembler maintaining a prescribed ratio between the value of the vehicles it produces in Canada and its sales of vehicles in Canada, together with a prescribed level of Canadian value added in its Canadian production. The production-to-sales ratio has the effect of requiring that an assembler wishing to import vehicles on a duty-free basis for sale in Canada produce vehicles in Canada. However, the vehicles produced need not be the same as those sold. So long as the ratio is maintained, an assembler entitled to Auto Pact benefits is free to supply the Canadian market with vehicles imported from any other country. This flexibility permits specialization by allowing a U.S. assembler in Canada, such as General Motors, to limit the number of model lines produced in Canada and to supply the entire Canadian and U.S. markets for those model lines from Canadian plants. The Canadian value added (CVA) requirement ensures that Canadian production amounts to more than mere assembly. The production-to-sales ratio and the CVA requirement are the so-called Auto Pact safeguards. If the safeguards are met, the assembler can import new vehicles and original equipment parts duty-free from anywhere, without regard to origin.[3]

The Auto Pact served Canadian interests well. However, the arrangement was inherently unstable. At the time that the Auto Pact was entered into, the Big Three completely dominated the Canadian assembling industry. By the mid 1980s, the Asian transplants were becoming a significant factor in the North American automotive market. Toyota, Honda, Hyundai and CAMI were all in the process of establishing plants in Canada. In the mid 1960s, the disparity in the relative efficien-

---

3 Not quite anywhere. Under the Motor Vehicle Tariff Order, 1988, which covers the assemblers producing in Canada during the Auto Pact base year, the countries from which duty-free importations may be made are those entitled to the benefit of Canada's MFN Tariff. This includes most countries in the world. Tires and tubes are excluded. See SOR/88-71, *Canada Gazette Part II*, Vol. 122, No. 2, Jan. 20, 1988, p. 615.

cies of the Canadian and U.S. industries was so great that the need for safeguards for the Canadian industry in a sectoral free trade arrangement was obvious. By the mid 1980s, this disparity had disappeared, and so, from the U.S. perspective, had the rationale for the safeguards. U.S. interests were sceptical about the utility of a regime which provided for unqualified access to the U.S. market but conditional access to Canada, particularly when that conditional access was about to be extended to transplant assemblers.

Effect of the Canada-U.S. Free Trade Agreement

In the Canada-U.S. Free Trade Agreement (FTA), which came into effect on January 1, 1989, Canada surrendered its future ability to use duty remission as a means of ensuring performance in Canada in return for assurance that duty-free access to the U.S. market would continue. Like the Auto Pact, the FTA provides for duty-free access for Canadian automotive goods to the U.S. market based solely on origin, but replaces the Auto Pact origin rule with the FTA rules of origin. The proposition that the FTA would provide more secure access to the U.S. market is based on two factors. First, the U.S. government always regarded the Auto Pact and its safeguards as a transitional arrangement, whereas the FTA was viewed as a long-term arrangement. Second, the free trade arrangement under the FTA is bilateral and applies to all goods as opposed to being unilateral and sectoral as under the Auto Pact. Many sectors of the U.S. economy would acquire a vested interest in the continued existence of FTA, making its cancellation much more difficult.

However, the FTA weakened existing Canadian programs in respect to its automotive industry and foreclosed certain future courses of action. The Auto Pact functions through duty remission, and without duty to remit, there is no incentive to meet the safeguards. The bilateral elimination of duties on all goods under the FTA will be complete by January 1, 1998, following which U.S. automotive goods will enter Canada duty-free solely on the basis of origin and without regard to whether Auto Pact safeguards are being met. Also, while the FTA permits duty remission under the Auto Pact and Canada's Auto Pact based duty remission orders to continue in perpetuity, Canada surrendered its ability to extend the program. While an exception was made for CAMI, the other transplants in Canada, Toyota, Honda and Hyundai will never be permitted to receive Auto Pact status.

The FTA requires the elimination of export-based and production-based duty remission orders which have been issued to various assemblers in Canada. Most notably, the production based duty remission orders granted to Honda, Toyota and Hyundai, which tie duty remission to CVA in domestic production of vehicles, must be eliminated by January 1, 1996.

Canada entered the NAFTA negotiations with its policy options curtailed by the FTA. However, the Auto Pact was still perceived as a significant element in Canadian automotive policy and the Canadian negotiators had a strong mandate to preserve it.[4]

The Canadian and Mexican Automotive Industries

The Canadian automotive industry is integrated with that of the United States. The Canadian industry has a strong assembling sector which is a consistent net exporter of finished vehicles to the United States. However, the Canadian parts sector is weaker, especially in high value added items such as engines, transmissions and body stampings.

The Mexican automotive industry is partially integrated with the North American industry. Many maquiladoras, Mexico's in-bond manufacturing plants, are owned by U.S. assemblers[5] and parts producers, and produce mainly low-cost labour-intensive items such as wiring harnesses and radios. Most of their production is exported to the United States or Canada.[6] While the maquiladoras are integrated with the U.S.

---

4 For a more detailed discussion of the effects of the FTA on the Auto Pact, see Jon R. Johnson, "The Effect of the Canada-U.S. Free Trade Agreement on the Auto Pact," in Maureen Appel Molot, ed., *Driving Continentally*.

5 See *The Mexican Auto Industry: A Competitor for the 1990's*, a study completed by the Automotive Parts Manufacturers Association in September, 1990 (the "APMA Study"). According to the APMA Study, General Motors owns 30 maquila plants with more than 30,000 employees. See p. 72.

6 Automotive parts production comprises about 39 percent of all maquiladora production. See *The New North American Order—A Win-Win*

automotive industry, they are not integrated with the rest of the Mexican automotive industry. Assemblers in Mexico produce engines in world-scale plants[7] for both the U.S. and Canadian markets.[8] Export plants such as the Ford plant at Hermosillo achieve high levels of productivity.[9]

However, assemblers' plants in Mexico are generally at least a decade behind plants in Canada and the United States,[10] and Mexican assembly costs are estimated as exceeding international costs by between 10 and 15 percent.[11] The assemblers cannot justify making the capital expenditures to upgrade because of the short production runs involved in serving the Mexican market and because the use of Mexican parts resulting from meeting content requirements makes the Mexican produced vehicles uncompetitive for export.[12] The Mexican auto parts

---

Strategy for U.S.-Mexico Trade, Clyde V. Prestowitz, Jr., Robert B. Cohen with Peter Morici and Alan Tonelson, p. 81. Maquiladoras are mostly foreign owned. While some maquiladora production can enter the Mexican market, most is exported to the United States.

7 James P. Womack, "The Mexican Motor Industry: Strategies for the 1990's," *MIT International Motor Vehicle Program International Policy Forum*, May 1989, p. 8.

8 Chrysler at Toluca and Saltillo, Nissan at Cuernavaca, Volkswagen at Puebla, Ford at Chihuahua and General Motors at Ramos Arizpe and Toluca. See APMA Study pp. 48-9, 51, 60, 71 and 72.

9 Womack, J., D.T. Jones, and D. Roos (1990), *The Machine that Changed the World*, p. 265.

10 Mark Scheinman, "Corporate Strategy, Globalization and the FTA: Mexico's New Role," a paper presented at a research workshop on "The Auto Industry: Responding to a Changing North American Trade Environment," sponsored by the Centre for Trade Policy and Law, Carleton University, October 3-4, 1991, p. 8.

11 Miguel Angel Olea, "The Mexican Automotive Industry in the NAFTA Negotiations," a paper presented at a research workshop on "The Auto Industry: Responding to a Changing North American Trade Environment, sponsored by the Centre for Trade Policy and Law, Carleton University, October 3-4, 1991, p. 16. The figure given for trucks is 20 percent.

12 The Hermosillo plant was established under a provision of the 1983 Automotive Decree that permitted an assembler to produce a line of

sector is protected and generally not competitive. These sectors of the Mexican automotive industry have not been integrated into the North American industry.

The Auto Pact and the Automotive Decree Compared

Mexican automotive policy[13] has been implemented through a series of decrees commencing in 1962 and culminating in the current Automotive Decree, which entered into force on November 1, 1990.[14] The Automotive Decree covers all vehicles except for tractors, buses and large trucks.[15] These vehicles are covered by the Autotransportation Decree.[16]

The Automotive Decree substantially liberalized previous Mexican rules governing the automotive industry. Domestic content requirements were reduced from 60 percent to 36 percent, and imports of vehicles were permitted for the first time in decades. However, the regulatory framework imposed by the Automotive Decree is consider-

---

vehicles for export and imposed local content requirements on the basis of a sliding scale. For example, if 80 percent of the production was exported, the domestic content requirement was 30 percent (as opposed to the usual 60 percent required under the 1983 Automotive Decree). See *North American Free Trade: Issues and Recommendations* by Gary Clyde, Hufbrauer, and Jeffrey J. Schott, p. 217.

13 For a good summary of the Mexican Automotive Decrees of 1962, 1972, 1977, 1983 and 1989 (the current Automotive Decree), see Hufbrauer and Schott, *North American Free Trade—Issues and Recommendations*, pp. 215-219.

14 The full name is the *Decree for the Development and Modernization of the Automotive Industry* ("Decreto para el Fomento y Modernizacion de la Industria Automotriz") (December 1989). See NAFTA Annex 300A, Appendix B, paragraph 1.

15 Gross vehicular weight exceeding 8,864 kilograms. See Article 2:IV of the Automotive Decree for the classes of vehicles covered.

16 The full name of which is the *Decree for Development and Modernization of the Autotransportation Vehicle Manufacturing Industry* ("Decreto para el Fomento y Modernizacion de la Industria Manufacturera de Vehiculos de Autotransporte"). See NAFTA Annex 300A, Appendix B, paragraph 18.

ably more restrictive than that created by Canada's Auto Pact based duty remission orders.

The Auto Pact and the Automotive Decree both require automotive assemblers to maintain a level of national value added in their domestic production of motor vehicles.[17] However, under the Automotive Decree, only parts supplied by members of the Mexican "auto parts industry" or "national suppliers" count in the calculation of an assembler's national value added. To be considered a member of the auto parts industry, 60 percent of a producer's total sales must be parts sold to the Mexican assembling industry. To be considered as a national supplier, the producer must be supplying the Mexican automotive industry with certain defined parts. Furthermore, for the parts supplied to be eligible for inclusion in an assembler's calculation of national value added, the supplier (whether a member of the Mexican auto parts industry or a national supplier) must maintain a 30 percent level of national value added in its own production. In addition, an auto parts industry supplier must be majority Mexican owned.[18] A national supplier can be majority foreign owned, but not by the assembler it is supplying.[19] Maquiladoras are neither members of the auto parts industry nor national suppliers, and parts produced by them cannot be included in the calculation of an assembler's national value added. Under the Auto Pact, the ownership of a Canadian parts producer and the content levels it achieves in its own production are irrelevant to determining whether

---

17 The calculation of CVA under Canada's Auto Pact duty remission orders is not comparable to the calculation of national value added under the Automotive Decree. In calculating CVA, only the cost of imported components count as foreign and virtually all other costs count as domestic. Under the Automotive Decree, only the domestic content of parts supplied by the auto parts industry and by national suppliers and of parts exported by these suppliers where the exportation has been promoted by the assembler count as domestic.

18 Hufbrauer and Schott state on p. 218 that a Mexican auto parts firm must be at least 60 percent Mexican-owned. However, see NAFTA Annex I—Mexico, p. I-M-33, which describes the relevant restriction as requiring 51 percent ownership.

19 See Hufbrauer and Schott, p. 218.

the parts supplied to an assembler are to be included in the assembler's CVA calculation.

Under the Automotive Decree, assemblers must maintain positive trade balances.[20] An assembler's ability to import new vehicles is determined by the amount of its extended trade balance (its trade balance modified by further adjustments, including a negative adjustment if the assembler fails to meet the content requirement).[21] Currently, an assembler in Mexico needs two units of positive value in its extended trade balance to import one unit of value of new vehicles. For 1994 and years following, the two units of positive value in the trade balance are reduced to 1.75. Furthermore, imports of new vehicles can comprise only 15 percent of total number of vehicles an assembler sells in Mexico. For 1993 and years following, this percentage increases to 20 percent. Restricting imports to a certain percentage of vehicles sold in Mexico

---

20 An assembler's trade balance is the sum of the foreign trade exchange value of exports of automotive products plus exports of parts and components that it promotes minus the value of direct and indirect imports of parts and components that a manufacturer incorporates into vehicles produced in Mexico for sale in Mexico. The formula is set forth in rule 9 of the Acuerdo que Determina Reglas para la Aplicación para Fomento y Modernización de la Industria Automotriz (the "Auto Decree Implementing Regulations").

21 Under the content requirement, the assembler's national value added from suppliers (i.e. the total invoicing to the assembler for parts and components supplied by national suppliers and the auto parts industry minus imports incorporated in parts and components acquired from national suppliers and the auto parts industry plus exports "promoted" by the assembler minus imports incorporated in exports promoted) (VANp) divided by the assembler's total national value added (i.e. the assembler's production in Mexico for sale in Mexico plus its trade balance) (VANt) must equal at least 36 percent. If VANp is less than 36 percent of VANt, the negative adjustment equals the excess of VANt over VANp/0.36. The other adjustments are transfers of trade balances from other assemblers plus net trade balances of maquiladoras controlled by the assembler (up to an amount equal to 20 percent of the assembler's direct and indirect imports) plus 30 percent of its investment in fixed assets plus its unused entitlement to import vehicles carried forward from previous years. The formula is set forth in rule 8 of the Auto Decree Implementing Regulations.

makes it impossible for an assembler in Mexico to specialize in the same manner as is possible under the Auto Pact for an assembler in Canada.

The Autotransportation Decree, which took effect on January 1, 1990 and covers buses and heavy trucks, is less restrictive. Assemblers are subject to trade balancing requirements, and during a transition period which expires for all vehicles by 1993, there is a 40 percent national value-added requirement.[22]

The Mexican negotiators were well aware that both the U.S. and Canadian negotiators had as an objective the complete elimination of the Automotive Decree and the Autotransportation Decree over a period of time. The Canadian position was complicated by the strong mandate given to its negotiators to preserve the Auto Pact. The Mexican objective in the negotiations was not to preserve the Automotive Decree or the Autotransportation Decree, but to extend the elimination over as long a period as possible.

Provisions of NAFTA

NAFTA contains the following provisions affecting automotive goods.

1. Elimination of tariffs on all automotive goods by January 1, 2003.
2. New rules of origin.
3. Continuance of the Auto Pact and Canada's duty remission program based on Auto Pact principles.
4. Phasing out of the Automotive Decree and other Mexican restrictions.
5. Treatment of Mexican-produced vehicles as "domestic" under the U.S. Corporate Average Fuel Economy ("CAFE").
6. Elimination of restrictions on the importation of used cars.

---

22 See Hufbrauer and Schott, p. 219.

Tariff Elimination under NAFTA

NAFTA will eliminate tariffs on all automotive goods traded among Canada, the United States and Mexico.

Complexities of Trilateral Duty Elimination

Tariff elimination under NAFTA will be more complex than under the FTA. Elimination of tariffs between the United States and Canada will continue on the FTA schedule to completion for all goods by January 1, 1998. However, tariff elimination on goods traded between Canada and Mexico and between the United States and Mexico will not commence until January 1, 1994 and, in the case of many automotive goods, will not be completed until January 1, 2003.

Many goods from Mexico are currently entitled to the benefit of Canada's General Preferential Tariff (GPT) and the U.S. Generalized System of Preferences (GSP). The Canadian and U.S. NAFTA tariff elimination schedules, as they apply to goods from Mexico, will use these rates as base rates.

Only "originating" goods will be entitled to preferential treatment under NAFTA. Origin will be determined in accordance with the NAFTA rules of origin. However, to be eligible for treatment under the FTA Schedule, an automotive good entering Canada will have to satisfy the NAFTA rules of origin applied as if Mexico were not a Party.[23] Similarly, to be eligible for treatment under the NAFTA schedule based on Canada's GPT rate, an automotive good entering Canada will have to satisfy the NAFTA rules of origin applied as if the United States were not a Party.[24] If the good satisfies the NAFTA rules of origin but neither

---

23 See NAFTA Annex 302.2(4). Mexican value added of up to 7 percent of the transaction value of the good is permitted.

24 See NAFTA Annex 302.4(5). U.S. value added of up to 7 percent of the transaction value of the good is permitted.

of these conditions apply,[25] the good will receive either the less favourable of FTA or NAFTA GPT based treatment or, in the case of a few automotive goods, treatment under a schedule based on Canada's most-favoured-nation rate of duty.[26]

U.S. Customs will distinguish between originating goods entitled to FTA treatment and those entitled to treatment under its NAFTA schedule. Rather than selectively applying the NAFTA rules of origin, the United States will distinguish between goods of Canada (eligible for FTA treatment) and Mexico (eligible for NAFTA treatment) on the basis of whether the good is eligible to be marked as a good of Canada or Mexico in accordance with the NAFTA marking rules.[27] There is no third category for joint production goods.

Elimination of U.S. Duties

Under NAFTA, tariffs on vehicles other than trucks and most automotive parts entering the United States will be eliminated forthwith upon NAFTA becoming effective on January 1, 1994. As a result, producers of these goods in Mexico will enjoy the same duty-free access to the U.S. market as Canadian producers, and Canadian assemblers and parts producers will no longer have this comparative advantage over their Mexican counterparts. The comparative advantage is not significant in respect to these goods.[28]

---

25 For example, an auto part in a semi-finished condition could be sent from the United States to a maquiladora plant for finishing. Unless the Mexican value added amounts to less than 7 percent, the auto part will not be eligible for FTA duty treatment. This good might be called a "joint production" good.

26 See NAFTA Annex 302.2(6).

27 See NAFTA Annex 302.2(10). Presumably the difference in treatment is because mixed U.S.-Mexican production will be a common occurrence while mixed Canadian-Mexican production will be relatively uncommon. While criteria for the marking rules are set forth in NAFTA Annex 312, the rules themselves have yet to be established.

28 Passenger vehicles are subject to duties of 2.5 percent. Vehicles other than trucks are subject to low rates of duty. Most parts are subject to duties of 3.1 percent. There is no GSP rate for most vehicles entering the United

U.S. tariffs on light trucks are being cut from 25 percent to 10 percent on January 1, 1994 and are then being reduced by 2.5 percent each year, with elimination complete by January 1, 1998.[29] U.S. tariffs on heavy trucks[30] are being phased out in ten equal stages, with elimination complete by January 1, 2003. The comparative advantage that Canadian assemblers have over their Mexican counterparts is significant with these vehicles, because the U.S. tariff being eliminated is 25 percent.[31]

Canadian Duties on Mexican Automotive Goods

With a few significant exceptions, Canada will not be granting immediate duty-free access to Mexican automotive goods. Tariffs on passenger vehicles will be reduced immediately by 50 percent and the remaining tariff will be eliminated in nine equal annual stages, with complete elimination on January 1, 2003. Tariffs on trucks with a gross vehicle weight not exceeding five tonnes will be reduced by 50 percent and the remainder will be eliminated in four equal annual stages. Tariffs on other trucks, truck tractors, and buses, will be eliminated over ten equal stages.

Canadian tariffs on automotive goods from Mexico will be eliminated over a variety of time periods. Tariff elimination will be immediate on some parts, while tariffs on others will be eliminated over five or ten stages. Tariffs on a number of parts which were being eliminated in ten stages under the FTA for goods from the United States (with complete elimination by January 1, 1998) will, under NAFTA for goods from Mexico, be eliminated in five stages with complete elimination by

---

States, and the MFN rate of 2.5 percent applies. There are some exceptions, such as public transportation type motor vehicles, which already enter the United States duty-free from Mexico under the GSP. Many parts from Mexico already enter the United States duty-free under the GSP.

29 See U.S. tariff subheadings 8704.21 and 8704.31. These are trucks with a gross vehicle weight of under 5 tonnes.

30 See U.S. tariff subheadings 8704.22, 8704.23, 8704.32 and 8704.90.

31 See U.S. tariff item 9903.87.00.

January 1, 1999.[32] Producers of these parts in Mexico will be in a position *vis à vis* the Canadian market which is substantially on a par with their U.S. counterparts, although the practical effect for these producers is negligible given that the vast majority of parts from both Mexico and the United States already enter Canada duty free under the Auto Pact. Tariffs on most engines will be eliminated immediately under the NAFTA schedule. Mexico is a significant exporter of automobile engines to Canada.[33]

Canadian tariffs on Mexican parts are not very high. For example, Canada's GPT rate on passenger automobiles is 6 percent. Under NAFTA, this will be reduced immediately to three percent, which will then be eliminated over nine equal annual stages. The base rate for most Mexican-produced parts will be in the 6 percent range.

Mexican Duties on Canadian Automotive Goods

The elimination of Mexican tariffs on vehicles imported from Canada will closely parallel the staging categories for the elimination of Canadian tariffs. Elimination of Mexican tariffs on Canadian parts will take place over a variety of time periods. In some cases, these will parallel those for the elimination of Canadian tariffs, but for many parts they

---

32 For example: locks, distributors, starter motors, generators, lighting or visual equipment, cassette decks, junction boxes, car bodies, safety seat belts, body stampings, mufflers and exhaust pipes, steering wheels, steering columns and steering boxes.

33 In 1991, the value of engines imported into Canada under tariff subheading 8407.34 (engines, spark-ignition reciprocating, displacing more than 1000 cc) was $204,548,000, of which only $3,393,000 (or 1.66 percent) was dutiable. The remaining engines would have been subject to duty had it not been for the Auto Pact. Once NAFTA enters into force, engines from Mexico will enter Canada duty free under the NAFTA schedule. Unless imported under the Auto Pact, engines falling under this subheading from the United States will be subject to duty until January 1, 1998. There are a few other parts upon which complete duty elimination will occur under NAFTA on January 1, 1994 but not under the FTA until January 1, 1998. These include ball bearings and windshield wipers and defrosters.

will not. All tariffs will be eliminated by January 1, 2003. As Mexican duties are generally quite high, Canadian and U.S. produced vehicles and parts will be significantly more competitive in the Mexican market.

The New NAFTA Rules of Origin

As indicated above, controlling access to the U.S. market was a priority for the U.S. negotiators. The U.S. negotiators wished to limit duty-free access by tightening the rules of origin. The task of the Canadian negotiators was to place reasonable limits on the tightening. Given the experience with the FTA rules, the Canadian negotiators placed a high priority on limiting the scope for unilateral and arbitrary application of the rules by U.S. Customs.

Origin under the Auto Pact

Under the old Auto Pact origin rule, the landed value of imported parts could not exceed 50 percent of the appraised duty value of the finished vehicle entering the United States. The test was applied on each vehicle with no averaging. The test required tracing of parts to the point that they were imported into Canada or the United States. Everything besides the landed value of imported parts included in the duty-appraised value counted in the producer's favour.

The FTA Rules

The Auto Pact origin test was never contentious so long as the only significant assemblers in Canada were the Big Three. However, at the time that the FTA was being negotiated, the Asian transplants had all established plants in Canada. The Auto Pact rule was seen as being too generous and the U.S. FTA negotiators pressed for a stricter rule of origin. The FTA content requirement counts only production costs and not other costs towards territorial value.[34] However, the FTA content requirement accounts for materials when acquired by the producer and no tracing of materials back through chains of suppliers is required. If

---

34 The expression "territorial" is used to convey the idea of "domestic," as if Canada and the United States were a single entity.

the producer acquires a material that is originating (determined by applying the FTA rules of origin to the material), the producer receives territorial credit for its entire price, and the value of any imported sub-materials is "rolled up" into that price. Similarly, if the material is non-originating, its entire price counts as non-territorial, and any territorial value added it may contain is "rolled down."[35]

Problems with the FTA Rules

The FTA content requirement was viewed as unsatisfactory by both Canada and the United States. The U.S. Congress was unhappy with the threshold percentage of 50 percent and required the President to negotiate a 60 percent threshold. Manipulation of roll-up was viewed in the United States as a means whereby the transplants in Canada could export vehicles into the U.S. market which technically met the origin rule but in fact contained low levels of true Canadian or U.S. value added. U.S. concerns with the FTA rule of origin were aggravated by the huge U.S. trade deficit in automotive goods with Japan.

The Canadians viewed the matter differently. The administration by U.S. Customs of the FTA rules of origin was considered arbitrary. There were endless (and, from a Canadian viewpoint, needless) disputes over what costs counted as production costs. The Canadian perception of U.S. arbitrariness culminated in a ruling by U.S. Customs in respect to Honda that only the costs of assembling operations performed with respect to several major engine assemblies counted as territorial, while the cost of machining and other processing operations

---

35 While the FTA test was unclear on the point, both Canadian and U.S. Customs authorities accepted the proposition that a vertically integrated producer could claim roll-up on an originating material which it produced itself. However, because of the cryptic wording of the FTA content requirement, the authorities in the two countries could not agree on the territorial credit to be allowed. In one of the rulings with respect to Honda, U.S. Customs allowed credit only for imported sub-materials whereas Revenue Canada would have allowed credit for all sub-materials. See U.S. Customs Ruling CLA-2:R:C:M 000131 JLV, dated December 12, 1991. See also Revenue Canada Customs and Excise Memorandum D11-4-12, Guidelines paragraphs 39-40.

performed in Ohio did not count.[36] The United States was seen as trying to obtain through administration the 60 percent threshold that it had failed to obtain through negotiation.

The United States entered the NAFTA negotiations looking for a tougher content rule, through a higher threshold and restrictions on roll-up. These demands were coupled with a wide perception in the United States that Asian transplant operations in North America had to be forced to achieve higher levels of North American content. In Canada, the use of the rules of origin in this manner as an instrument of industrial policy was viewed with scepticism. The only effect of a more stringent rule of origin would be to divert transplant activity from Canada to the United States, where the U.S. domestic market could be served without complying with the rules of origin. However, the concept of a stricter rule of origin found considerable support in Canada among some constituents of the automotive industry, most notably the parts producers.

The NAFTA Rules

Goods containing imported materials are considered to originate in a country if the production of the good in that country has resulted in the "substantial transformation" of those materials into something new and different. Like the FTA rules, the NAFTA rules of origin define the required transformation primarily in terms of prescribed changes in classification, with some goods being subject to the additional require-

---

36 See U.S. Customs Service rulings CLA-2 CO:R:C:M 000155 VEA and CLA-2 CO:R:I 000160 JLV. The particular version of the FTA content requirement upon which Honda was relying uses the expression "direct cost of assembling" rather than the more usual "direct cost of processing." See FTA Annex 301.2 Interpretation, paragraph 4. Although the two expressions are both defined to mean the same thing, namely production costs, U.S. Customs interpreted the defined expression "direct cost of assembling" as excluding processing costs. While in the author's view the U.S. Customs ruling was wrong, the unusual drafting technique of using two defined expressions to mean the same thing left the opening for the restrictive ruling.

ment of a content requirement.[37] However, with vehicles and major automotive components, the required transformation is defined primarily in terms of the content requirement. The operation of the NAFTA content requirement has been described elsewhere in this book. The unique features of the content requirement applicable to automotive goods are tracing, averaging and phasing to higher thresholds.

Tracing

For passenger vehicles, small trucks and buses (together with those of their parts which are subject to a content requirement), roll-up is eliminated. The producer must trace all materials which are imported under specified tariff provisions. These tariff provisions cover a wide range of parts and components used in vehicles.[38] Suppose that an assembler of passenger vehicles purchases an engine from a local supplier and the pistons in the engine were imported by an upstream supplier. The origin of the engine would be irrelevant. The assembler would have to ascertain the upstream supplier's transaction value of the imported pistons and that amount would count against the assembler,[39] together with the

---

37 Origin can be established by the content requirement alone in certain situations in which a change in tariff classification cannot occur.

38 See NAFTA Annex 403.1 for the specified tariff provisions. For these automotive goods, the numerator of the content requirement is the producer's "net cost" minus the value of all these imported materials. The denominator is the producer's "net cost." The contentious decision which denied Honda its processing costs in respect to engine assemblies could not occur under the NAFTA rules because there is no distinction made between processing and assembling costs. However, because of tracing, Honda will be applying the content requirement in a manner completely different from what it was doing under the FTA. While the rule in the FTA which used the expression "direct cost of assembling" has been modified to make it clear that there is no distinction between processing and assembling costs, Honda will no longer be relying on that rule to qualify its motor vehicles.

39 The specified tariff provision for the pistons is 8409 (parts of engines). (See NAFTA Annex 403.1.) If the metal from which the pistons were made was imported and the pistons were produced domestically, the tracing requirement would not apply, because the tariff provision under which the metal would be imported is not specified in NAFTA Annex 403.1. The transaction value is, essentially, the duty-paid value, and is subject to

transaction value of materials imported directly by the assembler under the specified tariff provisions. The tracing requirement applies to every component or assembly purchased by the assembler. This approach is very similar to the approach under the old Auto Pact test for origin.

The NAFTA rules adopt a less stringent version of tracing in respect to larger trucks and buses and specialty vehicles. Tracing is confined to the engines and transmissions and does not extend back to the stage at which materials are imported. NAFTA Annex 403.2 breaks down engines and transmissions into their constituent materials (such as, in the case of an engine, the cast block, the cast head, the fuel nozzle, the fuel injector pump, etc.). The producer must determine whether each of these materials is originating or non-originating by applying the applicable NAFTA rule of origin. Notwithstanding whether the engine or transmission itself is originating or non-originating, the value of those constituent materials which are non-originating count against the producer, along with the value of other non-originating materials contained in the vehicle. However, there is no roll-down of territorial value added contained in the engine or transmission if the engine or transmission itself is non-originating. Normal roll-up and roll-down apply with respect to other parts of the vehicle.

Consider the example above respecting the engine and the pistons, applied to a large truck assembler. The origin of the engine is irrelevant. Pistons are included in the list in NAFTA Annex 403.2, so the assembler must ascertain whether or not they are originating. If the upstream supplier imported the pistons, they would be non-originating and their value would count against the assembler. If the upstream supplier produced the pistons locally but they were non-originating, their value (or, if the assembler elects, the value of the non-originating materials contained in the pistons) count against the assembler. The assembler must obtain sufficient information from the upstream supplier to ascertain whether the pistons are non-originating and, if so, their value or the value of the non-originating materials they contain.

---

adjustment under certain circumstances.

Averaging

Under the FTA, motor vehicle manufacturers were entitled to average their calculation over a twelve-month period on the same class of vehicles assembled in the same plant. The classes of passenger vehicles were broken down on the basis of size, with trucks and buses each forming their own class.[40] The NAFTA rules retain averaging and extend its scope. The "class of motor vehicles" has been redefined into much broader categories. For example, all passenger vehicles are in a single class, regardless of size. A vehicle producer has a number of averaging options. The producer can average over the same model line within the same class produced within the same plant, or over the same class within the same plant, or over the same model line within one of the NAFTA countries. A special averaging rule permits CAMI to average with General Motors Canada. Averaging has been extended to automotive parts. Averaging is tied to the producer's fiscal year or, in the case of an OEM parts producer, to the assembler's fiscal year.

Phasing to Higher Thresholds

The threshold percentage in the NAFTA content requirement is being increased over a phase-in period. The applicable percentage for small trucks and buses, together with their engines and transmissions, will be 50 percent until the producer's fiscal year[41] beginning on the day closest to January 1, 1998, 56 percent from then until the producer's fiscal year beginning on the day closest to January 1, 2004, and thereafter 62.5 percent. The applicable percentage for tractors, larger trucks and buses and specialty vehicles together with their engines and transmissions, as well as most parts for all types of vehicles will be 50 percent until the producer's fiscal year beginning on the day closest to January 1, 1998, 55 percent from then until the producer's fiscal year beginning on the

---

40 See FTA Article 1005(2) and the definition of "class of vehicles" in FTA Article 1006. The classes of vehicles were taken from the classes of vehicles for labelling purposes in the U.S. Corporate Average Fuel Economy regulations. See 40 CFR section 600.315-82, subparagraphs (a)(ii) to (ix).

41 The tie-in to the producer's fiscal year is because of averaging, which has been discussed above.

day closest to January 1, 2004, and thereafter 60 percent. Notwithstanding the foregoing, the applicable percentage remains at 50 percent for any five-year period for a vehicle not previously produced by the producer which is produced in a new plant, and for two years following a refit. The applicable percentage for other automotive goods is 50 percent.

As the NAFTA content requirement as applied to automotive goods is so different in concept from the FTA content requirement, the threshold percentage of 62.5 percent or 60 percent under NAFTA is not directly comparable with the 50 percent FTA threshold.

General Observations

For passenger vehicles, the NAFTA rules are a return to the old Auto Pact tracing concept. The difference will be in the manner of enforcement. The Auto Pact rule was never rigorously enforced. U.S. Customs was vigorous in its enforcement of the FTA content rule as against transplant operations in Canada. There is no reason for believing that they will be any less rigorous in the enforcement of the NAFTA rules.

The Canadian parts industry was strongly in favour of tracing, and they achieved this objective in the NAFTA rules. However, much of the burden of tracing will fall on parts producers, as they will have to provide much more detailed information to their assemblers. In one sense, this should not present a problem to parts producers in Canada because they provide similar information to assemblers in Canada which are entitled to Auto Pact benefits. However, the information they compile for Auto Pact purposes is audited by Revenue Canada. The tracing information that they will be compiling for NAFTA purposes will be audited by U.S. Customs. Mexican parts producers also provide tracing data to assemblers under the Automotive Decree.

The NAFTA rules of origin represent a compromise. An excessively strong rule of origin would have been a disincentive to the transplant assemblers to continue manufacturing for the U.S. market in Canada. The NAFTA origin requirements are more stringent than those under the FTA and, as such, represent a tightening of access to the U.S. market. However, the NAFTA rules are not nearly as stringent as some in the negotiations were demanding,[42] and there is a substantial phase-in period before the final threshold percentages apply. The NAFTA rules should also be more predictable and less open to contentious interpretations. Producers in Canada may be better off with more stringent rules that are less capable of being capriciously administered. The extent to which this will be achieved depends largely upon the degree of effort made by the NAFTA parties in ensuring that the Uniform Regulations which are to be completed by the time that NAFTA enters into force are precise and workable.

One concern with the NAFTA rules of origin as applied to automotive goods is their complexity. The FTA had one version of the content requirement. NAFTA has four.[43] Applying these different methods and auditing their application (particularly the tracing requirements) could be very difficult, especially for producers producing goods with a variety of end uses.

Effect of NAFTA on the Auto Pact and Other Policy Options

NAFTA contains provisions similar to those in the FTA prohibiting duty waivers which are conditional upon satisfying performance requirements.[44] However, Canada and the United States are expressly permitted to maintain the Auto Pact, as modified by the FTA, and Canada is permitted to maintain the Auto Pact duty-remission orders which have been issued to the recipients listed in FTA Annex 1002.1 NAFTA has, in

---

42 See, for example, Prestowitz, et al. supra at p. 69. While the threshold percentage that they recommended of 60 percent is not higher than that ultimately agreed to, the only costs which would have counted as territorial were labour and materials. Ford and Chrysler were pressing for threshold percentages in excess of 70 percent.

43 Transaction value method (cannot be used for automotive goods), normal net cost method for non-automotive goods, full tracing net cost method for passenger vehicles, etc., partial tracing net cost method for trucks, etc.

44 See NAFTA Article 304. See also FTA Article 405, which is incorporated by reference in NAFTA Annex 304.2(c) to apply as between Canada and the United States as regards measures predating NAFTA entering into force.

effect, preserved the status quo insofar as the Auto Pact and Canada's Auto Pact duty-remission orders are concerned. The two tier system is perpetuated, with the Big Three and CAMI continuing to be entitled to Auto Pact benefits and the transplants not being permitted to receive such benefits.

Effect of Duty Elimination with Mexico

An Auto Pact assembler's sole incentive to meet the Auto Pact safeguards is duty remission. If there were minimal or no duty to remit, there would be no incentive to meet the safeguards and the Auto Pact would, for practical purposes, cease to exist. Duty remission on automotive goods will continue to be relevant for automotive goods imported from the United States until 1998 and from Mexico until 2003 for most vehicles and until 1999 or 2003 for many other automotive goods.[45] However, once duty elimination under NAFTA is complete, Mexico will be added to the United States as a country from which automotive goods can be imported into Canada duty free without meeting the safeguards. The question is whether free trade with both the United States and Mexico will reduce the benefits of duty remission so significantly that the Auto Pact safeguards will be ignored.

The continuing incentive to comply with the safeguards will be to save duty on vehicles and parts imported from third countries. Assemblers entitled to Auto Pact benefits will continue to have duty-free sources of new vehicles and parts other than the United States and Mexico. This advantage cannot be made available to their counterparts in the United States or Mexico so long as these countries choose to maintain external tariffs. How meaningful this advantage is depends on the volume of vehicles and parts imported from third countries, as opposed to the United States and Mexico, and Canada's level of external tariffs. Consider the following figures for the period January to December, 1991.

45 As discussed above, engines are a significant exception.

Imports of Automotive Goods into Canada
Under Selected HS Subheadings
Period January—December, 1991 (CDN $'000s)

	Duty Free	Duty Paid	Total Imports
United States	$21,472,158	$1,297,188	$22,769,346
Mexico	1,414,925	159,019	1,573,944
Third Countries			
Japan	1,134,132	3,376,134	4,510,266
Other	909,656	996,452	1,906,108
Sum	2,043,788	4,372,586	6,416,374
TOTAL	$24,930,871	$5,828,793	$30,759,664

Source: These figures are taken from *Imports by Commodity for 1991*, published by Statistics Canada.[46]

Canada's published import statistics do not identify the basis for the duty-free treatment. Accordingly, the following analysis is based on several arbitrary assumptions. It is likely that most of the duty-free

46 The HS (or Harmonized System) Subheadings are the following: 8301.20, 8407.31, 8407.32, 8407.33, 8407.34, 8408.20, 8409.91, 8413.30, 8483.10, 8483.20, 8483.30, 8483.40, 8511.30, 8511.40, 8511.50, 8512.20, 8512.40, 8539.10, 8544.30, 8701.10, 8701.20, 8702.10, 8702.90, 8703.10, 8703.21, 8703.22, 8703.23, 8703.24, 8703.31, 8703.32, 8703.33, 8703.90, 8704.21, 8704.22, 8704.23, 8704.31, 8704.32, 8704.90, 8705.10, 8705.20, 8705.30, 8705.40, 8706.00, 8707.10, 8707.90, 8708.10, 8708.21, 8708.29, 8708.39, 8708.40, 8708.50, 8708.60, 8708.70, 8708.80, 8708.91, 8708.92, 8708.93, 8708.94, 8708.99 and 9401.20.
All the subheadings except those falling under HS headings 8701 to 8705 (which are various types of completed vehicles) are taken from the list of automotive parts listed in NAFTA Annex 403.1 for tracing purposes. The only subheadings selected from that list are those which are solely or substantially comprised of automotive goods.

imports from the United States and Mexico were made by the Big Three. Therefore, it is assumed that these imports have been made under the Auto Pact. However, a significant portion of the duty-free imports from Japan would have been made by Toyota and Honda under their production-based duty-remission orders. Some of the duty-free imports from from third countries would have been made under Canada's export-based remission orders. In the absence of better information, it is assumed that 50 percent of the imports from Japan and 75 percent of the imports from other third countries were made under the Auto Pact. Based on these assumptions, the breakdown is as follows:

Assumed Duty-free Imports under the Auto Pact (CDN $'000s)

United States	$21,472,158	
Mexico	1,414,925	
Third Countries		
Japan	567,066	(50% of 1,134,132)
Other	682,242	(75% of 909,656)
Sum	1,249,308	
TOTAL	$24,136,391	

Of the foregoing items, 88.96 percent came from the United States, 5.86 percent from Mexico and 5.18 percent from third countries. Of these items from countries other than the United States, 53.11 percent came from Mexico and 46.89 percent came from third countries.

Based on the foregoing, it is apparent that without free trade with the United States and Mexico, the incentive to comply with the safeguards is overwhelming. Assuming a rate of 9.2 percent, duty saved on $24,136,391,000 is $2,220,547,970. Even assuming a rate of 6.0 percent (Canada's GPT rate on many automotive goods), the duty saved would be $1,448,183,460.

Removing the United States and Mexico still leaves $1,249,308,000 of Auto Pact imports. Assuming a duty rate of 9.2 percent, the duty saved is $114,936,340. Assuming a rate of 6.0 percent on all the non-Japanese imports, the duty saved is $93,104,590. On the basis of these figures, it would appear that there is still a considerable incentive to earn the duty remission by meeting the safeguards. As the automotive industry in Canada evolves and expands, sourcing from third countries may increase, which would strengthen the incentive.[47] However, diversion of sourcing from third countries to Mexico would weaken the incentive. The incentive would also be weakened by Canada lowering its external tariff. If the tariff on parts were lowered to correspond to the U.S. MFN rate on most parts of 3.1 percent, the duty saved on the 1991 volume of third-country imports would be only $38,728,550.

To the extent that the foregoing assumptions underestimate duty-free imports of automotive goods being made under Canada's production and export-based duty-remission programs, the foregoing estimates of duty saved are overstated. However, there are many other tariff subheadings under which goods for use in automotive production are imported besides the subheadings used for the above tables. These were not used because they include goods imported for non-automotive purposes. Therefore, the figures in the table understate the volume of imports of automotive goods and to that extent, the above estimates of duty saved are understated.

If Canada becomes the highest cost NAFTA producer and the additional cost to an Auto Pact assembler of complying with the safeguards by assembling vehicles and sourcing parts in Canada (as opposed to assembling vehicles and sourcing parts in the United States or Mexico) exceeds the duty saved through compliance, there will be no incentive to comply.

Effect of the Elimination of Duty Drawback

The elimination of duty drawback under NAFTA will have opposing effects on the incentive to comply with Auto Pact safeguards. On the one hand, elimination of duty relief through drawback will provide an

---

47 The scope for increased third country sourcing is limited by the need to satisfy CVA and NAFTA rules-of-origin requirements.

added incentive for Auto Pact assemblers to earn duty remission through complying with the safeguards. On the other hand, the elimination of duty drawback will increase pressure to lower the external tariff on automotive goods to U.S. rates.

Under the FTA, duty drawback on exports to the United States was to have been eliminated on January 1, 1994. NAFTA postpones this until January 1, 1996. Elimination of drawback for exports to Mexico from both the United States and Canada will commence January 1, 2001. Unlike under the FTA, Canadian exporters of goods to the United States will still be entitled to drawback of the Canadian duty up to an amount equal to the duty paid on the finished goods entering the United States. There will be U.S. duty payable on goods which are in FTA staging category "C," for which duty elimination is not complete until January 1, 1998, and on goods which do not satisfy the rules of origin.

The elimination of duty drawback for exports to the United States will adversely affect the transplant assemblers in Canada. The postponement of the elimination of duty drawback by two years will be helpful, but each transplant will still be receiving some duty relief under its production-based duty waiver. Under the FTA, these must be terminated by January 1, 1996, which coincides with the NAFTA deadline for the elimination of duty drawback for exports to the United States.

The NAFTA provision allowing drawback of Canadian duty on imported parts up to the amount of U.S. duty on the exported finished good could act as a disincentive for the transplants to satisfy the rules of origin. If the Canadian duty paid on parts exceeds the U.S. duty paid on the finished vehicles going into the United States, an exporting transplant will be in the same economic position whether its goods satisfy the rules of origin or not. This is possible because U.S. MFN rates for all vehicles, except trucks, is 2.5 percent while Canadian MFN rates on most parts is 9.2 percent. This seems a perverse result, given that the whole point in having a more stringent rule of origin is to increase North American sourcing by transplants.

The only way that the Canadian government can assist the transplants when drawback is eliminated is to lower external tariffs to U.S. levels. However, as indicated above, this will further weaken the incentive for Auto Pact assemblers to comply with the safeguards.

Other Policy Options

NAFTA is much more comprehensive than the FTA in its effects on policy options open to governments. For example, the NAFTA investment chapter prohibits conferring benefits on an investor (which could be an assembler or a parts producer of any nationality) which are conditional upon meeting performance requirements.[48] In the past, Canadian governments have granted subsidies to automotive firms for the construction of plants or the development of new products. These subsidies have been conditional on meeting a number of requirements, such as achieving levels of Canadian content. These policies are precluded under NAFTA.

The Effect of NAFTA on Mexican Automotive Policies

The U.S. and Canadian negotiators achieved their objective of dismantling Mexican automotive policies, but only after lengthy phase-in periods.

The Automotive Decree

NAFTA will eliminate the Automotive Decree by 2004. Up to that time, the Automotive Decree remains in effect but a number of its restrictions are eased or eliminated.

Trade Balance

In calculating its trade balance, the assembler will be required to include only a percentage of the imported parts and components in vehicles sold in Mexico rather than the entire amount. The initial percentage will be

48 See NAFTA Article 1106(3). The prohibited performance requirements are those related to purchasing domestic goods, achieving levels of domestic content, trade balancing requirements and export requirements. However, NAFTA Article 1106(4) expressly permits conditions relating to location of production, providing a service, training and employing workers, constructing or expanding particular facilities, or carrying out research and development. The provision is silent on world product mandate requirements.

80 percent for 1994 and will be phased down in more or less equal annual amounts to 55 percent in 2003.[49] This provision will enable assemblers to import more parts and components. For example, in 1999, when the applicable percentage is 66.10 percent, the importation of 1513 units of parts and components would have the same impact on the assembler's trade balance as the importation of 1000 units under the present rules.[50] Thus by 1999, an assembler's entitlement to import parts will have increased by 51.3 percent.

New Vehicle Imports

The limitation on annual imports of new vehicles to a prescribed percentage of vehicles sold in Mexico will be eliminated. In determining the total value of new vehicles that an assembler may import, the assembler will be permitted to divide its extended trade balance by the aforementioned percentages rather than by 1.75.[51] In 1994, the applicable percentage will be 80 percent. Dividing the extended trade balance by 0.8 rather than 1.75 will increase the ability of an assembler to import vehicles by 219 percent.[52] The value of the extended trade balance (upon which the ability to import new vehicles is based) is also enhanced by the more generous trade balance calculation just described.

Content Requirement

The 36 percent national value-added requirement will be reduced to 34 percent from 1994 to 1998, to 33 percent in 1999, to 32 percent in 2000, to 31 percent in 2001, to 30 percent in 2002 and to 29 percent in 2003.

---

49 The percentages are: 80 percent for 1994, 77.2 percent for 1995, 74.4 percent for 1996, 71.6 percent for 1997, 68.9 percent for 1998, 66.1 percent for 1999, 63.3 percent for 2000, 60.5 percent for 2001, 57.7 percent for 2002 and 55.0 percent for 2003.

50 1000 is 66.10 percent of 1513.

51 NAFTA Annex 300-A.2(14).

52 In 2003, the last year of the transition period, the applicable percentage is 55 percent (or 0.55) and the ability to import new vehicles will have increased by 318 percent over what would have been the case if 1.75 had been used.

Existing producers that did not satisfy the 36 percent content requirement for the 1992 model year may use the percentage that they did achieve for that year until that percentage is higher than the prescribed percentages. Thus if the percentage achieved for the 1992 model year was 32 percent, the assembler may use that percentage until 2001.[53]

For existing assemblers, the basis for calculating the percentage of value added is the higher of the assembler's Mexican production for sale in Mexico plus its trade balance (the current basis for the content calculation, or "VANt") and the assembler's reference value for the year that the calculation is being made.[54] The reference value is the lower of the assembler's current year domestic sales, and the average of its sales for the 1991 and 1992 model years (adjusted for inflation) plus a prescribed percentage of the excess of sales in the current year over that average amount.[55] The trade balance is not included in the reference value. However, the sales include imported vehicles and not just those produced domestically, so that the reference value could be higher than VANt. If this occurs, the assembler will require a higher level of domestic Mexican value added to satisfy the content requirement than would be the case if VANt is used. This provision affords some protection to the Mexican autoparts industry, given the more lenient trade balancing requirements and the significantly enhanced capability to import new vehicles. This more stringent rule will not apply to new assemblers.[56]

The national value added required of the auto parts industry and national suppliers will be reduced from 30 percent to 20 percent. A

---

53 Only Ford achieved the required percentage in the 1992 model year. The percentage which this relieving provision permits an assembler to use is calculated on a basis which includes purchases from independent maquiladoras. Under the current Automotive Decree, these are excluded but, as indicated below, under the NAFTA rules they will be included.

54 NAFTA Annex 300-A.2(5).

55 See NAFTA Annex 300-A.2(8). "Base value" is defined in NAFTA Annex 300-A.2(27). The prescribed percentage is 65% for 1994-97, 60% for 1998-2000, and 50% for 2001-03.

56 Those beginning production of vehicles after the model year 1991. (See NAFTA Annex 300-A.2(5).)

maquiladora can now qualify as a national supplier, provided that it is not owned by the assembler that it is supplying.

Other Requirements

The ownership restriction on enterprises of the auto parts industry is to be eliminated for investors of Canada and the United States, and their subsidiaries in Mexico, by 1999. Parts produced in Mexico by suppliers owned by such investors will be eligible to be counted in the determination of national value added. An enterprise's status as an investor of Canada or of the United States is based on its having substantial Canadian or U.S. business activities and not on ultimate ownership. Thus, Canadian and U.S. transplant enterprises, as well as those of the Big Three, have status as investors of Canada or the United States.

The restriction imposed on the sales of maquiladora production into the Mexican domestic market is to be phased out over seven years. One year after NAFTA enters into force, a maquiladora may sell up to 60 percent of its previous year's exports into the domestic market. This percentage will increase in five percent increments to 85 percent in the sixth year. The restriction will be completely removed in the seventh year.

Following January 1, 2001, the NAFTA drawback rules will apply to the maquiladoras. Duty deferred on materials imported from countries other than the United States or Canada will have to be paid at the time that the goods are exported to the United States or Canada. This will have little effect on U.S. owned maquiladoras but will have a substantial effect on maquiladoras owned by investors in third countries such as Japan or Germany.

Mexico is obliged to eliminate immediately its Autotransportation Decree, which covers larger trucks and buses. However, until 1999, there will still be restrictions on the importation of these types of vehicles. Mexico may restrict the number of vehicles imported by an assembler to 50 percent of the number of vehicles produced in Mexico,[57]

---

57 See NAFTA Annex 300A, Appendix B, paragraph 20. Note that the imported vehicles must be originating.

and the importing assembler must satisfy a 40 percent national value added requirement in its Mexican production.

NAFTA contains a general prohibition of import permit systems. However, Mexico is permitted to require import permits in respect to all types of vehicles. For vehicles covered by the Automotive Decree, the permit system may continue in force for ten years, and for vehicles covered by the Autotransportation Decree, the permit system may continue for five years.

CAFE Rules

The U.S. CAFE rules impose fuel economy requirements on vehicles sold in the United States. The rules split the fleet of each assembler into a domestic fleet and imported fleet. As to whether a car line is domestic or imported depends on its meeting a 75 percent content test.[58] The two fleets are treated exactly the same but the calculations for each fleet must be made separately. For the purposes of the test, Canadian production is considered domestic but Mexican production is considered imported. NAFTA requires that Mexican value added count as domestic, just as Canadian presently does. This rule will not commence for existing assemblers (producing before model year 1991) in Mexico, the United States or Canada until after 1997, and these assemblers may elect whether to have the rule apply until 2004, at which time the rule must apply. However, for assemblers establishing in Mexico after 1991 (including assemblers such as Honda with existing operations in Canada or the United States) and assemblers not operating in North America, the rule applies from the time that NAFTA comes into force.

Prior to the completion of the NAFTA negotiations, a number of commentators suggested that the Big Three would benefit from Mexican production being treated as "domestic" for CAFE purposes. This view was based on the fact that Mexican produced cars tend to be smaller and more fuel efficient entry level vehicles. If treated as "domestic," the lower fuel consumption of these vehicles would help offset the

58 See 40 CFR Ch.I (7-1-89 Edition), Section 600.511-80.

higher fuel consumption of U.S. and Canadian produced vehicles.[59] Ford undergoes several contortions to comply with CAFE. Its Crown Victoria, assembled in Ontario, has sufficient Mexican content to be considered imported while the Escorts manufactured at Hermosillo have sufficient U.S. content to be considered domestic.

The Big Three themselves did not advocate the change in status of Mexican production to domestic. In their letter to Carla Hills dated September 9, 1991, they stated, ". . . we wish to make it clear to the U.S. that our companies do not seek such a change in status of the CAFE designation of Mexican produced autos in NAFTA."[60]

The terms of NAFTA change the status of Mexican production, but only after a fairly lengthy lead time for existing assemblers in Mexico. This result is consistent with their wishes. Ford needs a period of time to adjust its sourcing practices in respect to vehicles such as the Crown Victoria and the Escort. Volkswagen is content that its fuel efficient Mexican-produced Golfs and Jettas count as "imported" for a number of years to offset the less fuel efficient Audis which it imports into the United States from Germany.

Used Cars

Canadian restrictions on used cars from Mexico will be phased out over ten years starting 2009. Mexican restrictions on used cars from Canada and the United States will be phased out over the same time period. In their September 9, 1991 letter to Carla Hills, the Big Three recommended that the Mexican embargo on imports of used cars be maintained to protect Mexico's new vehicle industry.[61] The fifteen year lead time in NAFTA gives a substantial time period for the Mexican new vehicle industry to adjust. The rationalization of the North American industry which will result from NAFTA should be complete by that time.

---

59 See APMA Study, pp. 113-4.

60 The text of this letter is reproduced in a Special Report dated September 23, 1991 of *Inside U.S. Trade*, An Inside Washington Publication. (See p. S-5.)

61 See September 9, 1991 letter, p. S-5, item #7.

There is still no rule for determining origin of used cars. While the North American versus foreign distinction may be obvious with older vehicles, the distinction may not be so clear with later model vehicles.[62]

Conclusion

NAFTA sets the stage for the full integration of the Mexican automotive industry into the North American automotive industry. Assemblers in Mexico will no longer have to satisfy Mexican demand with locally produced vehicles and will be able to specialize. The distinction in the Mexican parts between the maquiladoras and the auto parts industry will disappear. Subject only to the constraints imposed by the NAFTA rules of origin, assemblers in Mexico will be able to source parts from wherever they choose.

Assembling

James Womack suggests that Mexico could become an effective source of cheap entry-level vehicles for the U.S. and Canadian markets.[63] Womack and others draw an analogy with the entry of Spain into the European Community. Following its entry into the European Community, European assemblers used Spain as a source of entry-level vehicles, and Spanish production increased dramatically.

Some predict that Mexico will become the favoured low-cost production location for both North American and Japanese producers and that the Spanish experience will be replicated in Mexico. Ford's experience at Hermosillo has demonstrated that cost-effective production of

---

62 Consider a used car that was produced by a transplant in the United States for the domestic U.S. market. No certificate of origin would have been issued for the car when it was new because it was not exported. The car may contain a high level of non-North American content. It is not obvious that this car is North American. The exporter of this car will not be able to obtain the information necessary to satisfy the NAFTA content requirement.

63 James P. Womack, "The Mexican Motor Industry: Strategies for the 1990's," MIT International Motor Vehicle Program International Policy Forum, May 1989, p. 19.

vehicles is possible in Mexico. Some assemblers are currently making very large investments in new production capacity. Nissan is planning a "state of the art" facility at Aguascalientes for the production of 200,000 vehicles by 1995.[64] Volkswagen is increasing the capacity at its Pueblo plant to 300,000 vehicles a year from its current capacity of 150,000 vehicles.[65]

As to whether the dramatic increase in Mexican vehicle production depends on Mexico becoming an effective low-cost producer, Mexico has advantages in its lower labour costs, and Mexican workers have proven to be very effective at plants like Hermosillo. However, labour only represents about 10 to 15 percent of assembling costs.[66] Mexico does not have other cost advantages and, because of the lower quality of its infrastructure, has some real disadvantages. Cost effective vehicle production in Mexico depends not only on the willingness of assemblers to make large capital expenditures to upgrade existing plants and significantly increase their scale of operation,[67] but also on the willingness of the Mexican Government to solve infrastructure problems. Unless vehicle production becomes cost effective in Mexico, North American assemblers will serve the Mexican market from plants in Canada and the United States.

If Mexico becomes an effective low-cost producer and vehicle production expands dramatically, what will be the effect on vehicle assembly in the United States and Canada? According to the Womack scenario, Mexico would specialize in cheap entry-level cars and trucks for the entire North American market. Mexican small truck production for the U.S. market will become feasible with the elimination of the 25

---

64 See APMA Study, p. 51.

65 See APMA Study, p. 59.

66 Miguel Angel Olea, p. 14.

67 See Miguel Angel Olea, p. 17. Olea attributes part of the 10 to 15 percent cost disadvantage of Mexican assembling plants to inadequate scale of operations. He suggests that the scale of operations would have to reach 2.5 million units per year (roughly a four fold increase) or 500,000 units per assembler for assembling costs to be competitive.

percent U.S. tariff.[68] Plants in Canada and the United States would specialize in larger more expensive vehicles and would increase exports to the expanding Mexican market.

This optimistic scenario depends first upon the Mexican market being opened and second upon it growing significantly. NAFTA will open the Mexican market. Increased Mexican domestic demand for cars and trucks depends on whether the current policies of the Mexican government, including entering NAFTA, are successful in significantly raising the living standards of its 85 million people. Measures of the performance of the Mexican economy in recent years have been very positive, and projections of current growth rates suggest significant future improvement. Womack et al. predict that the Mexican market could expand from its current level of about 500,000 units to 2 million units by the year 2000.[69] However, some economists are very critical of the current Mexican government's export oriented policies, and suggest that the success of such policies depends on repressing wages, which in turn represses demand.[70]

If neither Mexican demand nor production capacity increases significantly, the effect of the integration of Mexico's automotive industry will have minimal effect on assembling in the United States and Canada. If Mexican production capacity increases dramatically but Mexican domestic demand does not, some of the excess production may be exported to the European Community and Asia. However, most of it will enter the North American market, with possible adverse consequences for assembling in both the United States and Canada.

The conclusions reached in an economic analysis of the possible effects of a NAFTA on the auto industry by Florencio Lopez-de-Silanes,

---

68 See Womack et al. (1990) p. 266, where he states that "... some way must be found around the 25-percent American tariff on pickup trucks." NAFTA will eliminate this impediment for assemblers in Mexico.

69 Womack et al. (1990), p. 266. See also Mark Scheinman, p. 4, who predicts that Mexican domestic sales of cars and trucks will probably surpass Canada's sometime between 1996 and 1998.

70 See, for example, David Barkin, *Distorted Development: Mexico in the World Economy*, 1990), pp. 113-115.

James R. Markusen and Thomas F. Rutherford[71] suggest that this negative scenario will not materialize. Lopez-de-Silanes et al. conclude that assembling by the Big Three in Mexico will almost double, but that assembling in Mexico by foreign firms will decrease by almost 25 percent.[72] Assembling by the Big Three will increase slightly in the United States and decrease slightly in Canada. However, assembling by foreign firms will increase by about 25 percent in Canada and decrease by about 35 percent in the United States.[73]

---

71 Florencio Lopez-de-Silanes (Harvard University and NBER), James R. Markusen (University of Colorado, Boulder and NBER) and Thomas F. Rutherford (University of Colorado, Boulder), *The Auto Industry and the North American Free Trade Agreement: Employment, Production and Welfare Effects*, First Draft, September 1992. Their model distinguishes between parts, engines and finished cars and between the Big Three and foreign firms. The analysis reports on three scenarios: (1) a free trade area with no content requirements and elimination of Mexican trade balancing requirements; (2) a free trade area with a content provision that must be satisfied for cars to be freely traded within North America; and (3) a free trade area with the content requirement and retention of the Mexican trade balancing requirement. The second scenario is closest to the terms of NAFTA and the conclusions reached by Lopez-de-Silanes *et al.* referred to in this chapter are those arising from the second scenario.

72 This conclusion is not consistent with the extensive investment plans made by Nissan and Volkswagen, referred to above.

73 See Lopez-de-Silanes et al. pp. 31-32 and Tables IX and X on pp. 37-38. One would have thought that the relatively stringent rule of origin would have had the opposite effect on foreign (i.e. transplant) assembling in Canada and the United States. It is not clear from the Lopez-de-Silanes *et al.* analysis whether it is assumed that the content requirement must be satisfied for all vehicles produced in the NAFTA free trade area, or just by those intended for export from one NAFTA country to another. U.S. transplant produced vehicles destined for the U.S. market do not have to meet the NAFTA rules of origin. Except for trucks, Canadian and Mexican produced transplant vehicles destined for the U.S. market which do not satisfy the rules of origin are only subject to a 2.5 percent duty.

Parts

As with assembling, significant increases in Mexican parts production depend upon Mexico becoming a low-cost producer. The Mexican auto parts industry is particularly vulnerable to the integration that will take place under NAFTA. These producers have been protected for a long time and they are not efficient. As the NAFTA provisions are phased in, they will be squeezed by the maquiladora parts producers operating in the domestic market and by the increasing volume of imported parts that will be permitted during the NAFTA phase-in period. When the ownership restrictions are eliminated in 1999, the existing Mexican auto parts industry will also face competition from foreign-owned domestic parts producers.

If the Mexican assembling capacity and domestic demand increase as much as some predict, there should be a substantial new market for parts produced in the United States and Canada. Given the emphasis on just-in-time inventory practices in modern vehicle assembly, the principal beneficiaries of this market will probably be U.S. parts producers located in California, Texas and other states bordering Mexico. Parts producers in Canada are a long way from assemblers in Mexico and Canadian-produced parts have to cross two borders to reach the Mexican market.

Lopez-de-Silanes et al. predict that Mexican production of parts will increase by about 22 percent but that Mexican production of engines will decrease by about 28 percent by the Big Three and by about 68 percent by foreign firms.[74] They suggest that the predicted decrease in Mexican engine production is consistent with the view that investment in engine production in Mexico was largely because of Mexican content and trade balancing requirements.[75] According to the analysis, parts production will decrease only marginally in Canada and increase only

---

74 Lopez-de-Silanes et al., Tables IX and X, pp. 37-38. Overall they predict net employment losses for Mexico but net welfare gains, mainly resulting from lower prices for vehicles.

75 Lopez-de-Silanes et al. p. 32. Note, however, the observation made by Prestowitz et al. at p. 81, that the General Motors Ramos Arizpe engine plant can deliver a V6 engine to an American assembly plant at a cost saving of $200 compared with an identical engine from GM's American engine

marginally in the United States. Engine production by North American firms will increase by about 7 percent in the United States and by about 15 percent in Canada.

The Transplants

Given some of the positions advanced during the NAFTA negotiations, the transplants did not fare too badly. However, in some significant respects, they will be operating at a disadvantage *vis à vis* the Big Three.

The NAFTA rules of origin are the same for all assemblers. However, the burden of compliance will fall most heavily on the transplants (which, in the case of Mexico, include one European manufacturer, Volkswagen) because of their ties to suppliers in third countries (Japan, Germany, Korea). Strict compliance with tracing could be difficult for all assemblers, and U.S. Customs can be selective in its enforcement practices. Over-zealous enforcement by U.S. Customs of the rules of origin against imported transplant vehicles could discourage transplant expansion in Canada and Mexico, but will not solve the Big Three's problems in the U.S. market with Japanese competition. As indicated above, precise and workable Uniform Regulations will narrow the scope for arbitrary enforcement.

The elimination of drawback will also affect the transplants more adversely than the Big Three. Both Mexico and Canada will have to significantly lower their external tariffs if their transplant assemblers are to be competitive with their U.S. counterparts.

The two tier structure continues in Canada, with only the Big Three and CAMI being entitled to Auto Pact benefits. However, the two tier structure proposed by the Big Three for Mexico, with a more favourable phasing out of Automotive Decree restrictions for existing assemblers (including Nissan and Volkswagen) did not materialize.[76] Nonetheless, transplants that do not already have operations in Mexico will suffer some disadvantages. Until the Automotive Decree is phased out completely, only assemblers with operations in Mexico will be entitled to

---

plants.

76 See the Big Three letter to Carla Hills dated September 9, 1992, referred to above.

import new vehicles into Mexico. Honda has a motorcycle plant in Guadalajara and is the transplant most likely to establish assembly operations in Mexico.[77] The Automotive Decree (as modified by NAFTA) would apply to a new Honda Mexican assembly operation in the same manner as to those of existing assemblers, except that the calculation of content would not be based on a reference value.[78] A new Honda assembly operation in Mexico would be able to import new vehicles into Mexico because a portion of its investment in new plant and equipment would be credited to its extended trade balance.

Lopez-de-Silanes et al. predict that the foreign firms will be the big losers as a result of a NAFTA. The principal reason is because the Big Three, which rely very heavily on North American parts and engines, will benefit from rationalization of their North American operations significantly more than foreign firms, which are much less dependant on North American engines and parts.[79] According to this analysis, the negative effect on foreign firms is considerably aggravated by the content requirement. With the content requirement, Lopez-de-Silanes et al. predict that foreign firm vehicle production will drop by about 25 percent and that foreign firm engine production will drop by almost 55 percent.[80]

---

77 See APMA Study, p. 81. The definition of "vehicle" in paragraph 4 of NAFTA Annex 300-A specifically excludes "motorcycle" so that Honda would not be considered as an "existing producer of vehicles." Para. 1 of NAFTA Annex 300-A requires each Party to treat existing producers no less favourably than new producers. Thus, if Mexico offered a favourable arrangement to Honda to induce it to invest, it would have to offer the same arrangement to the existing producers.

78 This would be advantageous to Honda.

79 Lopez-de-Silanes et al. p. 35.

80 See Lopez-de-Silanes et al., p. 40, Table XII. In a North American free trade area without a content requirement, the analysis predicts that foreign firm vehicle production would drop by only about one percent and foreign firm production of engines would drop by about 38 percent. The validity of these conclusions depends on how the assumptions made in the analysis respecting the content requirement compare with the requirement actually imposed by NAFTA.

Canada's Position

The effect on Canada of the integration of the Mexican automotive industry into the North American one depends on whether Mexico succeeds in becoming a low cost producer of vehicles and parts and whether the dramatic increase in the Mexican domestic demand for vehicles predicted by some occurs. If Mexico does not become a low cost producer of vehicles and parts, the effect on Canada will be minimal. If Mexico becomes a low cost producer of selected products (such as entry-level vehicles and labour-intensive parts) and the Mexican demand for vehicles expands dramatically, the Canadian assembling and parts industries could benefit. However, U.S. parts producers located in the southwest United States will be in a much better position to benefit from increased Mexican demand than their Canadian counterparts.

The least attractive scenario for Canada occurs if Mexico becomes an effective low cost producer of vehicles and parts but a dramatic increase in Mexican demand does not take place. So long as Canadian parts producers are competitive with Mexican, Canadian parts producers will continue to be in a better position to serve assemblers located in the northeast United States. However, if Canadian costs of parts production are significantly higher than Mexican costs, new investment in parts production will be made in Mexico, at Canada's expense.[81]

The conclusions of the Lopez-de-Silanes et al. analysis are mildly positive for Canada. They predict a small overall employment gain for Canada with a zero effect on welfare.[82]

Other things being equal, the Auto Pact will continue to provide an incentive for assemblers entitled to its benefits to meet the safeguards by assembling vehicles in Canada and purchasing Canadian parts.

---

81 The substantial protection given by the NAFTA investment provisions to investors from NAFTA countries will remove some concerns about investing in Mexico. In a reversal of past policy, Mexico has accepted the principle of prompt, adequate and effective compensation at fair market value in the event of an expropriation. See NAFTA Article 1110. The NAFTA investment provisions also contain investor/state dispute settlement procedures which will permit a U.S. or Canadian investor to bypass the Mexican judicial system in pursuing NAFTA rights.

82 Lopez-de-Silanes et al., p. 31.

However, if Canadian costs become greater than those in the United States and Mexico by any amount that is more than marginal, the incentives provided by Auto Pact duty remission will not prevent assembling and parts production from leaving Canada for the United States or Mexico.

Canada cannot prevent the integration of the Mexican automotive industry into North America by refusing to ratify NAFTA. Some suggest that the integration of the Mexican industry into the North American is well under way in any event and that NAFTA will merely facilitate the process.[83] If Canada refuses to ratify NAFTA, the United States and Mexico will probably proceed with a bilateral free trade arrangement. If this occurs, Canada will be exposed to the down side of NAFTA with none of its potential benefits.

83 See Michael Hart, *A North American Free Trade Agreement* (1990), pp. 118-119.

NAFTA: The Textile and Apparel Sector

Eric Barry and
Elizabeth Siwicki
Canadian Textiles Institute

Two Different Industries

ANTICIPATING THAT "TEXTILES" ISSUES WOULD be contentious, the three NAFTA participants established a separate negotiating group to deal with them. In the negotiations, the term "textiles" is a broad label covering issues affecting both the textile manufacturing industry and the clothing manufacturing industry. This verbal shorthand blurs the fact that these are different industries with different economic characteristics and structure and that "textile" negotiations can affect them in different ways.[1]

---

1 The textile manufacturing industry includes producers of man-made fibres plus producers of yarns, fabrics, and textile products. The clothing manufacturing industry produces clothing. Statistics Canada's Standard Industrial Classification groups textile manufacturers under SIC 18, Primary textiles industry; SIC 19, Textile products industry; SIC 3257, Motor vehicle fabric accessories industry. Clothing manufacturers are in

Canada's textile manufacturing industry has been transformed in the last 15 years. The key to its transformation has been substantial and sustained capital investment which has made it modern, efficient, decreasingly labour intensive and increasingly capital intensive, with rapidly growing productivity and better than average profitability.[2]

Shipments by Canadian textile manufacturers in 1989 were over $7.7 billion, making it the largest year in the industry's history. While shipments have declined since then because of the recession, the industry is well positioned to participate in the economic recovery.

While much new technology has appeared in clothing manufacturing, it is still essentially a labour intensive industry with relatively low capital investment.

Key statistics on both the textile and clothing industries are presented in table 1.

Table 1: Key Statistics

	Textiles (SIC 18, 19, 3257)	Clothing (SIC 24)
	($ million)	($ million)
Shipments (1991)	6,427	5,945
Investments in Last 10 Years (1981-1990)	3,851	526
Total Wages & Salaries Paid (1989)	1,713	2,042
Employment (1989)	(Number) 67,075	(Number) 112,177

Source: Statistics Canada.

SIC 24, Clothing industries.

2 Industry, Science and Technology Canada 1991, *Industrial Competitiveness; A Sectoral Perspective: Textiles*, p. 111-118.

As might be expected, the U.S. textile industry is a bit more than ten times the size of its Canadian counterpart. Shipments by American textile manufacturers in 1991 were valued at US$64.1 billion. Similarly, estimated shipments by U.S. clothing manufacturers in 1991 were valued at U.S.$52.9 billion.

The size of the Mexican textile industry is more difficult to gauge. An unpublished report by a leading consulting firm has estimated the value of 1988 shipments to be approximately Can$3 billion expressed in constant 1980 Can$ or about half of 1988 shipments by Canadian textile manufacturers measured the same way. No estimate was made of the value of Mexican clothing shipments.

Textile and Clothing Trade

Table 2 presents an overview of Canadian trade in textiles and clothing in 1991. Imports are substantially larger than exports for both industries but there is an important difference in import sources.

In value terms, about 73 percent of textile imports come from developed countries (56 percent from the U.S. alone) with 27 percent coming from developing or "low-wage" countries. By contrast, nearly 80 percent of clothing imports come from developing countries and only 10 percent from the U.S.

Again in value terms, textile manufacturers export three times as much as clothing manufacturers with 64 percent of textile exports and 86 percent of clothing exports going to the U.S.

Trade with Mexico has been tiny. In 1991 only 1 percent of textile imports originated in Mexico and over half of these entered Canada duty-free. Only 0.5 percent of clothing imports came from Mexico. Textile and clothing exports to Mexico were even smaller.

Imports of textiles into the U.S. in 1991 were US$7.3 billion. Textile imports account for a much smaller proportion of the U.S. market than is the case for textile imports into Canada. Textile imports from Mexico into the U.S. for the same year were US$206 million or 2.8 percent of all imports. With U.S. 1991 textile exports to Mexico totalling $536 million the U.S. enjoyed a positive textile trade balance with their southern neighbour.

Imports of clothing into the U.S. in 1991 were US$27.7 billion and occupied a share of market roughly similar to that occupied by clothing imports into Canada. Clothing imports from Mexico were only 2.4 percent of the U.S. total.

Table 2: Canadian Textile and Clothing Trade Data Overview (1991)

	Textiles ($ million)	Clothing ($ million)
Trade with All Countries		
Imports	2,972	2,215
Exports	1,069	329
Trade with the U.S.		
Imports from the U.S.	1,658	227
Exports to the U.S.	688	284
U.S. share of		
Imports	56%	10%
Exports	64%	86%
Trade with Mexico		
Imports from Mexico	31.6	11.5
Exports to Mexico	4.4	0.3
Mexican share of		
Imports	1.0%	0.5%
Exports	0.4%	0.9%
Trade balance with		
All Countries	-1,903	-1,885
U.S.	-971	58
Mexico	-27	-11

Source: Statistics Canada.

The Canada-U.S. Free Trade Agreement

It became apparent very early in the NAFTA negotiations that the Americans were taking advantage of them to renegotiate the FTA rules of origin for textiles and clothing. Therefore, a brief review of these is essential background for what happened in NAFTA.

The American textile and clothing industries opposed the FTA. The price they exacted from their government for their forced participation was a set of rules of origin designed to limit the use of third-country inputs in textiles and clothing that would qualify for FTA rates of duty.

For example, a fabric can be woven, dyed and finished in Canada but will not qualify unless it is made from Canadian or American yarn. Similarly, a garment can be cut and sewn or otherwise assembled in Canada but will not qualify unless it is made from Canadian or American fabric. Of course, the same rules apply to U.S. textile and clothing manufacturers. A more detailed comparison of the FTA rules of origin and how they were changed in NAFTA is presented later in this chapter.

Canadian textile and clothing manufacturers rely more on inputs from the rest of the world than do their U.S. competitors. In partial recognition of this, the FTA included exceptions to the rules of origin in the form of three tariff rate quotas or TRQs. These permit non-wool fabrics made from imported yarns or apparel made from imported fabrics to be exported to the U.S. at FTA rates of duty subject to the following annual limits:

- For non-wool fabrics and made-up textile articles (such as sheets or towels) up to 25,083,900 million square metre equivalents
- For non-wool apparel up to 41,806,500 million square metre equivalents
- For wool apparel up to 5,016,780 million square metre equivalents

There are important differences in the relief provided to the Canadian textile and clothing industries by these TRQ exceptions.

First, the review mechanisms are different. The non-wool fabrics and made-up textile articles TRQ provides for a review of its "quantitative elements" before the end of 1992, while the two apparel TRQs remain in place at least until the end of the FTA transition period or

January 1, 1998. Second, the fabrics and made-up textile articles TRQ level was set at a fraction of actual export levels, while the apparel TRQs represented a multiple (about six times) of apparel exports at the time.

The rates at which the TRQs have been utilized tell the story (see table 3). Textile manufacturers have heavily utilized their TRQ.

Clothing manufacturers, on the other hand, have not heavily utilized the non-wool apparel TRQ so that their ability to import non-FTA fabrics, make garments, and export these garments to the U.S. at FTA rates of duty has not been impeded at all. Clothing manufacturer usage of the wool apparel TRQ has been heavier although even in this area nearly half of the quota remains unutilized.

Table 3: TRQ Utilization

Year	Non-wool fabrics & made up articles (Negotiated level: 25,083,900 SMEs)		Wool apparel (Negotiated level: 5,016,780 SMEs)		Non-wool apparel (Negotiated level: 41,806,500 SMEs)	
	Utilization %		Utilization %		Utilization %	
1989	19,798,538	79%	997,383	20%	3,616,401	9%
1990	24,531,149	98%	1,006,310	20%	6,974,293	17%
1991	20,231,107	81%	2,549,850	51%	11,276,383	27%

Different NAFTA Positions

The Minister for International Trade was advised in September 1990 by the Canadian Textiles Institute that, if NAFTA was to happen, the textile industry and Canada needed to be part of it.

The textile industry did not perceive any short term threat or advantage stemming from free trade with Mexico but quickly reached the view that it was in its best long-term interests to participate in a trilateral NAFTA agreement. In September 1991, the Canadian Textiles Institute sent a detailed confidential submission to the International Trade Minister setting out the industry's NAFTA objectives.

The textile industry perceives its major challenge to be adjusting to the Canada-U.S. Free Trade Agreement. As the NAFTA negotiations got underway in late 1991, it became clear that the U.S. move to make the FTA rules of origin even more restrictive would impair the Canadian industry's access to the U.S. market. Canadian efforts to resist these U.S. initiatives, which were being supported by Mexico, were limited by our lack of negotiating leverage. Once it became obvious that the rules would be the way the Americans and Mexicans wanted them, Canada's efforts focused on seeking "compensation" in the form of expanded and extended tariff rate quotas.

The clothing industry took a different view which is best summed up in the official position of the Canadian Apparel Federation which opposed the U.S. demands for changes to the FTA rules of origin and urged the government:

> . . . to pursue a triangular strategy for textiles and apparel in the North American Free Trade Negotiations, by signing a bilateral agreement with Mexico, and keeping the provisions of the Canada-U.S. FTA, with some modifications . . .[3]

Canadian officials raised the possibility of a triangular approach for apparel at the negotiating table, but very much as a "last resort," preferring instead to continue to pursue a mutually acceptable trilateral agreement. The broader view was and remains that both industries are better off "in" the NAFTA agreement than "out" of it given the integration of the North American market and future prospects for an expanded "hemispheric" free trade area.

The end result was an agreement that makes everyone at least a little unhappy. This, at least in the trade policy bureaucracy, appears to indicate a successful negotiation.

The deal as it applies to textiles and apparel is complex and must be assessed not by looking at each of its specific elements, but, rather, by looking at the overall "package." For each sector, and for each partner, there are good things and there are bad things, but it is the balance of what has been achieved that is relevant.

---

3 *Canadian Apparel Manufacturer*, September/October 1992, p. 10.

The following pages describe the key NAFTA provisions applicable to textiles and clothing and highlight some of the areas where these differ from the FTA.

Rules of Origin and Tariff Preference Levels (TPLS)

The NAFTA rules of origin applicable to textiles and apparel are spelled out in detail in Annex 401 of the text. The relevant section is "XI: Textiles and Textile Articles" (HS[4] Chapters 50-63).

While most importers and exporters would consider the Tariff Preference Levels (TPLs) (explained and described in more detail later in this chapter) an integral aspect of determining which goods do or do not qualify for NAFTA rates of duty, these TPLs are actually described and itemized in an Appendix to a separate section of the text, "Annex 300-B: Textile and Apparel Goods," which is part of NAFTA Chapter 3.

Rules of Origin

Textiles and textile articles qualify for NAFTA rates of duty if they undergo specific manufacturing processes which are described by reference to a change in HS classification. Importers or exporters simply look up the HS heading or sub-heading under which the goods in question are classified to find the applicable rule.

Here is a simplified summary of the rules governing some commonly traded textile and apparel goods, along with an indication of where TPLs apply.[5]

Yarns (HS Chapters 50-55)

Silk, wool/hair or vegetable fibre yarns qualify if they are produced in the free trade area, regardless of the origin of the input fibres.

---

4 "HS" refers to the Harmonized Commodity Description and Coding System (Harmonized System).

5 The term "domestic" is used to denote materials produced in Canada, Mexico or the U.S.; the term "imported" is used to denote materials imported from outside the free trade area.

Cotton or man-made staple fibre yarns qualify if they are spun in the free trade area from domestic cotton or man-made fibres.

Man-made filament yarns qualify if they are extruded domestically.

TPLs apply in the case of cotton or man-made staple fibre yarns made from imported cotton or man-made staple fibres.

Woven Fabrics (HS Chapters 50-55)

Silk or flax (linen) fabrics qualify if they are woven in the free trade area regardless of the origin of the input yarns.

All other fabrics qualify if they are woven in the free trade area from domestic yarns.

TPLs apply to cotton or man-made woven fabrics classified in HS Chapters 52 through 55 containing imported yarns.

Knitted Fabrics (HS Chapter 60)

Knitted fabrics qualify if they are knitted in the free trade area from: domestic man-made filament yarns; domestic cotton or man-made staple fibre yarns spun from domestic cotton and man-made staple fibres; domestic wool/hair yarns (regardless of the origin of the wool/hair fibres); domestic vegetable fibre yarns (regardless of the origin of the vegetable fibres); or imported flax (linen) or silk yarns.

TPLs apply to cotton and man-made fibre fabrics knitted in the free trade area from imported yarns.

Nonwoven Fabrics (HS Chapter 56)

Nonwoven fabrics, including felts, qualify if they are made in the territory from: cotton, wool/hair or vegetable fibres regardless of their origin; or domestic man-made staple fibres or filaments.

Coated Fabrics (HS Chapter 59)

Most *coated fabrics* incorporating a woven substrate qualify if they are made in the free trade area from domestic woven fabrics. Coated fabrics incorporating a knitted substrate qualify even if this substrate is imported.

The main exceptions are *tire cord fabric* (HS 59.02) and *belting* (HS 59.10), which, in addition to the above requirements, also require input fabrics to be made in the free trade area from domestic man-made filament yarns or from domestic man-made staple fibre yarns made from domestic man-made staple fibres.

Carpets (HS Chapter 57)

Carpets qualify if they are woven, tufted or otherwise produced in the free trade area from domestic yarns. Jute yarns and jute woven fabrics (the latter used as carpet backings) can be imported. Other types of carpet backings must be domestic in order for the carpets to qualify.

However, there is a different rule applicable to some carpets traded between the U.S. and Mexico (detailed in an Appendix to "Annex 300-B"). This requires man-made fibre tufted carpets to be made from domestic man-made fibre yarns made from domestic man-made staple fibres, and felt carpets and carpet tiles to be made from domestic man-made staple fibres in order to qualify for NAFTA rates of duty.

Other Textile Made-Up Articles (HS Chapter 63)

Other textile made-up articles (such as sheets, blankets, towels, etc.) qualify if they are made from: domestic wool, cotton, man-made filament or most vegetable fibre fabrics made from domestic yarns; or domestic man-made staple fibre fabrics made from domestic yarns made from domestic fibres. Woven silk or linen fabrics, coated fabrics, or nonwovens can be imported.

TPLs apply to cotton or man-made fibre made-up textile articles made from non-originating inputs.

Apparel (HS Chapters 61 and 62)

Generally, *apparel* must be both cut (or knit to shape) and sewn or otherwise assembled in the free trade area from domestic fabrics made from domestic yarns. But there are exceptions.

Bras can be made from imported fabrics and still qualify. Man-made fibre sweaters traded between the U.S. and Mexico must be produced in the free trade area from domestic yarns made from domestic man-made staple fibres. In addition, there are several input fabrics which can be imported without disqualifying the garments. These include woven silk and linen fabrics; Harris tweeds; some cotton velveteens and corduroys; batiste fabrics; a variety of shirting fabrics; some circular knit fabrics; coated fabrics; and nonwovens.

TPLs allowing the use of imported fabrics, domestic fabrics made from imported yarns, or, in the case of knit-to-shape garments, imported yarns, apply to almost all apparel.

While a summary is helpful in providing an overview of the rules, importers or exporters should inform themselves of the specific rules covering the products they are trading as there are various technicalities not mentioned here that might apply.

Tariff Preference Levels (TPLs)

It is impossible to judge whether or not textiles or apparel goods qualify for NAFTA rates of duty simply by looking at the rules of origin. Importers or exporters must also consider the various "exceptions" that permit specified levels of textiles and apparel not meeting the rules of origin to also qualify for NAFTA rates of duty. These are referred to in NAFTA as Tariff Preference Levels (TPLs) and in the FTA as Tariff Rate Quotas (TRQs).

TPLs are detailed in Appendix 6.0 (B) "Annex 300-B: Textile and Apparel Goods." Specific levels apply to specific products traded between Canada and the U.S.; Canada and Mexico; and the U.S. and Mexico.

Two sets of TPLs cover apparel. One covers cotton and man-made fibre apparel (knitted and woven); the second covers wool apparel (knitted and woven). Details are provided in tables 4 and 5.

Table 4: Cotton or Man-Made Fibre Apparel (in square metre equivalent SMEs)

	From Canada	From U.S.	From Mexico
Imports into			
Canada	N.A.	9,000,000	6,000,000
U.S.	80,000,000*	N.A.	45,000,000
Mexico	6,000,000	12,000,000	N.A.

*Of which no more than 60,000,000 SMEs can be made from fabrics which are knitted or woven outside the free trade area.

N.A.: Not applicable.

Table 5: Wool Apparel (in square metre equivalents SMEs)

	From Canada	From U.S.	From Mexico
Imports into			
Canada	N.A.	919,740	250,000
U.S.	5,066,948*	N.A.	1,500,000
Mexico	250,000	1,000,000	N.A.

*Of which no more than 5,016,780 SMEs can be men's or boys' wool suits of U.S. category 443.

N.A.: Not applicable.

As mentioned previously, there are a number of apparel items traded between the U.S. and Mexico that do not have access to the TPLs. These are apparel made from denim, oxford cloth and some circular knit fabrics, and man-made fibre sweaters. These apparel items must either meet the applicable rules of origin or pay regular MFN rates of duty. This exception does not apply to these apparel items traded between Canada and Mexico, or Canada and the U.S.

Also covered by a TPL are goods imported into the U.S. from Mexico under U.S. tariff item 9802.00.80.60 (more commonly known as U.S. 807) up to a level of 25,000,000 SMEs. This TPL covers apparel made from fabrics which are cut in the U.S., sewn or otherwise assembled in Mexico, and returned to the U.S. with duty payable only on the Mexican value-added.

Another set of TPLs cover cotton and man-made fibre knitted and woven fabrics and made-up textile articles of HS Chapters 52 through 55, 58, 60 and 63. These allow up to the specified amounts of fabrics and made-up textile articles made from non-originating inputs to still qualify for NAFTA rates of duty. Details are provided in table 6.

Table 6: Fabrics and Made-Up Textile Articles (in square metre equivalents SMEs)

	From Canada	From U.S.	From Mexico
Imports into			
Canada	N.A.	2,000,000*	7,000,000
U.S.	65,000,000**	N.A.	24,000,000***
Mexico	7,000,000	2,000,000	N.A.

Notes:
*Applies to knitted fabrics (Chapter 60) only.
** With not more than 35,000,000 SMEs for knitted fabrics and textile articles, and not more than 35,000,000 SMEs for woven fabrics and textile articles.
*** With not more than 18,000,000 SMEs for knitted fabrics and textile articles, and not more than 6,000,000 SMEs for woven fabrics and textile articles.

N.A.: Not applicable.

Finally, there is a "spun yarn" TPL, which allows up to the specified amounts of yarns classified in HS headings 52.05 through 52.07 or 55.09 through 55.11 spun in the free trade area from imported cotton or man-made staple fibres to still qualify for NAFTA rates of duty. Details are provided in table 7.

Table 7: Cotton or Man-Made Fibre Spun Yarns (in kilograms)

	From Canada	From U.S.	From Mexico
Imports into			
Canada	N.A.	1,000,000	1,000,000
U.S.	10,700,000	N.A.	1,000,000
Mexico	1,000,000	1,000,000	N.A.

N.A.: Not applicable.

All TPLs applicable to imports into the U.S. from Canada are subject to an annual growth rate for 5 years starting in 1995. These are: 2 percent for spun yarns, fabrics and made-up textile articles, and apparel made from domestic fabrics made from imported yarns or knit to shape from imported yarns; and 1 percent for wool apparel and for cotton or man-made fibre apparel made from fabrics imported from outside the free trade area.

Finally, there is a provision for a review, after 5 years, of the TPLs and of any applicable growth factors.

How NAFTA Rules Differ from the FTA Rules

The concepts are identical. In both agreements, textile and apparel goods "originate" if they undergo specific manufacturing processes in the free trade area. In both agreements, there are exceptions (albeit called by different names: TPLs in NAFTA; TRQs in the FTA) to the rules that allow "non-originating" goods to qualify for preferential rates of duty up to specified levels.

The main changes from the FTA origin rules are NAFTA requirements:

- that cotton or man-made fibre spun yarns (HS Chapters 52 and 55) be made from domestic fibres. The FTA allowed imported fibres
- that knitted cotton fabrics (HS Chapter 60) be made from domestic yarns made from domestic fibres. The FTA allowed imported cotton fibres
- that tire cord fabrics (HS 59.02) and belting (HS 59.10) be made from domestic man-made filament yarns or domestic man-made staple fibre yarns made from domestic fibres. The FTA allowed imported yarns
- that textile articles (HS Chapter 63) be made from domestic pile and terry fabrics as well as domestic knitted fabrics. The FTA allowed these to be imported
- that apparel be made from domestic fabrics made from domestic yarns or knit-to-shape from domestic yarns. The FTA allowed the yarns to be imported

While these changes require more domestic processing in order for goods to "originate," there are also changes that provide for more liberal rules for certain products, mainly in the apparel area. These include previously described exceptions for apparel made from a variety of specified fabrics as well as an exception for one yarn type used in sheer curtains.

As for TRQs/TPLs, the basic challenge for Canada in the negotiations was to achieve adjustments to the FTA TRQ levels covering its exports to compensate for what are generally regarded as more restrictive rules of origin in NAFTA as compared to the FTA. For example, FTA apparel TRQs covering "non-wool" apparel have been replaced with higher NAFTA TPLs to accommodate trade potentially affected by the rule changes. A spun yarn TPL was introduced to compensate for the new rule covering cotton or man-made staple fibre yarns. An increased fabrics and made-up textile articles TPL level is the result of a combination of factors, including rule changes and an FTA provision calling for renegotiation of the FTA TRQ level covering these goods before the end of 1992.

Other changes include growth factors for TPLs covering Canadian exports to the U.S.; specific review clauses covering rules of origin and TPLs; new provisions allowing rules of origin exceptions for goods that are mutually agreed to be "in short supply;" and new provisions allowing changes to TPL access for goods that are deemed to be "in ample supply."

Duty Drawback

Under the FTA, most exporters using imported (from third countries) inputs had been scheduled to lose duty drawback after January 1, 1994. There are only two exceptions: citrus fruits and apparel exported at MFN rates of duty.

NAFTA represents an improvement over the FTA as far as duty drawback is concerned. The new agreement extends the period during which full duty drawback will be available for two years beyond the FTA expiry (i.e. to January 1, 1996) for Canada/U.S. trade and allows for full duty drawback on trade with Mexico until January 1, 2001.

It also provides for continued duty drawback beyond these dates on the basis of a formula that permits exporters to draw back the lesser of (a) duties paid on non-NAFTA inputs used in the production of goods exported to another NAFTA country, or (b) duties paid to that NAFTA country on the exported product. In other words, an exporter cannot get more drawback on inputs than is paid on the exports in which they are incorporated.

The "lesser of" formula effectively means that exporters will not be able to claim drawback on inputs used in "originating" NAFTA exports once these become duty-free at the end of their respective transition periods. However, they will continue to be able to claim either full or partial drawback on inputs used in "non-originating" exports, as these will still be dutiable at regular MFN rates of duty.

Tariff Elimination

Tariffs on textiles and apparel traded between Canada and the U.S. will continue to be reduced as scheduled under the FTA.

Some textiles and apparel traded between the U.S. and Mexico will become duty-free immediately. Most tariffs will be reduced over a 6-year period, and some (but not many) over a longer period.

Most tariffs on textiles traded between Canada and Mexico will be reduced to zero over an 8-year period, as follows: a 20 percent reduction in the first year; no reduction in the second year; five 10 percent annual reductions; and a final 30 percent reduction in the last year. Some textile tariffs will reduce over 6 years; others (mostly those already-accelerated under the FTA) will go to zero immediately. Clothing tariffs will be reduced over a 10-year period.

As was the case in the FTA, NAFTA contains an "acceleration" clause which will permit a faster phase-in period for goods mutually agreed between two or more of the parties.

Also as in the FTA, there is a "tariff snapback" provision (Section 4 of "Annex 300-B: Textile and Apparel Goods") which allows a party to temporarily suspend the NAFTA rate of duty (i.e. return to MFN rates of duty) for specific products under specific conditions. Such actions require compensation (normally these would be equivalent tariff reductions on other products) to the affected Party by the Party taking the action.

Quotas, or Quantitative Restraints

The U.S. has agreed to eliminate its MFA[6] quotas on "originating" imports from Mexico immediately. There is a phase-out period for quotas covering "non-originating" goods. These provisions are detailed in Schedule 3.1.1 in Appendix 3.1 to "Annex 300-B: Textile and Apparel Goods."

Canada has no existing quotas with Mexico.

NAFTA also contains a provision (Section 5 of "Annex 300-B: Textile and Apparel Goods") allowing the imposition of temporary quantitative measures as an "emergency action." This permits the U.S. or Canada to take an action against Mexico, or Mexico to take an action against the U.S. or Canada. However, any actions by the U.S. against Canada or vice versa remain governed by Article 407 of the FTA, which is commonly interpreted as precluding quantitative restrictions. The NAFTA Section 5 safeguard applies only to "non-originating" goods; no quantitative safeguards are permitted on "originating" goods.

What Lies Ahead?

Agreements of the magnitude of the FTA and NAFTA set forces in motion and experience indicates that the outcome is usually surprising.

The successful negotiation of the Canada-U.S. Free Trade Agreement was a watershed for the textile manufacturing industry. Up to 1989, the industry exported about 8 percent of what it made. About half went to the U.S. and the remainder went all over the world.

The reality of the FTA and the need to adapt acted as a psychological trigger and firms began to look beyond the domestic market. In 1990, with a recession in Canada and the U.S. with textile duties down by only two-tenths, and with a high Canadian dollar, textile exports to the U.S. increased by 28 percent. In 1991, exports held that gain and increased by another 15 percent. In 1992 they increased by yet another 30 percent.

In 1989 Canadian textile exports to the U.S. were $464 million. In 1992 they approached $900 million. In 1993 they will pass the $1 billion mark.

---

6 "MFA" refers to the Multifibre Arrangement.

Many Canadian textile companies have set as an export target 50 percent of what they make. Some reached that goal in 1992. A few are exporting as much as 80 percent of their production. The growth has resulted almost entirely from exports to the U.S. but firms have begun to venture into non-North American markets for the first time.

Most of these firms could probably have been successful in U.S. markets without the FTA but generally they hadn't tried. The FTA was the psychological trigger necessary for them to make the effort.

In 1987, no one would have forecast increased Canadian textile exports to the U.S. of the magnitude that have occurred. In fact the FTA has caused textile trade between the two parties to grow to the benefit of both parties.

On the clothing side, it was widely assumed in 1987 that the Canadian market would be flooded with U.S. garments. This has not happened. Canada had a positive balance of clothing trade with the U.S. before the FTA. Since the FTA this positive balance has continued to grow at an increasing rate.

Textile and clothing trade between the U.S. and Canada began to increase before the FTA was really in effect. Interestingly enough this phenomenon is repeating itself with NAFTA. Exports of textiles from Canada to Mexico have grown by 85 percent in the first half of 1992 while exports of clothing have more than doubled. Imports of both textiles and clothing from Mexico have begun to increase too. While the absolute numbers are still tiny, NAFTA is giving early indications of a trade expanding effect even before it has come into existence.

Toward a More Open Agriculture in North America

Thomas Grennes
North Carolina State University

Introduction

THE NORTH AMERICAN FREE TRADE AGREEMENT (NAFTA) can be expected to increase the average incomes of residents of the United States, Mexico, and Canada. By increasing net wealth, the trade agreement can be distinguished from tax and transfer programs that merely take from one group and give to another. This chapter will analyze the effect of NAFTA on trade and specialization in the agricultural sector. In addition to the benefits from creating additional trade, the possible disadvantages of trade diversion will also be analyzed. The effect of freer trade on worker displacement and the environment will also be considered.

Distinctive Features of Agricultural Trade Policy

The agricultural sector has particular significance in NAFTA and the Uruguay Round of GATT negotiations because agriculture has been left out of previous rounds of trade liberalization. As a result, the average level of protection in agriculture is higher than in other sectors of the economy in the high income countries of OECD.

Agriculture is also distinguished by the form of its trade protection. Import quotas are more important here than in other sectors of the economy. The United States has requested waivers from the GATT rules for its agricultural import quotas every year since the 1950s. The quotas are authorized by domestic legislation (Section 22 of the Agricultural Adjustment Act of 1933) to restrict imports that would interfere with domestic price support programs (Johnson 1973, p. 34). Prior to the recent market-oriented reforms in Mexico, 100 percent of import categories were covered by licensing. The coverage of licenses has been reduced substantially, but the use of licenses for agricultural products remains more important than for other products (Grennes et. al.).

Non-border instruments of protection are more common for agriculture than for other products. Prices of final products have been controlled at the consumer and producer levels, and many input prices have been controlled as well. Production and marketing controls have been used, and land use has been restricted. Marketing orders in the U.S. restrict the size and grade of products that can be offered to consumers. The Mexican agricultural agency, CONASUPO, intervened at all levels of agricultural activity including the farm level, food processing, and retail sales.

Another distinctive feature of agriculture is the importance of border regulation to protect human health and the health of domestic plants and animals. An ongoing trade policy issue is whether sanitary and phytosanitary measures at the border serve legitimate domestic purposes or whether they are being used as non-tariff barriers to trade. One standard for legitimacy is whether imports and domestic products are treated equally. Even if equal treatment is given, differential standards across countries give rise to complaints of unfair trade by producers in the country where standards are higher (K. Anderson). In particular, American producers have complained about unfair competition with

Mexican growers who can legally use DDT and other chemicals that are illegal in the U.S.

Specific Features of the August 1992 Agreement Affecting Agricultural Trade

The agricultural sector is politically sensitive to liberalization, and this was acknowledged by the longer transition period (15 years) granted for certain products both for the U.S. and Mexico. Special treatment was given to sugar, frozen orange juice concentrate, peanuts, and certain fruits and vegetables (asparagus, broccoli, cantaloupe, and cucumbers) for the U.S. and for corn, dry beans, and milk powder in Mexico. Corn is important in Mexico both as a food staple and as a major source of income for some of the poorest farmers. Land tenure is also politically sensitive because the *ejido* system is associated with land reform and peasants' rights achieved by the Mexican Revolution. Mexican agriculture is also significant as the main source of illegal migrants to the United States. The fact that Mexico and Canada signed a separate bilateral agreement on agriculture is further evidence of the special features of the sector.

The U.S.-Canada free trade agreement remains in effect for those two countries. Canada and Mexico signed a separate bilateral agreement that excluded certain products (dairy and poultry) from liberalization.

The features of the agreement announced August 13th were not significantly different from what was expected at the time negotiations began in June 1991. The United States and Mexico agreed to eliminate all tariffs, import quotas, and licenses on all agricultural products beginning January 1, 1994. The barriers would be phased out over a period of up to 15 years that would vary by product. No changes in domestic policies, including U.S. marketing orders and deficiency payments, would occur.

All import licenses and import quotas would be eliminated, including products covered by Section 22 of the Agricultural Adjustment Act (sugar, peanuts, cotton, and dairy products). The current quotas would first be converted into tariff quotas, and then the quotas would increase each year until they were no longer binding. Under a tariff quota no tariff is levied on the first Q units of imports, but a tariff is applied to each unit beyond Q. The initial tariff-free quantities and tariff rates applicable to additional quantities were chosen to approximate the current levels of protection of existing quotas. The United States will retain a global quota on sugar, and planned increases in the Mexican sugar quota would be offset by a reduction in the quota for the rest of the world.

Sanitary rules would be based on scientific evidence and trade disputes would be evaluated by trade panels composed of representatives of the three countries. The countries agreed to eliminate export subsidies (except to counter subsidies by non-member countries) and to structure domestic policies so they would not distort trade. It will not be easy to continue current domestic policies and avoid trade distortion. If per unit production subsidies stimulate grain production in the U. S., they will increase U.S. exports. U.S. grain programs have paid per unit deficiency payments based on the difference between a target price and the market price. As long as payments (current or expected future) to farmers increase with current output, production will be stimulated and trade will be distorted. However, if payments were based entirely on historical output (past acreage and past output per acre), deficiency payments would be equivalent to lump sum payments, and they would have a neutral effect ("decoupled") on production and trade (see Grennes 1988a, 1988b).

A characteristic of all free trade areas is that traders have an incentive to import into the member country with lower tariff rates and re-export to the member country with higher tariffs against non-members. This problem does not exist with a customs union. Rules of origin are designed to discourage re-exports. For example, frozen orange juice concentrate can be imported duty-free to the U.S. from Mexico only if it is entirely made from NAFTA orange juice. For peanuts, the rules of origin are more restrictive for U.S.-Mexican trade than for U.S.-Canadian trade. In the latter case, peanuts could be imported by Canada from non-member countries and re-exported duty-free to the U.S. as peanut butter. However, peanut butter can be exported from Mexico to the U.S. duty-free only if the peanuts are certified to be entirely of North American origin.

The problem is a general one. If the domestic price for a product is kept above the world price by domestic policy, agents have an incentive to import the product in some form. In the case of sugar, the domestic price of which has been as high as five times the world price, imports of sweetened products have increased significantly. At one point it was profitable—and legal—to import sweetened instant ice tea into the U.S. from Canada, separate the sugar and tea, and re-sell the sugar in the U.S. In the case of Mexico, that it processes sugar is not sufficient to allow its sugar to enter the U.S. free of duty. However, confections made with sugar from non-member countries may be exported from Mexico to the U.S. free of duty. Stringent rules of origin also apply to dairy products imported from Mexico.

In the case of horticultural products, safeguards against "import surges" are provided. U.S. marketing orders that restrict the size and grade of products are allowed by the agreement.

A fund with contributions from both the U.S. and Mexico for cleaning up environmental damage in the border area is included. U.S. standards for chemical residue on fresh fruits and vegetables remain in effect. Violations by Mexican suppliers will result in earmarking the violators for future monitoring.

These are the main features of the agricultural section of the NAFTA agreement of August 13th, 1992. The precise effects vary by product, region, and country, but the net economic effects will be beneficial for all three countries. From the perspective of all the residents of the countries some comments on the August 13th agreement are appropriate before conducting a more detailed analysis:

a. The U.S.-Mexico agreement is comprehensive in the sense that it eliminates all border protection and all agricultural products. Canada and Mexico excluded certain products from trade liberalization and they signed a separate agreement for agriculture.

b. The long transition period for certain products is intended to soften the adjustment problem for certain workers and firms, but the delay also reduces the benefits from liberalization. The present value of $1 of benefits (at a 4 percent interest rate) deferred 10 years is $.676, and deferral for 15 years reduces benefits to $.555 per $1.

c. The agreement says little about the terms under which new members would be allowed to join NAFTA. The inclusion of a formal accession clause would make the agreement appear more outward-looking.

d. Domestic content provisions could become a more significant barrier to trade. The traditional practice of U.S. customs officials was to consider a product produced in a country if a substantial transformation of components occurred in that country, regardless of the precise domestic content of the product.

Formal Studies of NAFTA

A number of quantitative studies of NAFTA have been done using formal economic models. Some have focused on macroeconomic effects, while others have studied particular sectors of the economy. Exact results have varied depending on the nature of the model and its parameters and on the assumptions about the precise features of the trade agreement. A common result of nearly all the macro-economic models is that real income would rise in all three countries as a result of NAFTA, and the largest benefits would accrue to Mexico. A representative result is that real GDP would rise by 1.6 percent in Mexico, 0.7 percent in Canada, and 0.1 percent in the U.S. (Brown, Deardorff, and Stern).

Most of the studies show rather small increases in income, but Kehoe (1992) suggests that traditional models may seriously understate the gains from trade liberalization. A country's productivity growth can be stimulated by importing more specialized inputs and developing new final products as a result of learning-by-doing. He cites the literature on endogenous growth and the favourable economic growth experience, of Spain when it joined the European Community.

A detailed model of the agricultural sector appears in Grennes et. al. (1992), and it was used to analyze the economic effects of a NAFTA. The formal model consists of 29 agricultural products for the United States, Mexico, and a residual rest-of-the-world category. Canada was not treated separately because a free trade agreement between the U.S. and Canada already exists, and the volume of trade between Canada and Mexico is very small. Less than 2 percent of Mexico's imports come from Canada. The simulation was carried out (based on data for 1988) by removing all border trade barriers between the U.S. and Mexico but retaining trade barriers against the rest of the world. Domestic policies in the U.S. (for example, deficiency payments) and Mexico were also assumed to remain in place. The assumed changes in trade policy were approximately the same as those contained in the actual agreement of August 12, 1992, although no attempt was made to model the transition period. The weighted average rate of protection in 1988 was 5 percent for the U.S. and 24 percent for Mexico. These rates include border protection only, so deficiency payments were excluded from the measure of protection. The rates for broad commodity groups were:

Commodity	United States	Mexico
Grains/oilseeds	0	32
Livestock, meats, dairy	2	13
Horticulture	23	14
Other	1	8
All 29 commodities	5	24

The rates indicate that each country had the highest rate of protection for the product for which its partner had a comparative advantage. Mexico had a 32 percent rate for grains and oilseeds, and the U.S. had a 23 percent rate of protection against horticulture.

The simulation results should be interpreted as showing what would happen to trade after the U.S. and Mexico removed all trade barriers against each other (beyond the transition period) but retained barriers against non-members.

Table 1 shows a larger increase in U.S. agricultural exports to Mexico ($482 million) than agricultural imports from Mexico ($166 million). The increase in net exports of the U.S. is partly due to the higher initial level of protection in Mexico.

In terms of broad product categories, there would be an increase in U.S. exports of grain and oilseeds of $430 million (see Table 2). The biggest component of this category is corn (see Table 3). U.S. corn exports to Mexico are expected to increase by 65 percent, but exports to Mexico are a small percentage of U.S. corn production. Consequently, U.S. corn production will rise by only 0.3 percent and the U.S. corn price will rise by 1.1 percent. Because Mexico is a much smaller country, removal of the corn tariff will have a much bigger effect on production, consumption and the price of corn in Mexico.

Table 1: Changes from BASE in Agricultural Exports due to NAFTA

Exporter	Importers (Millions of dollars)			
	U.S.	Mexico	Rest of World	Total Exports
United States	—	482	-59	423
Mexico	166	—	5	171
Rest-of-World	3	-39	—	-36
Total	169	443	-54	558

There would be an increase in U.S. imports of horticultural products of $104 million (Table 2), especially tomatoes. Most tomato imports occur in the winter months, and they compete with Florida production. U.S. production of tomatoes is expected to decrease by 0.7 percent and the price in the U.S. is expected to decrease by 1.9 percent. (Table 4). A paper by Buxton and Roberts (1992) contains roughly similar results for the effect of NAFTA on the U.S. fresh tomato industry: a slight decrease in price (-1.3 percent) and a decrease in production (-1.9 percent). Decreases in production of other fruits and vegetables in the U.S. are expected, but no product is expected to experience a production or price decrease in excess of 2 percent (Table 4). There would also be an increase in exports of beef, pork, and poultry by the U.S. and an increase in both exports and imports of live animals. Hence, the prediction is that NAFTA would bring about a kind of magnification of the current pattern of trade with Mexico.

Table 2: Changes From BASE in Agricultural Exports by Commodity Group

Exporter	Importers (Millions of dollars)			
	U.S.	Mexico	ROW	Total Exports
United States				
Grains, oilseeds	—	430	-61	369
Livestock, meats, dairy	—	49	0	49
Horticulture	—	1	2	3
Other	—	3	-1	2
Total	—	482	-59	423
Mexico				
Grains, oilseeds	2	—	9	11
Livestock, meats, dairy	56	—	0	57
Horticulture	104	—	-6	98
Other	3	—	2	5
Total	166	—	5	171
Rest of World				
Grains, oilseeds	12	-38	—	-25
Livestock, meats, dairy	5	0	—	5
Horticulture	-16	0	—	-15
Other	3	-1	—	-1
Total	3	-39	—	-36

Possibility of Trade Diversion

A potential problem with NAFTA and all free trade areas is that an inefficient pattern of trade could result from exempting Mexican products from U.S. tariffs, while retaining tariffs in the U.S. against the rest of the world. American importers could switch from a lower cost (under a uniform tariff) non-member source to a higher cost Mexican source due to the discriminatory tariff policy. Since the U.S. acquires only 6 percent of its imports from Mexico currently, it would be possible to divert many U.S. imports from the rest of the world to Mexico and lower real income. In the simulation, however, trade diversion does not occur for U.S. imports, since U.S. agricultural imports from the rest of the world do not decrease (Table 1).

Table 3: Changes From BASE in Agricultural Production, Consumption and Prices for Select Grains and Oilseeds in Mexico and the United States*

Country/ Commodity	Production	Consumption	Price
Mexico			
U.S. corn	—	64.0	-33.2
Mexican corn	-7.3	-7.3	-15.9
U.S. other coarse grain	—	50.1	-32.3
Mexican other coarse grain	-10.9	-13.9	-15.8
United States			
U.S. corn	0.3	-0.8	1.1
U.S. other coarse grain	1.7	-2.1	2.3

*U.S., Mexican, and Rest-of-World corn are assumed not to be homogeneous but, instead, are imperfect substitutes. Thus all three types of corn are available in each country or region, but the United States produces only U.S. corn and Mexico produces only Mexican corn.

In terms of individual products, the only significant case of trade diversion is frozen orange juice concentrate. Total U.S. imports of frozen orange juice concentrate would increase by 8000 tons as a result of an increase in consumption of 6000 tons and a decrease in production of 2000 tons. The net increase in U.S. imports is the sum of an increase in

Table 4: Production, Consumption, and Price Responses for Horticultural Commodities

Country/ Commodity	Production (Percent)	Consumption (Percent)	Price (Percent)
Mexico (Mexican produced)			
Melons	2.4	-0.6	1.3
FCOJ	18.8	-13.4	12.2
Cucumbers	6.6	-1.3	3.6
Onions	3.8	-0.7	2.1
Green Peppers	1.6	-0.2	0.9
Tomatoes	1.8	-0.4	1.0
United States (U.S. produced)			
Melons	-0.5	-0.6	-0.7
FCOJ	-0.3	-0.4	-0.3
Cucumbers	-2.0	-2.2	-2.4
Onions	-0.8	-10.0	-1.0
Green Peppers	-1.5	-1.8	-1.9
Tomatoes	-0.7	-0.9	-1.9
United States (Mexican produced)			
Melons	—	10.8	-4.0
FCOJ	—	32.1	-9.2
Cucumbers	—	10.8	-5.2
Onions	—	13.7	-5.8
Green Peppers	—	10.2	-5.1
Tomatoes	—	10.2	-6.1

imports from Mexico of 12,000 tons and a decrease in imports from Brazil of 4000 tons. Thus, removing the U.S. tariff against Mexico results in trade creation of 8000 tons and trade diversion from Brazil to Mexico of 4000 tons (see Grennes et. al. p. 42). Frozen orange juice concentrate is the only agricultural product for which significant trade diversion was detected. The results indicate that trade diversion would not be as serious a problem as it was when Greece, Spain, and Portugal joined the European Community. (Plummer (1991a, 1991b), Winters).

It is also possible for Mexico to substitute tariff-exempt imports from the U.S. for tariff-eligible imports from the rest of the world (ROW). This kind of trade diversion did not show up either in terms of a large reduction in total imports from ROW or a reduction in imports of particular products. One reason why this kind of diversion is unlikely to occur is that the U.S. already accounts for 70 percent of Mexico's agricultural imports. Thus, U.S. exporters are already the lowest cost source even without a tariff advantage.

Erzan and Yeats have explicitly modeled the possible trade diversion from NAFTA. The value of trade created would be nearly four times the value of trade diversion. Of the limited trade diversion, most of it would occur outside Latin America. Brazil would be the biggest loser within the region and agricultural products would be the category with the most diversion within the region. However, the main conclusion from their work is that trade creation would dominate trade diversion.

Regional and Multilateral Approaches to Trade Liberalization

An important question is whether NAFTA and the expansion of regional trading blocs will contribute to faster worldwide trade liberalization or whether regionalism will be an impediment to broader liberalization. This issue has particular importance for agriculture because of the Common Agricultural Policy (CAP) of the European Community. The highly protectionist CAP has transformed the EC from a net importer of grain and many other agricultural products to a net exporter. The grain policy that combines a variable import levy and an export subsidy ("restitution") has been described as the new Corn Laws. The adverse effects of the CAP have increased as membership has grown (Plummer 1991a, 1991b, Winters and Hamilton). Intransigence by the EC on agricultural trade reform has prevented a general agreement on a much broader range of trade issues in the Uruguay Round negotiations. Thus, the EC as a regional approach to organizing agricultural trade has been a significant barrier to multilateral trade liberalization.

A necessary condition for a free trade agreement to contribute to multilateral free trade is that trade creation must dominate trade diversion. The arrangement must also satisfy the GATT condition of not raising tariffs against non-members. It should also be outward-looking in the sense of allowing fairly free entry of new members, provided they satisfy the rules of NAFTA. Easy accession of new members to a NAFTA would be roughly consistent with a kind of conditional most-favoured-nation principle, i.e., membership extended to one trading partner would also be extended to other trading partners. In that case, excluded trading partners whose exports might be diverted by NAFTA could avoid the trade diversion by joining the arrangement. The use of this kind of conditional most-favoured-nation principle was successful in promoting freer trade in the latter half of the nineteenth century, in absence of the GATT or a comparable international institution (Irwin). As the number and size of customs unions and free trade areas increase it might be prudent to clarify and tighten the GATT rules concerning what constitutes an acceptable preferential arrangement. Openness could be achieved by requiring customs unions and free trade areas to admit all prospective members who satisfy the stated economic conditions of membership. In the case of NAFTA, Caribbean countries who would be harmed by giving Mexico privileged access to the U.S. sugar market could avoid trade diversion by becoming members.

In terms of negotiating costs, it is easier to reach agreement among three countries than among 150 countries. The Uruguay Round stalled after six years of negotiation but the NAFTA agreement was reached in just over one year. With respect to new members it would be desirable to include an access clause ("docking") in NAFTA, stating the conditions under which new entrants could join. Establishing the rules in advance would reduce the cost of negotiating with new members. A weakness of the NAFTA agreement is that it is largely silent on the issue of future access by non-members, and an explicit statement about access would make NAFTA look less like an exclusive club to non-members. However, one can expect the Congress to be reluctant to give up its prerogative of judging new members on a country-by-country basis.

Some logical conditions of membership that could be included would be commitment to a market economy and absence of foreign exchange controls. Inducing some Latin American countries to meet these conditions could provide benefits to the prospective members that would be as large or larger than the benefits from removing trade barriers. Unilateral policy reform by Latin American governments has been and can be an effective policy. Chile and Mexico are two examples (see Goldin and van der Mensbrugghe).

NAFTA and Western Hemisphere Free Trade

NAFTA could be expanded into a Western Hemisphere Free Trade Agreement. The Enterprise for the Americas Initiative announced by President Bush in June 1990 is a formal invitation to move in that direction. Whether this larger regional bloc would lead to higher world income could be judged by whether it results in net trade creation and whether it remains accessible to prospective new members. There is a greater potential for trade diversion in the broader arrangement than in NAFTA, but it does not appear to be a serious problem for the countries of the Americas. Trade creation is expected to dominate (see Erzan and Yeats).

In general, the importance of trade diversion varies by country and product. A necessary condition for diversion is that the low cost supplier of a member must be excluded from the agreement. In addition, the member country must retain a tariff on the product against non-members. An example would be including Brazil but excluding Argentina, its main current supplier of wheat (see Grennes et. al.). For many important Latin American agricultural exports such as coffee and bananas, this problem does not exist because the products already enter the U.S. duty-free. Thus, as residents of a member state, Mexican growers of coffee and bananas gain no advantage over non-members.

Sugar is a greater potential problem, but only if the U.S. retains a global quota. If it does, greater imports from members will reduce imports from non-members. This could be a serious problem if certain

Caribbean sugar producers are excluded from the agreement, and spokesmen for those governments have already expressed their concern about diversion of sugar trade. However, the source of the problem would be the global U.S. sugar quota, not the free trade agreement. The U.S. sugar program has been one of the most wasteful agricultural programs in terms of costs imposed on sugar buyers and perverse incentives given to U.S. sugar growers. In the recent past, the sugar program provided incentives for American farmers to incur $5 in costs to produce another unit of sugar when additional sugar could have been imported for $1. A disadvantage of a quota over a tariff is that a quota does not limit how high a domestic price can rise relative to a comparable world price. In the Uruguay Round discussions, U.S. negotiators have proposed phasing out global import quotas on all products. If this occurs, the possibility of diversion of sugar trade from a WHFTA would be smaller. The ultimate protection against trade diversion is to allow the lower cost non-member supplier to join the free trade agreement. For this reason it is important to make NAFTA or a broader Western Hemisphere trading arrangement accessible to new members.

Environmental Consequences of NAFTA

Environmental degradation is a frequently cited criticism of NAFTA. In this regard, it is important to distinguish between environmental problems that existed before NAFTA from those that are related to freer trade. Air pollution in Mexico City and water pollution along the U.S.-Mexico border are legitimate environmental issues, but they should not be attributed to NAFTA. Congressman Gephardt's proposal to "clean up the border" by imposing a special tariff (euphemistically named a "cross-border transactions tax") is a mistake, because it penalizes the wrong activity. Tomatoes grown in Sinaloa and exported to the U.S. and corn grown in Iowa and exported to Mexico do not contribute to border pollution, and the essence of NAFTA is to encourage this kind of mutually profitable and environmentally clean trade. The appropriate remedy for pollution is to correct the problem at its source rather than to penalize an unrelated activity like trade.

Food safety and protecting the health of plants and animals are legitimate concerns for consumers and agricultural producers on both sides of the border. However, the issues are not closely related to NAFTA. If NAFTA fails, the problems remain. If NAFTA is ratified, the volume of trade will increase, but the basic issues will remain. For example, U.S. standards for chemical residue on fruits and vegetables are applicable to both domestic products and imports, and U.S. standards will remain in effect under NAFTA. It is always difficult to determine the optimum standards for food safety, but NAFTA will not lower those standards in any way.

With regard to protecting the health of plants and animals, all trading countries have border measures (sanitary and phytosanitary standards) to exclude importation of diseased plants and animals. There are enforcement problems, including the possibility of using the standards as non-tariff barriers to trade. Long before NAFTA was discussed, the U.S. enforced rules against importation from Mexico of cattle with hoof-and-mouth disease and avocadoes subject to a certain plant disease. The NAFTA agreement would not make it more difficult to enforce such standards. The agreement does provide that standards should be scientifically based, which is the same position taken by the U.S. government in its trade discussions with the European Community.

Another environmental issue that has been linked with trade is the use of some chemicals by Mexican growers that are not legal in the U.S. Several aspects of the issue should be clarified. First, American consumers are protected against unsafe Mexican products by restrictions on the allowable chemical residue on fruits and vegetables. U.S. standards apply both to chemicals that are legal in the U.S. and those that are not. Second, if the chemicals are dangerous to the health of Mexican workers or if they pollute the Mexican environment, they constitute a legitimate domestic problem in Mexico with or without NAFTA.

Third, spokesmen for American farmers have claimed that differential standards across countries put American producers at a competitive disadvantage in competing against imports or in other markets. They call for trade barriers that would result in a "level playing field" or "fair trade." Relative costs are affected by different environmental standards, but differences do not justify interfering with trade. Many other standards also differ across countries; some are lower than in the U.S. and others are higher. Mexico also has a lower legal minimum wage law and different standards for the use of child labour. Other countries have more restrictive standards than the U.S. in terms of allowing the sale of meat from animals that were fed growth hormones, allowing factories to produce on Sunday, and worker safety laws.

International differences in standards influence relative costs in the same way that costs are affected by differences in wages, the price of capital goods, laws, and taxes. The politically popular expression "level playing field" and the analogy between trade and a game with a winner and a loser is fundamentally misleading. When trade occurs, both parties win. Furthermore, an important source of gains from trade is the existence of differences in costs. There is also a more pragmatic reason for American agricultural lobbyists to oppose restricting imports because of lower standards in some exporting country. The European Community has already restricted beef imports from the U.S. by claiming higher standards for food safety. Germany and Italy have higher standards than the U.S. for chemical residue on tobacco. American products of biotechnology are also vulnerable to similar import restrictions.

NAFTA and Employment

Some opposition to NAFTA has been based on concern about worker displacement due to imports or relocation of plants to Mexico. Some concern is justified in the sense that all economic change, no matter how great its net benefits to society, harms someone. Because NAFTA will produce more winners than losers, it is possible to enjoy the benefits of freer trade and also compensate the losers. Compensation would distribute the gains from freer trade more evenly. Candidates of both political parties for President and the Congress in the U.S. advocate some form of trade adjustment assistance in conjunction with NAFTA. The fact that some workers would have to change jobs should not justify opposing NAFTA and depriving the gainers the benefits of more favourable trading opportunities. Restricting imports to save particular jobs is analogous to allowing Luddite workers to destroy machines that threatened their jobs.

In the agricultural sector NAFTA would result in more jobs in the export sector, including grains and oilseeds, and fewer jobs in the import competing sector, including horticultural products. Since agriculture as a whole is expected to expand, one would expect more agricultural employment with NAFTA than there would otherwise be. However, the case for or against NAFTA should not be based on the number of jobs created or destroyed in a particular industry. To put the trade-employment relationship into perspective, it should be noted that any changes in agricultural employment attributable to changes in trade policy have been completely dominated by domestic changes in technology and demand. Millions of agricultural jobs have been destroyed in this century for reasons completely unrelated to international trade. In 1900, most Americans were employed in agriculture, but today less than 4 percent of American workers are employed in agriculture. The fact that new circumstances make particular jobs redundant is not a convincing reason to oppose freer trade or economic progress in general.

A larger agricultural labour market adjustment problem exists in Mexico. The biggest increase in imports will be in corn (See Table 3), which is currently produced by many small inefficient producers (Robinson et. al., Levy and Van Wijnbergen). To ease the adjustment problem the transition period is 15 years and a tariff quota will be in place during that period.

How many Mexican workers will be displaced by additional corn imports is an interesting question, but it is not easy to answer. Many corn producers participate in the communal operations of *ejidos*, and they would be adversely affected by cheaper corn imports. However, a recent constitutional reform has eliminated many of the restrictions that had contributed to inefficient production. Producers are now allowed to own land, lease land, hire additional labour, choose between crops and grazing, and enter into contracts with foreign investors. Relaxing restrictions on the use of *ejido* land lowers the cost of growing corn and makes it more difficult to determine the net effect of freer trade. Some of the workers displaced from corn production will be absorbed by the expanding fruit and vegetable sector and by food processing, but expansion of employment depends on complementary investment. For fruits and vegetables investment in water projects is essential. Expansion of facilities to produce tomato paste is an example of food processing financed by American investment.

Ratification Process

The NAFTA must be ratified by the legislatures in all three countries, but the political situations are quite different. In Mexico the President's party has a large majority in the legislature. In Canada the parliamentary system gives a majority to the Prime Minister in the Parliament, but the government and the U.S.-Canada free trade agreement are currently unpopular. Although the economic gains to people benefiting from NAFTA exceed the losses to other people in all three countries, it remains to be seen whether the agreement will be ratified. It is well-known that the U.S. Congress tends to be more protectionist than presidents of either party. The fact that members of Congress are elected by particular districts rather than the entire country leads them to subordinate national interests to parochial interests at times. For example, the military budget may not be cut even if a majority favours a reduction, because each member vigorously opposes closing bases or defense plants in his own district. Small but powerful special interest groups that would be harmed by NAFTA can exert disproportionate influence on the Congress.

Another factor favouring protectionism is the fact that benefits from trade liberalization tend to be spread evenly among the population, but the costs tend to be much more concentrated. The smaller number of losers makes it easier for them to form a coalition and lobby effectively before the Congress. The small number of sugar growers has made it easier to form an effective lobby. For example, there might be 1000 people in a Congressional district who would gain $1 each from trade liberalization. Because the gain per person is small, no individual has a strong incentive to commit his time and money to influencing his Congressman. At the same time, two people in the district may lose $100 each from freer trade, and each one has a strong incentive to commit time and money to oppose trade liberalization. In this case, the Congressman is vulnerable to the protectionist pleas of the special interest group that would lose $200 even though there would be a net gain of $800 to residents of the district as a whole. The fact that the percentage of income spent on food declines with affluence (Engel's Law) weakens resistance to special interest pleas for agricultural protection in high income countries. Special interest groups could block NAFTA just as

Western European agricultural groups have successfully led the opposition to agricultural reform in the GATT negotiations for many years.

Conclusion

The NAFTA presents a rare opportunity to increase the prosperity of residents of the United States, Mexico, and Canada. It would allow producers in each country to specialize in making their best products. The trilateral agreement could be extended to other countries of the hemisphere, and the regional agreement could stimulate worldwide trade liberalization.

Increasing competition in world agricultural markets would be an impressive achievement after many decades of failed negotiations. In terms of specific products, the U.S. is expected to increase exports of grain, oilseeds, and meat to Mexico. At the same time Americans are expected to increase imports of horticultural products, especially fruits and vegetables.

Trade diversion is not expected to be an important problem for the members of NAFTA. Some workers are expected to be displaced from current jobs, but trade adjustment assistance has been proposed to ease the adjustment of particular workers. In addition a lengthy transition period (up to 15 years) has been included for products that are most vulnerable to import competition.

Some legitimate environmental problems exist, but they existed before NAFTA was proposed, and they will not be aggravated if NAFTA is ratified. The pre-NAFTA standards for protecting against excessive chemical residue on fruits and vegetables and for preventing imports of plant and animal diseases remain in effect. To the extent that NAFTA stimulates economic growth in Mexico, it will provide Mexicans with greater capacity and will to improve the environment.

Although the August agreement represents a step toward a more open world economy, it does contain certain protectionist features. Deferring the removal of trade barriers for 15 years for certain products reduces the present value of the benefits of trade reform. The absence of conditions and procedures for the accession of new members makes the NAFTA appear to be an inward-looking arrangement. For several products NAFTA introduces domestic content rules that are more restrictive than they have been in the past. Finally, Canada and Mexico excluded certain agricultural products from trade liberalization.

Although NAFTA presents an opportunity to expand agricultural trade based on comparative advantage, its impact is likely to be smaller than the effects of other changes in member countries. The U.S.-Canadian agreement is more important to Canada than freer trade with Mexico. Broader economic reform in Mexico will have a greater effect than preferential trade with its neighbours. In the U.S. long-term growth in agricultural productivity dominates the effect of additional trade with Mexico.

References

Anderson, Kym, and Richard Blackhurst, eds. *The Greening of World Trade Issues*. Ann Arbor, MI: University of Michigan Press, 1992.

Bradford, Colin, Jr., ed. *Strategic Options for Latin America in the 1990s*. Paris: OECD, 1992.

Brown, Drusilla, Alan Deardorff, Robert Stern. "A North American Free Trade Agreement: Analytical Issues and a Computational Assessment." Paper presented at the Conference on North American Free Trade, Center for Strategic and International Studies, Washington, June 27-28, 1991.

Buxton, Boyd M. and Donna Roberts. "Economic Implications of Alternative Free Trade Agreements for the U.S. Fresh Tomato and Tomato Paste Industries." Paper presented at annual meeting of American Agricultural Economic Association, Baltimore, August 1992.

Erzan, Refik, and Alexander Yeats. "U.S.-Latin America Free Trade Areas: Some Empirical Evidence." in Sylvia Saborio, ed. *The Premise and the Promise: Free Trade in the Americas*. New Brunswick, N.J.: Transactions Publishers, 1992.

Grennes, Thomas. "Domestic Agricultural Programs: The Case for Multilateral Decoupling." *Choices*, First Quarter, 1988a, pp. 9-11.

Grennes, Thomas. "Farm-Support Policies Compatible with Trade Liberalization." *World Economy* 11, March 1988b, pp. 109-117.

Grennes, Thomas, Julio Hernandez Estrada, Barry Krissoff, Jaime Matus Gardea, Jerry Sharples, Constanza Valdes. *An Analysis of a United States-Canada Mexico Free Trade Agreement*. IATRC Commissioned Paper Number 10, November, 1991.

Grennes, Thomas, and Barry Krissoff. *Agricultural Trade in a North American Free Trade Agreement*. August 1992.

Goldin, Ian, and Dominique van der Mensbrugghe. "The Forgotten Story: Agriculture and Latin American Trade and Growth." In Colin I. Bradford, Jr., ed. *Strategic Options for Latin America in the 1990s*. Paris: OECD, 1992.

Grossman, Gene, and Alan Krueger. *Environmental Impacts of a North American Free Trade Agreement.* Princeton University, 1991.

Hufbauer, Gary C. and Jeffrey J. Schott. *North American Free Trade: Issues and Recommendations.* Washington: Institute for International Economics, 1992.

Irwin, Douglas. "Multilateral and Bilateral Trade Policies and the World Trading System: An Historical Perspective." Prepared for World Bank-CEPR Conference on "New Dimensions to Regional Integration." Washington, D.C., April 2-3, 1992.

Johnson, D. Gale. *World Agriculture in Disarray.* London: Macmillan, 1973.

Karr, Albert. "Bush to Offer Plan to Broaden Job Training." *Wall Street Journal,* August 24, 1992, p. A3.

Kehoe, Timothy J. *Assessing the Economic Impact of North American Free Trade.* University of Minnesota, May 1992.

Krissoff, Barry, Liana Neff, and Jerry Sharples. "Estimated Impacts of a Potential U.S.-Mexico Preferential Trading Arrangement for the Agricultural Sector." IATRC Working Paper 92-1, March 1992.

Levy, Santiago and Sweder Van Wijnbergen. "Maize and the Mexico-United States Free Trade Agreement." Washington, World Bank, February, 1991.

Lipsey, Richard G. "Getting There: The Path to a Western Hemisphere Free Trade Area and Its Structure." In Sylvia Saborio, ed. *The Premise and the Promise: Free Trade in the Americas.* New Brunswick, N. J.: Transaction Publishers, 1992.

Low, Patrick, ed. *International Trade and the Environment.* World Bank Discussion Paper No. 159, Washington, April 1992.

Pasour, E. C., Jr. *Agriculture and the State: Market Processes and Bureaucracy.* The Independent Institute, Oakland, California, 1990.

Plummer, M. "Ex-Post Empirical Estimates of the Second Enlargement." *Weltwirtschaftliches Archiv* Band 127 Heft 1991a, pp. 171-82.

Plummer, M. "Efficiency Aspects of the Accession of Spain and Portugal to the EC." *Journal of Common Market Studies,* 29 (March 1991b): 317-23.

Robinson, Sherman, and Mary E. Burfisher, Raul Hinojosa-Ojeda, and Karen Thierfelder. "Agricultural Policies and Migration in a U.S.-Mexico Free Trade Area." Giannini Foundation Working Paper No. 617, December 1991.

Saborio, Sylvia, ed., *The Premise and the Promise: Free Trade in the Americas*. New Brunswick, N.J.: Transaction Publishers, 1992.

Winters, L. Alan, and Carl Hamilton. "Opening Up International Trade with Eastern Europe." *Economic Policy* (April 1992): 78-116.

World Bank. *World Development Report 1992*. New York: Oxford University Press, 1992.

The Financial Sector in NAFTA: Two Plus One Equals Restructuring

John F. Chant
Simon Fraser University

THE FINANCIAL SECTOR PROVISIONS OF THE North American Free Trade Agreement (NAFTA) cannot be judged on the same terms as the rest of the Agreement. They differ substantially in form and substance from other provisions because of the distinctive nature of trade in financial services. Like the rest of the Agreement, the financial sector negotiations for NAFTA could build on the accomplishments of the Canada-U.S. Free Trade Agreement (FTA) and, indeed, this part of the Agreement fully embodies all the equivalent provisions of the FTA. But in the case of the financial sector, the FTA was very much a bilateral agreement, dealing with each country's concerns about the other's policies. The addition of accession, provision for the extension to third parties, to the objectives of NAFTA required that the financial sector provisions would have to be recast in a multi-lateral framework. This paper provides an assessment of the major provisions of Chapter 14: Financial Services of

NAFTA in terms of providing for freer access in the supply of financial services between the participating countries.

The Financial Sector: A Special Case

The financial sector presents difficulties in free trade negotiations for a number of reasons:

1. trade in financial services, like trade in many other services, differs substantially from trade in goods
2. regulation shapes the financial sector to a greater degree than most other parts of the economy, and
3. Canada and the U.S., in particular, have adopted different, and even incompatible, approaches to regulation of their financial sectors.

Trade in Financial Services

Much trade in financial services requires different relationships between suppliers and their customers than most trade in goods. At one extreme, some financial services, such as underwriting of securities for large corporations and governments, require a presence in neither the country of the issuer nor the country of the buyers. U.S. securities firms, for example, have been active suppliers of underwriting services to Canadian issuers. At the other extreme, other securities industry services, retail brokering in particular, require a presence near the customers. Similar contrasts can be found in banking. The market for loans to large corporations extends world wide and can be conducted through representatives rather than subsidiaries and branches. Retail deposit-gathering and consumer loans, on the other hand, require a supplier to be located near the customer.

These differences between trade in services and trade in goods with respect to the importance of cross-border trade requires that the financial sector negotiations have a different emphasis than the negotiations for trade in goods. For some financial activities where a presence near the customer is not required, the relevant issue in trade negotiations will still be freedom in cross-border transactions. But for much trade in financial services, the right of establishment and the powers of established institutions will be far more important than cross-border trade.

Pervasive Regulation

Trade negotiations for the financial sector must take into account the heavy degree of regulation governing this sector in almost every economy. Heavy regulation, in itself, need not unduly complicate the trade negotiations. If two countries pursued similar approaches to regulation, financial institutions from one country might be able to operate in the other country under home country rules, the approach followed by the European Community.[1] Negotiations will become complicated to the degree that the regulations of the negotiating parties differ. In this case, it will be difficult to equate the treatment of foreign and domestic institutions between the negotiating parties.

The problem of regulation is particularly acute for Canada-U.S. financial sector negotiations because two countries have adopted contrasting approaches to the regulation of their financial institutions. These differences for the regulation of banks can be summarized as follows:

Canada	**U.S.**
Strict entry requirements, few banks	Easy entry, many banks
Ownership restrictions	Fewer restrictions on ownership
Powers set by rule	Many powers determined case by case
Allowed to be in securities business	Prohibited from securities business

1 See Key (1990) for a careful description of the European Community's approach to the financial sector.

The negotiations were further complicated because they took place at the time when Mexico, the third country, was returning its state-owned banking system to private hands. Otherwise, the Mexican approach to regulation more closely resembles Canada's.

Differences in the level of government responsible for regulation will also complicate trade negotiations. National governments negotiate and are bound by trade agreements. Nevertheless, some activities that are subject to negotiation will be the responsibility of other levels of government. The impact of agreements between national governments will thus be limited when the activities subject to negotiation are either shared with or subject to the authority of lower levels of government. Despite a commitment by a national government to provide national treatment, these efforts will make little difference when the regulations of lower level governments serve as an obstacle to trade in financial services and remain unchanged despite the Agreement.

Provincial governments in Canada and state governments in the U.S. both have major areas of responsibility with respect to regulating the financial sector. In Canada, provincial governments regulate the securities industry and share responsibility with the federal government for regulating trust and loan companies. More significantly, in the U.S., state governments share responsibility with federal government for the regulation of banks.

Differences in financial regulation will pose difficult enough problems in normal times. These problems are exacerbated when existing regulations are undergoing reform, as is the case in all three countries. Thus, it will be doubly difficult to determine the combined effects of these reforms together with liberalized treatment of international suppliers. It is even more difficult to integrate prospective reforms into a bargaining stance when the possibility of their implementation remains uncertain.

The problems for financial negotiations arising from reform can be illustrated by the consequences of the removal of barriers to the ownership of securities firms by banks in Canada. Before the change in Canadian regulation, the U.S. treatment of Canadian securities firms had been on the same basis as domestic firms. The change in Canadian regulation permitted the ownership of securities firms by commercial banks. This change meant that Canadian practice became very much at odds with that in the U.S. where the Glass-Steagle Act generally prohibits banks from engaging in the securities industry either directly or indirectly through subsidiaries. The resulting changes in ownership of the security firms threatened to alter their status in the U.S. because, with their ownership by banks, strict application of the Glass-Steagle Act would have forced them out of almost all securities activities in the U.S. Thus, despite the absence of any change in U.S. policies, Canadian securities firms, because of their changed ownership, no longer conformed with the U.S. rules and would be forced to leave the U.S. market if nothing were done

Free Trade in the Financial Sector: What Does It Mean?

The concept of "free trade" lacks an obvious meaning when applied to the financial sector. A free trade agreement in this sector can embody different levels of commitment from the participating countries ranging from freedom for cross-border trade through an assurance of the right of establishment together with the assurance of national treatment to the creation of a common market with full harmonization of regulation.

The first level, freedom of cross-border trade which implies the absence of obstacles to the trade in goods and services, had not been a significant issue in the FTA negotiations because it had been generally assured by the liberal approaches taken by each country with respect to the freedom of financial flows. For Canada and the U.S., financial institutions had been able to offer services to customers in the other country. In absence of foreign exchange controls, residents of either country could generally hold deposits, securities and other financial instruments issued in the other country. The remaining obstacles to cross-border trade in financial services arose mainly from a lack of tax harmonization and, at times, from specific tax measures aimed at stemming cross-border flows. In the NAFTA negotiations, the question of cross border transactions became more important. Mexico had just removed foreign exchange controls, but still maintained rules that restricted the ability of foreign suppliers to meet domestic demands for financial services.

The most extreme commitment, a "common market" in financial services with fully harmonized regulation, was also not an issue in the negotiations, even though such an approach had been adopted by the member states of the European Community. The harmonization of regulation required for a common market for financial services would be feasible only where differences in regulation are slight and are not issues of national commitment. These conditions were absent for the FTA negotiations. Both Canada and the U.S. were committed to their own distinct approaches to regulation. While innovation, internationalization and the break-down of differences between institutions were all forcing a reassessment of regulation in each country, neither country had any disposition to move closer in any formal way toward the other's approach. With cross-border trade generally assured and a common market in financial services beyond reach, the financial sector negotiations of both the FTA and NAFTA, despite different approaches, have focused on the right of establishment subject to national treatment.

The Background of the FTA: Chapter 17

The NAFTA negotiations in the financial sector, like those in most other sectors, did not take place on a clean slate. Already, Canada and the U.S. had set a pattern through FTA negotiations that provided a starting point for many of the more difficult problems posed by the financial sector.

The financial sector components of the FTA are relatively simple and are contained in the four pages of provisions of Chapter 17. Significantly, the preamble to the Chapter states that provisions are intended

> to preserve the access that our respective financial institutions have to each other's markets...[and] both Canada and the U.S. have agreed to continue liberalizing the rules governing their respective financial markets and to extend the benefits of such liberalization to institutions controlled by the other party. This statement sets the scope for the agreement clearly. The framers of the agreement did not intend to move toward a harmonized and integrated financial sector. Rather they intended to preserve and extend the existing integration of their financial market in face of changing regulation that, despite its liberalizing intent, threatened to cut the supply of some financial services between the two countries.

The commitments taken on by the two parties in the FTA were significantly different from each other. The U.S. commitments taken in Article 1702 cover banking powers with respect to government securities, branching powers, and the consequences of amendments to the Glass-Steagle Act for the preservation of the powers of Canadian banks in the U.S. The Canadian commitments set out in Article 1703, in contrast, eliminate for United States persons the restrictions and requirements that apply to foreign persons and foreign-owned institutions.

The financial sector provisions of the FTA very much reflected their origins as part of a bilateral treaty. The commitments under the Agreement reflected the concerns of each party about the financial policies of the other.

The U.S., as part of its continuing world-wide program to liberalize limits to the foreign operations of U.S. banks, had been pressuring Canada to open its banking system to U.S. banks to a greater degree than possible under the 1980 Bank Act. The Treasury had earlier lobbied the Canadian authorities to raise the 8 percent ceiling on the share of foreign banks and were successful in having it raised to 16 percent in 1984. In the FTA, the U.S. succeeded in having any distinction between U.S. and domestic ownership removed from Canadian banking legislation.

The benefits received by Canada were defensive. The status quo had been disturbed by regulatory changes in both countries that jeopardized the position of Canadian institutions in the U.S. Exemption from Glass-Steagle provisions under the FTA preserved the ability of securities firms associated with banks to underwrite and deal in Canadian government securities in the U.S., a power threatened by their ownership by banks. Similarly, the protection of interstate banking powers through the FTA allowed Canadian banks to maintain their U.S. operations intact.

Experience with the FTA in practice has emphasized two significant shortcomings of the agreement. First, the FTA was an agreement between national governments and did not bind lower level governments. Second, the FTA contained assurances of equal treatment of the other country's financial institutions that applied to formal reform measures, but in the event did not govern effective reform carried out through the exercise of discretion by regulators.

The problem of divided jurisdiction was apparent at the time of the FTA negotiations. Provincial governments in Canada and state governments in the U.S. both have major responsibilities for regulating the financial sector. Thus, despite the commitment of the national governments to provide national treatment, the FTA made little difference where the regulations of lower level governments serve as obstacles to equal treatment.

The second problem was less apparent at the time of the negotiations and has since gained importance as a result of Canada's concern about the different consequences of the two countries' approaches to regulation. In Canada, reliance on rule tends to extend new powers to all institutions, whereas in the U.S., widespread use of discretion grants powers to institutions case-by-case. These differences became exacerbated with the failure of the recent initiatives for reform in the U.S. that appear to have ruled out any prospect for substantial reform in the near future.

The issue of the differences in approach to regulation gained importance when it became apparent that the safeguards for Canadian banks and their subsidiaries with respect to the Glass-Steagle Act have not been effective in securing equal powers. *The Wall Street Journal*, November 13, 1991, p. A8 reports

> Now, with the broad banking bill defeated and one in the Senate likely to die, too, the Federal Reserve Board is free to continue granting securities powers to strong banking companies. So far it has authorized three U.S. bank holding companies, J.P.Morgan, Bankers Trust and the relatively small Dauphin Deposit Corporation in Harrisburg, Pa., to underwrite bond and equity offerings. More than a dozen others, including Citicorp and Chase Manhattan Corp., can underwrite corporate debt issues but not stock deals.

These developments suggest that the powers of U.S. banks in the securities area are being changed substantially by the discretion of the regulators without changes in laws.

The importance of the erosion of the FTA safeguards will depend on the relative weights of discretionary versus legislative measures in future changes of U.S. banking regulation. The continuing failure to reach agreement on banking law reform suggests that future changes will be brought about through discretion. Thus, the negotiated safeguards with respect to regulation will not serve to protect the interests of Canadian securities firms in the U.S. to the degree that might have been expected.

The Financial Sector in NAFTA

NAFTA's Chapter 14 on financial services differs substantially from the FTA in its approach to freer trade in the financial sector. The latter did not provide an overall framework and dealt strictly with each country's concerns about the other's treatment of its financial institutions. Distinctly different measures were embodied in the two countries' commitments.

The FTA approach to trade in the financial sector would have been awkward and unwieldy for any agreement designed to extend beyond two countries to embrace a third or, just as important, for an agreement created with the prospect of future expansion to other countries. Accordingly, the NAFTA financial services chapter goes well beyond specific concerns that might arise in Canada-Mexico-U.S. negotiations and establishes a framework for dealing with the range of issues that could arise from this sector in any multi-national negotiation.

Each country had a separate agenda with respect to the financial sector provisions of NAFTA. The U.S. saw the NAFTA negotiations as opening up Mexican financial markets to U.S. financial institutions at a critical stage in their development. Moreover, the increased access to Mexican markets would be another step in the U.S. agenda started in the early 1980s directed toward the opening of financial markets throughout the world. Canada, on the other hand, had more modest ambitions. The NAFTA negotiations were for Canada an extension of the defensive measures in the FTA and centred on fine-tuning the protection of Canadian financial businesses achieved earlier in the FTA. In particular, the Canadians hoped to patch up weaknesses that had become apparent in the protection of the activities of Canadian financial institutions in the U.S. Finally, for Mexico, the financial sector required a trade-off between concessions necessary to gain benefits in other areas and the preservation of a national presence in a financial system made vulnerable as a result of its return to the private sector.

Chapter 14 of the NAFTA includes two separate elements: the general framework agreed upon by the parties which is contained in the body of Chapter 14 and the specific reservations to the agreement which are to be declared by each party in Annexes to Chapter 14. The overall impact of the Agreement on trade in financial services will depend on both the character of the general framework and the limitations imposed by each country's reservations.

Chapter 14: The Framework

The financial services chapter of NAFTA provides a careful declaration of principles with respect to openness of the financial sector, together with safeguards to permit participating parties to maintain distinct approaches to the regulation of their financial sectors. Chapter 14 deals with the following key issues:

- safeguards that protect each party's approach to regulation (Article 1403: Regulatory Measures)
- the supply of financial services from outside a country (Article 1405: Cross-Border Trade)
- the terms and conditions under which financial institutions from one country can operate in another country (the related issues of Article 1404: Establishment and Article 1407: National Treatment)
- the settlement of disputes in the financial sector (Article 1413: Consultations, Article 1414: Financial Services Committee, Article 1415: Dispute Settlement, and Article 1416: Investment Disputes in Financial Services)

Regulatory Safeguards

The NAFTA, like the FTA before it, was intended to open the participants' financial sectors to the supply of services through cross-border trade or establishment by financial suppliers from the other countries without interfering with national approaches to financial sector regulation. This objective is completely justified given the overall purpose of the NAFTA: the Agreement aims for a free trade area and not an EC-type common market. The financial sector counterpart to free trade in goods requires the participants to assure openness to suppliers in the other countries while being able to preserve distinct national approaches to regulation.

The need to preserve differences in approach to regulation was vital to any financial market agreement involving Canada and the U.S. because these countries have long maintained distinctly different, even incompatible, approaches to the prudential regulation of their financial sector. Mexico, with the return of all of its commercial banks to the private sector, has adopted its own approach, one that is closer to the Canadian approach.

Article 1403: Regulatory Measures assures that the participating countries can preserve their own approaches to regulation and maintain autonomy with respect to stabilization policies that impinge on the financial sector. All three areas of prudential concern—the protection of individuals, the protection of institutions and the protection of the system—are each provided for in parts (a), (b) and (c).

This Article also deals with a politically sensitive issue for both Canada and Mexico: national sovereignty with respect to monetary and exchange rate policy. It declares that the participating countries are not restricted by anything in the financial services part of the Agreement from pursuing "non-discriminatory measures of general application taken by any public entity in pursuit of monetary and related credit policies or exchange rate policies (p. 14-2)." Thus, the Agreement does not interfere with any country's ability to carry out stabilization policies in its perceived national interest when these policies are conducted in a non-discriminatory way.

Cross-Border Trade

Cross-border trade refers to transactions by which financial suppliers supply their services from their home country to customers in another country. Issues of cross-border trade were given little attention in the FTA because the degree of interference with freedom of trade in these services between Canada and the U.S. has been rare in its extent and duration. The issue of cross-border trade had to be treated more comprehensively with expansion of the financial sector agreement to Mexico, a country with a recent history of substantial interferences to cross-border trade in financial services. The issue will become even more important when the extension of the Agreement to additional countries is contemplated.

The Agreement declares the general principle that freedom of cross-border trade requires each party to permit its residents and nationals to purchase financial services from suppliers of other parties located anywhere in the free trade area. On the other hand, the cross-border provision states explicitly that it does not entail any obligation on the parties to permit providers either to do business or to solicit in their territory. In practice, the Agreement falls short of realizing the general principle. Apparently in deference to the problems of Mexico's transition, Article 1405.1 only prevents any party from restricting any further cross-border trade permitted at the time the Agreement takes effect. For the longer run, the Agreement provides for further consultation on future liberalization of cross-border trade.

Establishment and National Treatment

Many financial services, in common with other services, require a physical presence near the customer in order to provide the services effectively. Thus, the ability to supply these services in another country would be severely limited without right of establishment. Moreover, foreign suppliers, once established, must be able to operate on comparable terms to domestic suppliers. Many financial provisions of the FTA, especially the Canadian commitments, dealt explicitly with the terms of establishment and national treatment.

Establishment

Negotiators of the establishment provisions of NAFTA faced an important and contentious issue: the form under which a supplier can establish in another country. Canada has consistently required foreign banks to operate through the establishment of separate Canadian subsidiaries in order to create greater transparency for regulators. The U.S., in contrast, has permitted foreign banks to operate through branches of the parent bank. Moreover, many U.S. bankers have argued strenuously that the "branch approach" provides a more efficient means for expanding into another country.

The result turned out to be a compromise between these two positions. In the immediate application of the Agreement, the Canadian position prevailed. While Article 1404 states that "financial services providers of a Party should be permitted to establish financial institutions in the territory of another Party in the juridical form determined by the provider (p. 14-2)," it continues to specify that the participation of the external providers be "through separate financial institutions as may be required by that Party (p. 14-2)." In the longer run, the U.S. position may ultimately prevail: once U.S. banking regulation has been reformed to permit the expansion of commercial banks from the other parties throughout the U.S. by subsidiaries or branches, the Parties will reconsider market access "with a view to adopting arrangements permitting investor choice as to the juridical form of establishment by commercial banks (p. 14-4)."

The Establishment Article also incorporates one of the key commitments made by Canada in the FTA. The parties agree not to apply foreign ownership requirements to financial services providers from the other parties. In the Canadian case, this means that subsidiaries of U.S. and Mexican banks are not subject to the ceiling on the aggregate activities of foreign banks and are freer in their operations than the subsidiaries of other foreign banks.

National Treatment

Establishment alone does not assure that foreign firms are able to serve another country's needs for financial services. They must also be free to supply their services once they become established. The National Treatment provisions determine the operating conditions for those institutions that have been permitted to operate under the Establishment Article.

The Parties could have adopted either of two alternative approaches to the national treatment. *De jure* national treatment assures only that foreign institutions receive equal treatment under the law. Nothing in *de jure* national treatment guarantees that foreign institutions will not be harmed by seemingly equal legal treatment that effectively limits them because of their different circumstances. The alternative approach, competitive national treatment, requires that the differential impact of the law on domestic and foreign institutions does not place foreign institutions at a disadvantage in their ability to compete.

The NAFTA clearly embodies the broader concept of competitive national treatment. While defining national treatment as "treatment no less favourable than that accorded by a party (p. 14-5)" to its own nationals, the Agreement requires that policies, whether providing different or identical treatment, must offer "equal competitive opportunities," the condition that foreign providers not be disadvantaged relative to domestic suppliers.

The Agreement also specifies that fulfilment of the requirement will be judged on opportunities and not outcomes. To do otherwise would constitute failure to recognize the inherent advantage that national institutions generally have in terms of knowledge of the market and public recognition. This measure avoids reliance on criteria such as "differences in market share, profitability and size (p. 14-5)," as the sole basis for meeting the conditions, though these factors can be seen as possible evidence of a lack of competitive national treatment.

Dispute Mechanism

The application of many of the principles of the financial sector portion of NAFTA must rely on interpretation and may be both subjective and arbitrary. As Canadian banks have already discovered from their experience under the FTA, even the results of most careful negotiations may fail to meet their expectations in practice. With respect to these problems of interpretation and perception, the NAFTA goes well beyond the FTA in adding much needed provisions for dealing with possible disputes in the financial sector.

On the whole, the dispute settlement provisions follow the general provisions in Chapter 11 with allowance for the needs of the financial sector. In the early stage of a problem, a party may request consultation regarding any matter in the Agreement and expect sympathetic consideration. The Agreement also provides for a Financial Services Committee to supervise implementation, to consider issues referred to it and to participate in dispute settlement. This Committee also meets once a year to assess the functioning of the financial services agreement. Finally, the Agreement fills a major gap of the FTA by making disputes in the financial sector subject to the Dispute Settlement Procedures (Chapter 20). Under this procedure, disputes will be referred to a Tribunal consisting of panellists drawn from a roster of individuals with expertise in the financial sector. If the complaint is upheld by the Tribunal, the complaining party may suspend benefits in the financial services sector.

Reservations

The movement from a bilateral agreement to a trilateral agreement changed the significance of general commitments made under the Agreement. Under the FTA, each country made specific commitments tailored to meet the other country's concerns about access to financial markets in that country. Such an approach had little need for statements of exceptions because limits could be set in the specific commitments themselves.

NAFTA, as a multilateral agreement, required a different approach. Rather than making specific commitments, the participants agreed on a set of general principles. Thus, the measures in the Agreement must be designed to incorporate the greatest commitment to openness that any of the parties would be prepared to make. While in some areas, this commitment would be set by the status quo, in others it would be determined by the willingness of one of the parties to make concessions at some future date. The different circumstances of the three countries means that their willingness to make each general commitment would differ. As a result, the final agreement might include commitments to openness beyond those currently acceptable to any party and certainly would include more commitments than those acceptable to every party. Thus, a mechanism was required by which countries could avoid those general commitments that they were not prepared to make.

Annex VII of the agreement contains the schedules that set out the exceptions to the agreement registered by the three parties. Schedule A sets out the reservations to the agreement of both federal and provincial or state governments and Schedule B states the areas where the parties reserve the right to derogate (or reverse) provisions of the agreement in the future.

As might be expected, the text devoted to the reservations to the Agreement differed substantially from country to country. Canada, at one extreme, presented a single reservation of the national government, whereas the U.S. presented eighteen and Mexico, twenty-six.

Canada

Canada's sole reservation restricted the purchase of reinsurance by Canadian insurers from non-resident reinsurers to no more than 25 percent of the risks undertaken by the original insurer.

The lack of explicit reservations by Canada in the draft of the Agreement overstates the degree of acceptance of the Agreement by Canadian authorities. The September 8th draft of the Agreement does not include the reservations that will be registered by provincial authorities. While these reservations will not affect the federal jurisdiction of banking, a number of provinces retain restrictions that limit foreign ownership for both insurance companies and trust and loan companies.[2] These restrictions will be unaffected by NAFTA if they are registered as reservations.

U.S.

The U.S.'s reservations cover a wide range of issues:

- citizenship and residence requirements for bank directors
- exemption from bank ownership requirements for U.S. governments that do not apply to foreign governments
- the need for home country reciprocity in order for an institution to gain status as a primary dealer in government debt or trustee under an indenture for debt securities
- restriction on foreign insurance companies providing surety bonds on government contracts

On the whole, these reservations will have only minor impacts on the business of Canadian and Mexican financial firms in the U.S.

More important is a major reservation with respect to the application of Article 1407 (National Treatment) to banking. Under the agreement, the U.S. maintains provisions of the Bank Holding Company Act of 1956 and the International Banking Act of 1978 by which

> Federal authorities may not approve the establishment of, or acquisition of an interest in, a bank subsidiary within a state by a foreign bank that has a full-service branch or bank in the

2 For further discussion of provincial treatment of foreign institutions, see Senate (1990), pp. 50-51 and Economic Council (1990), pp. 89-92.

> United States, unless the measures of the host state expressly permit the transaction. (Annex VII, Part A, United States, VII-U-3)

Annex A elaborates that foreign banks are excluded from owning banks under some regional holding company laws and are excluded from being an eligible bank owner in some states. As a result, foreign banks cannot be assured of the same treatment as domestic bank holding companies based in the same state in terms of their ability to expand into other states.

This reservation has particular significance in light of the continuing breakdown of the barriers to interstate banking. It potentially places at a competitive disadvantage any Canadian and Mexican banks that wish to expand nationally or even establish a presence nationally. The actual impact of this provision will depend on the prevalence of such restrictive approaches among the states.

The reservations that will be added by the U.S. states to the September 8th draft of the Agreement will be considerably more significant for the overall thrust of the Agreement than the comparable reservations of the Canadian provinces. As in Canada, U.S. states are able to control the activities of insurance companies in their jurisdiction. In addition, the states share jurisdiction with the federal government with respect to banking and have the ability to control entry by banks into their state.

Mexico

Mexico's reservations, while numerous, focus on two themes: limitations to Articles 1404 (Establishment) and 1407 (National Treatment). The limitations to Establishment restrict foreign investment in existing financial institutions, whereas those to National Treatment prohibit foreign government ownership in an extensive list of financial institutions.

The most significant ownership limitations apply to financial holding companies and commercial banks (less than 30 percent foreign ownership), securities firms (less than 30 percent total foreign ownership and less than 10 percent for individual foreign investments), and insurance companies, financial leasing companies, bonding companies and financial factoring companies (less than 50 percent foreign ownership). In none of these cases does the restriction apply to investments in new establishments permitted under the Agreement.

More important in the Mexican case than the reservations is the set of comprehensive transitional exceptions. These exceptions reflect the Mexican's fears that their financial industry might become dominated by large foreign firms or by an overall foreign presence before domestic institutions are able to complete their transition to private ownership. They take the form of special reservations to a number of Articles of the Agreement that apply up to the earlier of January 1, 2000, or six years from the entry into force of the Agreement.

Specifically, the individual size of foreign financial affiliates is controlled by the ceilings shown in Table 1 for limiting the authorized capital of each institution relative to the total capital of all institutions in the same industry. These ceilings will apply throughout the entire transition period and will govern both internal growth and acquisitions.

Table 1: Maximum Capital of Individual Financial Affiliates

Type of Financial Institution	Maximum Individual Capital (Percent of Aggregate Capital of all Institutions)
Commercial Banks	1.5%
Securities Firms	4.0%
Insurance Companies	
Casualty	1.5%
Life and Health	1.5%

Source: Annex VII VII-M-29.

The aggregate capital limits for all financial sectors other than insurance are set at the initial levels shown in Table 2 for the first year of the agreement. These limits shall be increased annually by equal increments to reach the final limit by the last year of the transition.

Table 2: Maximum Aggregate Capital of Foreign Financial Affiliates

Type of Financial Institution	Percentage of Total Capital	
	Initial Limit	Final Limit
Commercial Banks	8%	15%
Securities Firms	10%	20%
Factoring Companies	10%	20%
Leasing Companies	10%	20%

Source: Annex VII VII-M-30.

As an additional safeguard to these transitional limits, Mexico also retains the right to freeze, at any time in the first four years after the end of the transition period, the aggregate capital of foreign affiliates for commercial banks and securities at their current levels if the aggregate of capital of foreign affiliates in these sectors exceeds 25 percent of the capital in banking or 30 percent in the securities industry. These extended ceilings have a maximum duration of another three years.

The Financial Sector in NAFTA: An Assessment

There are two perspectives for judging the financial sector provisions of NAFTA. First, it can be considered in terms of what it offered to the participants through opening up trade in financial services. Second, it can be evaluated as base for accession in terms of its suitability for extension to other countries.

The outcome balanced the interests of the three parties. Each party achieved its objectives to a substantial degree. Of the three parties, Canada appears to have fared the best in the short run. It gained an added safeguard for the U.S. activities of its financial institutions in the form of a dispute mechanism that has a good chance of being effective. The U.S. gained its benefits primarily in the long run. The agreement, despite transitory safeguards, will eventually open fully the financial system of a country of 85 million, one that had previously been firmly closed to the participation of foreign financial institutions. Access to Mexican financial markets will be more valuable to U.S. banks than to Canadian ones because of the greater involvement of their customers in the Mexican economy. Nevertheless, this opening will only take place after a transition during which the expansion of financial institutions from the U.S. and Canada will be strictly controlled. Finally, Mexico obtained a variety of benefits. Ultimately the opening of its financial sector will increase the sources of finance for its domestic industry by assuring it access to foreign financial institutions in competition with domestic sources. At the same time, the Agreement sheltered its financial system from substantial foreign competition during the sensitive period of its transition to private ownership.

The NAFTA financial sector provisions were much more than a reworking of the FTA provisions to include a third country. While the FTA was clearly a bilateral agreement dealing with two parties' concerns about the treatment each would give to the other's financial industry, NAFTA was crafted around principles expressing the requirements for freedom of trade in financial services. Its design permits countries to accept the agreement at different stages of financial development and work toward the eventual opening of their domestic financial markets to international competition. As a multilateral agreement, the NAFTA financial sector provisions offer potential benefits to countries other than Canada, Mexico and the U.S. by providing a framework in which a variety of financial sector needs can be met if these countries choose to join an expanded NAFTA.

References

Canada, *The Canada-U.S. Free Trade Agreement: Trade Securing Canada's Future.*

Canada, *North American Free Trade Agreement Draft Legal Text*, September 8, 1992.

Chant, John F., "Free Trade in the Financial Sector: Expectations and Experience," Studies on the Economic Future of North America, The Fraser Institute and Centre for International Studies, University of Toronto, 1991.

Cranston, R., ed. *The Single Market and the Law of Banking*, London: Lloyd's of London Press, 1991.

Economic Council of Canada, *Globalization and Canada's Financial Markets*, Ottawa, 1989.

House of Commons, *Bill C-130: An Act to Implement the Free Trade Agreement between Canada and the United States of America*, May 24, 1988.

Key, Sidney J. and Hal S. Scott, *International Trade in Banking Services: A Conceptual Framework*, Washington, 1991.

Senate of Canada, *Canada 1992: Toward a National Market in Financial Services*, Eighth report of the Standing Senate Committee on Banking, Trade and Commerce, May 9, 1990.

Ungerer, H., J. J. Hauvonen, A. Lopez-Claros and T. Mayer, *The European Monetary System: Development and Perspectives*, Washington: International Monetary Fund, 1990.

NAFTA and Energy: A Bridge not far Enough?

G. C. Watkins
DataMetrics Limited &
University of Calgary[1]

Introduction

THE NORTH AMERICAN FREE TRADE AGREEMENT (NAFTA) is intended to make the continent one economic zone.[2] In effect, it would supersede the U.S.-Canada Free Trade Agreement (FTA). However, outstanding FTA obligations between Canada and the United States not embraced by NAFTA remain.

This paper deals with energy under NAFTA. It consists of four main sections. Section I provides background energy information for the

---

1 I am indebted to helpful comments from André Plourde, University of Ottawa, and Steven Globerman, Simon Fraser University.

2 See NAFTA, "Overview," p. i.

three countries. Section II describes the provisions of the NAFTA agreement as they relate to energy. Section III assesses the treatment of energy under NAFTA. Concluding remarks are made in Section IV.

Direct energy trade between Canada and Mexico is minor and likely to remain so. Thus the significance of NAFTA for Canada lies in other aspects—what it does in the fulcrum energy market of the U.S.; what effect it has on the FTA; and what opportunities it provides for trade related to energy services.

Energy trade between the U.S. and Mexico is mainly one way—from Mexico to the U.S.—although of late the U.S. has been moving some natural gas to Northern Mexico. From a U.S. perspective NAFTA can be seen primarily as a vehicle that may open up energy related investment and service opportunities in Mexico and would enhance the development of Mexico's energy resources.

Mexico imports little energy but does have very considerable oil exports to the U.S., to which access would be secured under NAFTA. At the same time, modest participation by the U.S. and Canada in the Mexican oil and gas industry under NAFTA would represent a new departure for Mexico.

We shall see that the kind of arrangements prevailing for energy under the FTA have not been accepted by Mexico under NAFTA. Indeed, Mexico has been able to impose what is tantamount to an "exclusion zone" for some Mexican energy activities, an acknowledgement of its especial sensitivity—emanating mainly from Mexico's Constitution—to energy issues. This may be unfortunate. But the agreement is not immutable and its evolution could well see some relaxation of the energy provisions to yield further benefits from greater integration of North American energy flows and developments. Then the objective of a single economic zone would be achieved. In the meantime, the Agreement would open up opportunities for exports of Canadian and United States energy equipment and services to Mexico.

North American Energy Flows and Related Features

Several Tables in this section show energy flows among Canada, the United States and Mexico over the last decade or so. In addition, information is provided on the magnitude of fossil fuel reserves and the structure of energy demand in the three countries.

Oil

Both Canada and Mexico export substantial amounts of crude oil to the U.S.; flows in the other direction are minor or nil (see Table 1). In the

Table 1: Crude Oil Flows between Canada, U.S.A., and Mexico* (000 barrels/day)

Year	U.S. from Canada**	Canada from U.S.***	U.S. from Mexico	Canada from Mexico
	(1)	(2)	(3)	(4)
1980	455	99	533	0
1981	447	62	522	52
1982	482	58	685	54
1983	547	17	826	57
1984	630	16	748	45
1985	770	23	816	32
1986	807	24	699	18
1987	848	17	655	17
1988	999	14	747	11
1989	931	26	767	11
1990	934	18	755	12
1991	1,033	4	807	15

* Crude oil and equivalent.
** Includes US product imports from domestic and offshore sources.
*** Includes exchanges with the United States.
Note: There are no Mexican imports from Canada or the U.S.

Source: Cols (1) & (3) Crude Oil Imports into the US = US Dept. of Energy, *Monthly Energy Review*; Cols (2) & (4) Crude Oil Imports into Canada = Canadian Petroleum Association *Statistical Handbook*.

first half of the 1980s Canada imported noticeable amounts of Mexican oil into eastern Canada, but as the decade progressed these fell to modest levels.

Table 2: Significance of Oil* Flows among Canada, U.S.A., and Mexico

Year	Canadian exports as a % of Canadian production	Canadian exports to U.S. as a % of U.S. demand	Mexican exports to U.S. as a % of Mex. production	Mexican exports to U.S. as a % of U.S. demand	All U.S. oil imports as a % of U.S. demand
1980	25.7	2.7	25.0	3.1	40.4
1981	27.8	2.8	20.5	3.3	37.3
1982	30.6	3.2	22.8	4.5	33.4
1983	32.9	3.6	28.0	5.4	33.2
1984	35.3	4.0	24.8	4.7	34.5
1985	42.3	4.9	27.0	5.2	32.2
1986	44.6	5.0	25.3	4.3	38.2
1987	44.3	5.1	22.7	3.9	40.1
1988	49.8	5.8	25.9	4.3	42.7
1989	47.4	5.4	26.5	4.4	46.5
1990	47.5	5.5	25.4	4.4	47.2
1991	52.1	6.2	25.8	4.8	45.6

*Crude Oil and Equivalent

Note: Mexican production includes NGLs, and virtually all Canadian oil exports are to the United States.

Sources: Canada: Canadian Petroleum Association, *Statistical Handbook*; U.S.: Dept. of Energy, *Monthly Energy Reviews*; Mexico: BP, *Statistical Review of World Energy*, June 1991 and *Oil and Energy Trends*, various issues.

Canadian oil exports as a proportion of total Canadian production have doubled since 1980 and currently represent about one-half of domestic output. Growth in oil exports was particularly noticeable in 1985 when the Canadian oil production sector was deregulated. In contrast, the share such exports represent of U.S. demand for oil is quite minor at around six percent, notwithstanding the fact that at present close to one-half of total U.S. oil demand is met by imports (see Table 2).

Exports of Mexican crude oil to the U.S. have been quite stable since the early 1980s and constitute about one quarter of Mexican production of liquid hydrocarbons. Similarly to Canada, about 50 percent of Mexican production of some three million b/d of liquid hydrocarbons is exported. In terms of volume, Mexican oil exports to the U.S. are about 80 percent of Canada's. Of late, Mexico has imported 100,000 b/d of gasolines (about 10 percent of the value of crude exports), indicating a lack of appropriate Mexican refining capability. Mexico is also a net importer of fuel oil.

Natural Gas

Natural gas flows between the three countries are displayed in Table 3. Fluctuations in Canadian exports to the U.S. have been primarily policy induced. The decline in the early 1980s was mainly attributable to the high export prices set by the Canadian federal government.[3] The strong recovery of export volumes after 1984 primarily reflected price deregulation. Indeed, Canadian exports to the U.S. have increased by a factor of about 2.5 in 1991 over the nadir in 1983.

Overall, Canadian natural gas exports currently account for 40 percent of total Canadian production (see Table 4). But in the context of the aggregate U.S. natural gas market they play a quite modest albeit growing role, with exports rising from five percent of U.S. consumption in 1985 to nearly 10 percent last year. On a regional basis, Canadian imports assume more importance, for example satisfying about 25 percent of Californian natural gas consumption. Since 1985, Canada has accounted for virtually all U.S. natural gas imports.

---

3 See Watkins and Waverman, 1985.

While gas flows have been predominantly in one direction—from Canada to the U.S.—deregulation has spawned increases in natural gas imports into Canada from the U.S.; virtually no gas was imported into Canada during the regulated era. In contrast, the past four years have seen noticeable volumes of U.S. gas enter Canada, with current annual shipments of about 20 BCF, mainly into Ontario.

Exports of Mexican natural gas to the U.S. peaked in 1981. Such movements—and total production of Mexican gas—fell sharply after 1982 with the contraction in upstream investment as financial con-

Table 3: Natural Gas Flows between Canada, the U.S.A., and Mexico (BCF)

Year	U.S. from Canada	Canada from U.S.	U.S. from Mexico	Mexico from U.S.
1980	797	0.1	0	4.3
1981	762	0.1	105	3.3
1982	783	0.2	95	1.7
1983	712	0.1	75	1.6
1984	755	0.1	52	1.8
1985	926	0.2	0	2.2
1986	749	9.2	0	1.9
1987	993	3.3	0	2.1
1988	1294	21.2	0	2.3
1989	1382	42.4	0	17.0
1990	1512	24.7	0	15.7
1991	1860	19.6	0	60.2

Note: There are no Mexican gas imports into Canada or exports from Canada.

Sources: Cols. (1) to (4) = American Gas Association, *Historical Statistical Data for Gas Utilities*; except 1988-1991 cols. (1) and (2) = National Energy Board, *Annual Report 1990*; and cols. (2)& (4), 1991 = U.S. Dept. of Energy, *Natural Gas Imports/ Exports* (short term).

Table 4: Significance of Natural Gas Flows among Canada, the U.S.A, and Mexico

Year	Canadian exports as a % of Canadian production	Canadian exports to U.S. as a % of U.S. demand	Mexican exports to U.S. as a % of Mex. production	Mexican exports to U.S. as a % of U.S. demand	All U.S. gas imports as a % of U.S. demand
1980	25.4	4.0	0.0	0.0	5.0
1981	24.8	3.9	7.1	0.5	4.7
1982	25.0	4.3	6.1	0.5	5.2
1983	23.7	4.2	5.1	0.4	5.5
1984	23.2	4.2	3.8	0.3	4.7
1985	26.4	5.4	0.0	0.0	5.5
1986	22.5	4.6	0.0	0.0	4.6
1987	27.5	5.8	0.0	0.0	5.8
1988	31.4	7.2	0.0	0.0	7.2
1989	32.1	7.4	0.0	0.0	7.4
1990	34.7	8.1	0.0	0.0	8.2
1991	39.7	9.6	0.0	0.0	9.0

Note: All Canadian exports of natural gas are to the United States.

Sources: Canada: Canadian Petroleum Association, *Statistical Handbook*; U.S.: Dept. of Energy, *Monthly Energy Reviews*; Mexico: BP, *Statistical Review of World Energy*, June 1991; and *Oil and Energy Trends*, various issues.

straints resulting from falling oil prices and the Mexican external debt crisis took hold.[4] Mexico absorbed small amounts of U.S. gas until the end of the 1980s; 1991 saw a substantial jump as demand from Mexican border states rose sharply. Note that the existing Mexican south to north pipeline has limited capacity and is fully utilized.[5]

Electricity

Table 5 shows electricity flows between Canada and the U.S. Up until 1989, the bulk of this trade constituted Canadian exports of electricity to the U.S. However, trade flows have become more balanced recently, in part because of Ontario Hydro's policy of buying electricity from the U.S. to cut emissions likely to provoke acid rain.[6]

Of late, Canadian exports of electricity are appreciably less than in the early 1980s. Exporting utilities have had relatively little surplus available, given low water conditions in some provinces and restrictions on fossil-fuelled generation in Ontario.

Supplies of Canadian electricity play an even smaller part in the U.S. market than oil and gas, accounting for less than two percent of U.S. consumption during the 1980s although, as with natural gas, they are more noticeable regionally (for example in New York State). In 1991, Canadian electricity exports amounted to no more than about one percent of total U.S. demand.

No information was available on electricity flows between the U.S. and Mexico, but if any were recorded they would likely be minor.

---

4 A two BCF/day pipeline project to export Mexican gas to the U.S. was never completed as pricing disputes were not resolved (see Foss and Johnson, 1991).

5 Foss and Johnson, 1991, p.158.

6 National Energy Board, 1991, p.17.

Table 5: Electricity Flows between Canada and the U.S.A.

Year	Canadian imports from U.S. (GW.h)	Canadian exports to U.S. (GW.h)	Canadian exports as a % of Canadian production	Canadian exports to U.S. as a % of U.S. demand
1980	2,930	30,181	8.2	1.4
1981	1,497	35,372	9.3	1.6
1982	2,856	34,226	9.1	1.6
1983	3,179	38,410	9.7	1.8
1984	2,343	41,436	9.8	1.8
1985	2,693	43,016	9.6	1.9
1986	4,957	38,934	8.5	1.7
1987	3,471	47,427	9.8	1.9
1988	6,331	34,029	7.0	1.3
1989	8,745	22,089	4.6	0.8
1990	15,543	18,128	3.9	0.7
1991	n/a	24,614	5.0	0.9

Note: No information is available on electricity flows between the U.S. and Mexico, but they likely would be negligible or nil; n/a = not available.

Source: Statistics Canada, *Electric Power Statistics II*; and *Canadian Economic Observer*.

Coal

As Table 6 shows, coal trade is predominantly one way—from the U.S. to Canada—with Canada importing in excess of ten times more coal than it exports to the U.S.[7] Indeed, prior to 1981 Canadian exports of

7 U.S. coal imports are equivalent to almost 20 percent of Canadian coal

coal to the U.S were negligible. Most of the coal imported into Canada has traditionally supplied the steel and electricity generation industries in Ontario. Mexican coal production is minor; no cross border movements are reported.[8]

Table 6: Coal Flows between Canada and the U.S.A.

Year	Canadian imports from U.S. (000 short tons)	Canadian exports to U.S. (000 short tons)
1980	17,447	neg
1981	16,319	74
1982	17,028	78
1983	16,110	151
1984	20,186	210
1985	16,388	292
1986	14,469	404
1987	15,667	954
1988	19,019	1,130
1989	15,824	1,321
1990	14,258	1,295
1991	14,964	907

Note: No information is available on coal flows between the U.S. and Mexico, but these likely would be minor; neg = negligible.

Source: Statistics Canada, *Canadian Economic Observer*.

production.

8 Mexican coal production in 1991 was 15 million tonnes (Canada's and the United States' were 71 and 895 million tonnes, respectively); the Mexican coal reserves to production ratio is in excess of 100. Sources: BP, *Statistical Review of World Energy*; Statistics Canada, *Canadian Economic Observer*; and U.S. Dept. of Energy, *Monthly Energy Review*, various issues.

Fossil Fuel Reserves

What of the size of current proved remaining reserves of fossil fuels for the three countries? These numbers are shown in Table 7. Mexico's oil reserves exceed those of the U.S. and Canada in combination. The combined natural gas reserves of Mexico and Canada are roughly equivalent to those of the U.S. The proved coal reserves of the U.S. dwarf those of the other two countries. Note that estimates of Mexican reserves of both oil and gas are subject to controversy.[9]

Table 7: Fossil Fuels Reserves, 1980

Country	Oil (B Bbls)	Gas (TCF)	Coal (MM Tonnes)
Mexico	52.0	72.7	1,856
United States	33.9	166.2	260,295
Canada	8.1	97.6	6,760

Source: BP, *Statistical Review of World Energy*, June, 1991.

Energy Consumption

There are some significant differences in the structure of energy consumption among the three countries. Table 8 shows data on energy demand for the latest year for which Mexican information was available (1988). The U.S. places somewhat greater reliance on coal and oil than does Canada, which relies more heavily on natural gas and electricity. In contrast to both her northern neighbours, Mexico relies much more heavily on oils and less on electricity—a reflection in part of significant differences in stages of economic development.

9 Although estimates of Mexican proved oil reserves are subject to more than normal levels of uncertainty, it is likely they are still in the region of 50 billion barrels—but numbers as low as 35 billion barrels have been suggested; see *Oil and Gas Journal*, February, 1992, p. 17. On natural gas, see Foss and Johnson, 1991.

Table 8: Share of Secondary Energy Consumption, 1988

Country	Petroleum	Natural Gas	Electricity	Coal and Other
United States	42.7	23.1	10.4	23.8
Canada	39.5	25.5	15.4	19.6
Mexico	60.3	21.7	7.1	10.9

Sources: United States: U.S. Dept. of Energy, *Monthly Energy Review*. Canada: Energy, Mines and Resources, *Energy Statistics Handbook*. Mexico: Baker and Associates, *Prospects for Increased Gas Trade with Mexico*, June 6, 1991.

In summary, both Mexico and Canada ship substantial amounts of oil to the U.S., yet in combination they only account for about 10 percent of the U.S. market. Canada also ships a large proportion of its natural gas production to the U.S., but again only satisfies some 10 percent of U.S. consumption, although that share has been growing of late and assumes more significance on a regional basis. Trade in electricity and coal is minor. Mexican and Canadian oil and gas reserves exceed those of the U.S. The structure of energy consumption in Mexico is slanted more towards oils, compared with the U.S. and Canada.

Energy Related NAFTA Provisions[10]

The energy provisions of NAFTA parallel those of the FTA and thus remain in large measure an extension and clarification of rights and obligations under the General Agreement on Tariffs and Trade (GATT).[11] All rights and obligations under the U.S.-Canada Free Trade Agreement (FTA) of January, 1989 are to be "reflected in one form or another in the new agreement" (NAFTA "Overview," q.v). In effect, NAFTA takes priority over the FTA. Certain provisions of the FTA

10 This Section is predicated on the October 7, 1992 version of the NAFTA text.

11 Mexico joined the GATT in 1986.

would be suspended where NAFTA repeats or amends FTA obligations.

This Section focuses both on the specific energy provisions of NAFTA (Chapter 6, NAFTA) and mentions other elements, such as the disputes mechanism, arrangements for government procurement and the like which also affect trade in energy and related services.

NAFTA provides a long-term framework for energy trade among the three countries. Moreover it by no means erases the border between the United States and Canada—which may afford some comfort to economic nationalists. And in the case of Mexico the border is not only visible but remains paramount in the energy context.

Before looking at Chapter 6 of NAFTA dealing specifically with energy, I mention pertinent aspects of the "Preamble" and "Objectives" of the Agreement. The "Preamble" refers to the three governments being resolved to creating expanded and secure markets, to reducing distortions to trade, to building on other agreements and to promoting sustainable development.[12] Cited objectives include elimination of trade barriers, promotion of "fair competition" and increased investment opportunities, provision for elimination of disputes, and establishment of a framework for further cooperation.[13]

Allusion is also made to relations with other extant agreements. Specifically, the parties affirm their existing rights and obligations with respect to each other under the General Agreement on Tariffs and Trade (GATT) and to other relevant agreements. In the event of any inconsistency between the provisos of NAFTA and other agreements, NAFTA prevails except as otherwise provided.

The Energy Chapter

Chapter 6 of NAFTA is entitled "Energy and Basic Petrochemicals;" the corresponding Chapter in the FTA (Chapter 9) was simply called "Energy." The distinction resides in Mexico's dirigiste policy towards the

12 See NAFTA, "Preamble."

13 NAFTA, Chapter 1, Article 102(1).

energy sector, as discussed later.[14] The ultimate intent of Chapter 6 is to entirely replace the corresponding Chapter of the FTA.

Scope

The parties confirmed their respect for their constitutions. This caveat did not appear in the FTA and has to do with the exclusive reservation on "strategic" grounds of the energy sector to the state under the Mexican Constitution. This relates both to resource ownership and exploitation. Mexican sensitivity to constitutional issues concerning energy accounts for the fact that the treatment of the Mexican energy sector under the Agreement does not parallel that between the United States and Canada.

These concerns go back to the 1917 Mexican Constitution which reinstated the traditional Spanish rule of sovereign ownership of mineral rights (Article 27). It also defined "forbidden zones" for any foreign ownership of lands or waters. At present, Mexico's sovereign ownership of resources includes "all natural resources of the continental shelf and marine shelf of the islands." Since its inception in 1917, article 27 has been amended, with each amendment extending the reach by exploitation of state owned resources by state owned entities (see Kimball Jr. [1990]).

The apparent scope of energy goods covered by NAFTA is marginally less generous than that covered by the FTA. The difference arises partly from the reclassification of certain products. And, as outlined later, Mexico has excluded many energy materials. Such Mexican exclusions do not apply to trade between Canada and the U.S.

However, the scope of NAFTA is in one way seemingly broader than the FTA in that it refers specifically to measures relating to investment and services associated with energy and petrochemicals. No such mention is made in the FTA's energy chapter, although provisions for services (but not investment) are subsumed elsewhere in that Agreement.

---

14 Throughout the Chapter the phrase "energy" used in the FTA is generally replaced by the phrase "energy and basic petrochemicals."

Quantitative Import and Export Restrictions

As in the FTA, the GATT prohibition of restrictions on trade in energy and basic petrochemicals is affirmed in NAFTA. In the event that one of the three NAFTA countries imposes export or import restrictions on energy and basic petrochemical trade with other countries, the other two NAFTA countries cannot be used as a conduit to circumvent the restriction (Article 603(3)). And where a party to the Agreement imposes import restrictions on non-parties, consultation with other signatories is required to avoid distortive impacts (Article 603(4)).

NAFTA allows parties to administer a system of import and export licensing for energy and basic petrochemicals if consistent with the Agreement. Allowance is also made for parties to designate monopolies or state enterprises, but such bodies are not to frustrate the intent of the Agreement nor to introduce anti-competitive practices in non-monopolized markets (Articles 1502 and 1503).

NAFTA permits Mexico to issue import and export licences to reserve foreign trade in certain goods to PEMEX, in recognition of the latter's monopoly position. These goods include virtually all refined petroleum products plus bitumen, oil shale and tar sands, and LPGs (Annex 603.6). However such restrictive licences are still subject to trade rules under the Agreement, and under the GATT for that matter.

The Agreement (Article 605) repeats the clause in the FTA (Article 904) that allows governments to impose export restrictions on other parties on the grounds of: i) conservation of exhaustible resources; ii) supply shortages; iii) price stabilization; and iv) national security. In turn, these provisos were fashioned on those in the GATT agreements, although the definition of what constitutes a national security criterion is more lax under the GATT. Moreover—and this is critical—the definition of "national security" differs as between Canada and the United States, and as between Mexico and the other two parties. These aspects are mentioned below.

Article 605 in NAFTA also repeats the key energy caveat introduced in the FTA: if supplies were restricted to one of the parties under any of the first three reasons (conservation, supply shortages and price stabilization), the share of total supply available for export purchase may not fall below the average level in the previous 36 months. This was the contentious "proportionality" provision of the FTA—which put some flesh on the GATT skeleton—but did not constitute a supply obligation.[15] Until such time as the conditions that might invoke the proportionality clause become apparent, its significance will remain hazy.

Note that the proportionality provision refers to *government* actions to restrict exports. There is nothing to stop *markets* constraining exports. Canadians could outbid Americans even for the proportional share of supply. Restrictions are not to disrupt "normal channels" of supply nor to involve imposition of higher prices on exports via licence fees, taxation and minimum prices.

However, an Annex to the Agreement reveals that Article 605 is bilateral: it only applies to trade between Canada and the United States. It does not hold for Mexico, although presumably the vaguer GATT measures remain. In short, Mexico has been able to opt out of the more precise expression of the GATT limitations on energy export restrictions established under the FTA—although these provisions would be reaffirmed between the U.S. and Canada.

National security is seen as possible grounds for import or export restrictions, but the actions to be taken are quite tightly specified, much more so than under GATT (Article 607). But again Mexico is exempt from these provisions and their narrow scope. Instead, broad provisions on national security (Article 2102)—which refer to the Agreement not precluding any party taking actions deemed necessary to protect its "essential security interests"—apply.

One interpretation of the U.S.-Canada arrangements on supply restrictions is to view them as reciprocal trade-offs. Canada granted "proportionality" for the conservation, supply shortages and price stabilization criteria to assuage U.S. concerns emanating from Canada's export restrictions in the regulated era of 1970 to 1985. The U.S. granted a narrow interpretation of national security to meet Canadian concerns about any revival of U.S. import constraints imposed under the guise of national security in the 1950s and 1960s. Mexico did not agree to "proportionality" and so did not qualify for (and perhaps did not wish) a tight national security criterion.

---

15 The relevant GATT provisions are a lot more vague, referring to general exceptions allowing the imposition of import and export controls in certain situations; see Articles XI:2(a) and XX(g), (i) and (j) of the GATT.

Pricing Provisions

Article 603(2) of Chapter 6 refers to the abolition of minimum and maximum export and import price requirements. This embellishes the corresponding clause in the FTA, which did not allude specifically to maxima.[16] Prohibition of export taxes in the FTA is confirmed in NAFTA (Article 604).

Other Features

Energy regulatory measures within the member countries are to observe GATT strictures awarding most favourable national treatment for traded *vis-à-vis* domestic goods across provincial or state boundaries (Article 606 and Article 301). No specific provision is made under NAFTA for direct consultation if regulatory actions are seen by either party as discriminatory (in contrast to the FTA). However, NAFTA provides for energy regulatory bodies to "avoid disruption of contractual relationships to the maximum extent practicable" (Article 606(2)). While this is a soft "best efforts" type provision, nevertheless it was not in the FTA and thus represents a new obligation, one possibly urged by Canadian negotiators with an eye on ongoing disputes involving the California Public Utilities Commission—on which more later (see Section III). And it goes beyond a mere invitation to consult.

Perhaps of greater import is the definition of "energy regulatory measure" under NAFTA as any measure by "federal or *subfederal* [emphasis added] entities that directly affects the transportation, transmission or distribution, purchase or sales, of an energy or basic petrochemical good" (Article 609). What this definition does is make more explicit the need for provincial and state regulators to adhere to the obligations visited on the federal government by NAFTA. In other words, NAFTA obligations are to trickle (or cascade) down to state and provincial regulators.

Certain specific measures in the FTA between the U.S. and Canada laid out in Annexes in the FTA are reaffirmed in NAFTA (Article 608). These include the export of albeit only limited volumes of Alaskan oil to Canada, Canadian exemption from U.S. uranium enrichment regula-

16 This amendment is simply one of clarification.

tions, U.S. exemption from Canadian uranium upgrading policies, and elimination of certain Canadian price tests on the export of energy goods.[17]

NAFTA also repeats the article in the FTA that permits parties to indulge themselves in incentives for oil and gas exploration and development to "maintain the reserve base" (Article 608 (1)). And NAFTA reaffirms the primacy of the International Energy Program (IEP) on the sharing of oil supplies in the event of an emergency, at least between Canada and the United States (Annex 608.2). Mexico is excluded because it is not a signatory to the IEP.

Mexican Reservations

There is an important Annex in the Agreement (Annex 602.3) which defines the scope of the energy materials and activities over which the Agreement holds sway in the case of Mexico. The Annex is restrictive. It reserves to the Mexican State the exploration, exploitation, refining, processing and pipelining of crude oil, natural gas and basic petrochemicals.[18] It also reserves to the Mexican government all trade in energy and basic petrochemicals, including refined petroleum products. However, in the case of natural gas and basic petrochemicals, where end-users and suppliers find cross border trade "may be in their interests" these entities shall be permitted "to negotiate supply contracts." Such contracts may take the form of individual contracts between the "state enterprise and each of the other entities." The Annex also allows state enterprises to negotiate performance clauses in service contracts.

In Mexico, the generation, transmission, distribution, and sale of electricity is viewed as a public service and a "strategic area reserved to the state" (Annex 602.3 1(c)). However, opportunities are seen for private investment in Mexican electricity generation in terms of produc-

---

17 See FTA, Annex 902.5 and 905.2. The key price test eliminated was that relating to the least cost alternative; beforehand, the Canadian export price was not to be less than the least cost alternative energy supplies in the market involved.

18 The basic (protected) petrochemicals are butane, ethane, heptane, hexane and pentanes; fifteen petrochemicals are now open to foreign investment (see the list in the *Globe and Mail*, August 14, 1992, p. B-3).

tion for own use (self generation), co-generation and independent power production. But any surplus power is to be sold to CFE (Mexico's state-owned electricity firm). All nuclear power generation and associated activities are reserved to the Mexican state, without exception. However, independent power producers, CFE and electric utilities in the other two NAFTA countries have the right to negotiate power purchase and sale contracts.

In short, private investment is not permitted in "reserved" Mexican energy activities and any cross (Mexican) border trade in them is confined to contracts approved by the Mexican authorities (Annex 602.3). However, contract approval is not required for non-reserved activities.

Dispute Mechanisms and Government Procurement

Dispute mechanisms are dealt with in detail elsewhere in this volume.[19] The summary below focuses on those aspects that might be of particular relevance to energy. If a dispute, for example, about national security provisions between two countries arose and was not resolved bilaterally, the Free Trade Commission established under NAFTA would enter the fray and at this stage the other country could become involved. And arbitration could be invoked. There are also new provisions to help prevent one party's domestic laws delaying decisions. In the energy context this may well have relevance to disputes associated with the role of sub-federal agencies.

Trans-border investment in energy between Canada and the United States is sizeable and hence the recasting of the investment chapter in NAFTA (Chapter 11) in more generic and explicit terms than in the FTA has significance. It now includes procedures for resolving certain types of conflicts along the lines similar to Canada's foreign investment protection measures. And Canada may still review foreign acquisitions, as provided in the FTA. But, in large measure, Mexico's reservations on energy and petrochemicals exclude it from Chapter 11 provisions. However, if Mexico did choose to admit investment then Chapter 11 provisions would apply, including arbitration. In short, the protection

---

19 See the chapter by Gilbert Winham elsewhere in this book.

for investors is more comprehensive than under the FTA. And in particular, provisions for placing foreign investors in Mexico on the same footing as domestic investors do represent a significant departure from traditional Mexican doctrines. This may be a harbinger of more foreign investment in Mexico's energy sector.

Involvement by a state enterprise in regulation would elevate it to the level of the government, where it would acquire the associated NAFTA government obligations (Chapter 15). This could be especially relevant to the activities of PEMEX. NAFTA also reaffirms in large measure the facilitation of temporary entry for business and technical persons afforded under the FTA (Chapter 16). This could have significance for any enhanced trade in energy services (see later).

NAFTA is intended to liberalize government procurement to provide non-discriminatory opportunities for suppliers from each of the Parties (Chapter 10). The procedures for procurement are covered in NAFTA with greater precision and obligation than under the current GATT code or under the FTA. The crucial point is that while Canada and the U.S. are signatories to both the GATT code and the FTA, Mexico—absent NAFTA—is not. NAFTA enhances the obligations applying to Mexican procurement procedures. This represents a very considerable change and one that offers opportunities for the U.S. and Canadian energy industries if Mexico were able to embark on a widespread energy investment program.

In summary, the energy provisions of the FTA are preserved in NAFTA and modestly strengthened or clarified in areas such as dispute settlement, the application of NAFTA provisions to "lower tier" regulators, and encouraging contractual observance. However, while Mexico has basically accepted the energy pricing provisions of the FTA—prices cannot discriminate against exports—it has largely opted out of the quantitative FTA provisions governing energy trade. Under the FTA, trade is to take place without government interference; and where restrictions are imposed there is provision for maintaining the share of exports in total supply. Under NAFTA, these arrangements do not apply to Mexico, although they are maintained for trade between Canada and the United States. To a degree, then, NAFTA has enshrined Mexico as a "distinct society" in terms of energy trade and obligations.

Assessment of the Energy Component of NAFTA

In broad terms, then, the FTA measures governing energy trade between the U.S. and Canada would be reaffirmed under NAFTA. The significance of these provisions at least for Canada and the U.S. remains more long than short run, given the deregulation of energy trade between the U.S. and Canada that dates back to 1985. I shall argue below that the significance of the energy arrangements is in all likelihood mainly long term in the case of Mexico as well, at least for energy commodity trade.

Mexico has been able to absent itself from some important provisions. The desire for exclusion arises from the role of energy resources under the Mexican constitution. Not only are all in-situ energy resources owned by the state, but the government via PEMEX is the sole owner of the petroleum industry that exploits the in-situ resources.[20] PEMEX was established by decree as the only supplier of oil and gas and the only entity allowed to trade in oil and gas. The Agreement acknowledges and sustains this position, although there is some slight nibbling away at the edges in the case of trade in natural gas. Too much should not be made of Mexico's ownership of resources. After all, provincial governments in Canada enjoy a similar position. It is more the exclusivity provisions for investment and trade that are liable to erode any gains that may flow from greater integration of the energy economies of the three countries. This is discussed further below.

It is easy to suggest that Mexico's opting out privilege is a major flaw in the deal. Yet it is only in the last five years or so that Mexico has made fundamental changes in its economic policies, of which NAFTA is itself evidence. None but an inebriated optimist would expect NAFTA to trigger abrupt changes in the whole way that Mexico's energy sector is organised. As it is, some loosening of the straightjacket has been

---

20 Energy's role in Mexico's fiscal structure is important: it generates about one third of the total federal government revenues, while accounting for a similar proportion of federal public investment (see Baker and Associates [1991].

achieved. The list of petrochemicals on Mexico's protected list has been reduced from 20 to five. Some natural gas and electricity trade may take place without direct intervention by the Mexican government. Investment and the supply of services may be welcome in previously inhospitable areas, although this may mainly concern drilling or field development contracts rather then production sharing agreements.[21] And the mere existence of NAFTA should create a more stable business environment. It is over the long term that a successful trade agreement would encourage gradual relaxation of remaining constraints. And it is then that more benefits may emerge.

The individual energy commodities, the scope for the supply of energy services, and other aspects are discussed in more detail below.

Oil

The firm grip that the Mexican government would retain on the disposition of Mexican oil mutes market imperatives that could encourage a more efficient system of oil supplies in North America. And this does not just apply to Mexico. The U.S. in 1980 blocked the export of Alaskan oil, reserving it for the domestic market.[22] (As an aside, the U.S. has complained about its trade deficit with Japan, yet paradoxically it has prevented Japan from purchasing Alaskan oil—which Japan would readily absorb.)

Forcing Alaskan oil into the lower mainland U.S. market has introduced distortions. Any surplus Alaskan oil production after satisfying U.S. west coast demand is delivered to the U.S. Gulf Coast. For Alaskan oil to compete in this artificial incremental market, the additional freight costs must be absorbed upstream. And since there is no FOB price discrimination for Alaskan oil, the landed price of Alaskan oil on the U.S. west coast market is below the world price. In turn, this effectively

---

21 The latter would seem to be precluded by the Mexican Constitution.

22 Amendments to the (U.S.) Export Administration Act, 1979. NAFTA does provide for export of a modest amount of Alaskan oil to Canada, although this stands in stark contrast to the generous access for the U.S. to Canadian supplies.

makes Canadian heavy oil unattractive on the west coast, forcing it to seek other markets in the U.S., or in the Pacific Rim.[23]

If the U.S. could place more reliance on Mexican oil during an emergency—as might apply if Mexico were eventually to accede to a proportionality type clause—then the U.S. might feel able to lift the export ban on Alaskan crude, although it would seem that the ban was partly imposed to mollify the domestic shipping lobby, rather than for strict security reasons.[24] Then a more efficient distribution of North American oil would prevail, with possibly more Mexican and Canadian heavy crudes sold in the U.S., while Alaskan crude might move to the Far East. At the same time, relaxation by Mexico of its marketing monopoly would provide more market sensitive opportunities for utilization of Mexican oil in the U.S. and in Eastern Canadian refineries, although this would require installation of more upgrading capabilities in these plants, given a preponderance of heavy gravity Mexican crudes. But as the Agreement stands, none of these things would happen.

The U.S. market is the crucible in which Canadian and Mexican supplies of mainly heavy oil compete, especially in the Great Lakes area and to the south of it. In the absence of NAFTA and in the presence of a U.S.-Mexican agreement, over the long term Canada might find Mexican oil in a preferential position in the U.S. market, one where Canadian marketers would have diminished recourse in the event of trade disputes. This is an example of NAFTA helping to protect the position of

---

23 Current (September 1992) price relationships are as follows. The price of Alaskan crude in the Gulf of Mexico is set by world prices of about US$19/barrel (27°API). Tanker rates (U.S. bottoms) for the Gulf to Alaska are some $4/barrel. This yields an Alaskan netback of $15/barrel. The laid down cost of Alaskan crude at Los Angeles (via U.S. bottoms) is $18.65/barrel. The laid down cost of Canadian heavy (26.5°API) at Los Angeles is about $19.50/barrel. And the netback from 27°API crude delivered to Japan is $16.70/barrel (all in US $). Sources for oil prices and tanker rates: Energy, Mines and Resources Canada; Alaskan Government, Oil and Gas Division; National Energy Board, *Reasons for Decision*, TransMountain Pipe Lines, Tolls RH-3-91, June 1992; and Bloomberg, *Oil Buyers Guide*, September 28, 1992.

24 Note that Mexico has supplied substantial amounts of oil for the U.S.'s strategic petroleum reserves (SPR).

Canada in the U.S. market in comparison with a situation where the U.S. and Mexico had an Agreement excluding Canada. Of course, this comment would apply to all of Canada's trade with the U.S.

Natural Gas

The picture for natural gas is similar to oil in that the scope for a more efficient distribution of gas could be curtailed by constraints on the development of Mexican resources. However, as mentioned before, the Agreement does insert a chink in the door of exclusivity. This is the provision that would allow end-users and suppliers to write bilateral contracts, although Mexican government approval would still be required.

But it is over the longer term that a burgeoning demand for natural gas in Mexico—perhaps stimulated by NAFTA itself and by greater emphasis on environmental quality—would encourage a further opening up of Mexican markets and supply capabilities. In more detail: with NAFTA Mexico may become more receptive to proposals made in the past to develop Mexican gas resources. These include extension of a gas pipeline in northern Mexico to Tijuana, and construction of a gas-fired de-salination plant in the Baja, California. The Gulf of Cortez is an area known to contain natural gas, yet development has been precluded by PEMEX budget restrictions. NAFTA would provide a framework for some erosion of the PEMEX tutelage and hence could allow more gas development projects to go forward. However, prospective declines in Mexican gas production available for commercial consumption may spur foreign participation in Mexican development in any case without any major legal restriction through NAFTA.[25]

To the extent more U.S. gas moves to Mexico—and there are expectations that by the year 2000 one bcf per day would be delivered to the Mexican border states[26]—Canadian companies would enjoy more opportunity for gas exports to the U.S. And of course the development of new gas markets in Mexico would assist in absorbing remaining surplus

---

25 See Baker and Associates [1991].

26 Current volumes (summer 1992) amount to some 250 mmcfd.

gas deliverability in Canada and the U.S. and so enable the industry in both these countries to operate on a more balanced basis. Thus NAFTA may provide a framework for more efficient linking of gas markets and supply "nodes," and would reinforce long run efficiencies that the FTA tends to stimulate.

Slack drilling efforts over the past five years or so suggest imports of natural gas by Mexico will persist (and grow) for some time yet. Their longevity will depend critically on the ability of Mexico to raise capital for investment in natural gas development and transmission. Ultimately, Mexico will need increased domestic gas production to meet its targets. And over the long run favourable reserves to production ratios for Mexico *vis-à-vis* the United States suggest current trends will be reversed, possibly early in the next century. At that time, pipeline projects currently contemplated to bring U.S. (and maybe Canadian) natural gas to Mexico could be reversed to ship Mexican gas to the U.S. (see Foss and Johnson [1991]).

Recent comments by Adrian Lajous of PEMEX support the picture sketched above. He sees liberalized trade encouraging importation of U.S. gas by Mexico, with sharply higher imports in the second half of the 1990s necessary to tide Mexico over a period of flat domestic production. At the same time there will be a need in Mexico to accelerate the development of natural gas infrastructures by foreign participation in service contracts, leading to greater integration. And emerging Mexican demand will siphon off some southwest U.S. gas production, providing more opportunities for eager Canadian marketers.[27] Indeed this eagerness has already reached as far as Mexico, with the recent announcement of the first direct sales of Canadian gas to PMI, the gas purchasing arm of PEMEX.[28]

---

27 Comments as reported in the *Financial Post*, September 15, 1992, p.5.

28 The October 1992 deal between Western Gas Marketing Ltd. and PMI is only for 30 days (but is renewable). The routing of the Canadian gas to northern Mexico is convoluted but does demonstrate the ability of Canadian gas to flow to Mexico by exchange even under prevailing transmission systems.

Electricity

Although a Mexican state monopoly exists, apparently free trade across the border effectively prevails.[29] Any such electricity flows are in one direction at present—from the U.S. to Mexico. The ability under NAFTA to negotiate contracts between independent producers and the Mexican electric monopoly would smooth the path of any cross border transactions. However, the impact of NAFTA is more in terms of the fillip it may provide for U.S. and Canadian electrical equipment supplies than on transborder flows of electricity itself. Such opportunities, among other things, are discussed below.

All these comments on the outlook for various energy resources assume a liberal evolution of the Agreement over time. What does NAFTA mean for energy flows among the three countries as it is currently written? Prospective flows between Canada and the U.S. remain much as they would be under the FTA: deregulation made the FTA in large measure superfluous over the short term, but over the long term it will stimulate energy trade while by no means erasing the U.S.-Canadian border. In the case of Mexico, NAFTA would secure access by Mexican oil to the U.S. market and by providing a better framework for medium term reliance on natural gas imports it could free up some oil supplies for export. But overall, the impact of NAFTA as currently drawn up on energy commodity flows between Mexico and the U.S. and on Canadian energy flows is *de minimus*—at least over the balance of this decade.

Trade in Energy Related Goods, Equipment and Services

While this paper has to do with energy *per se* and not with the goods and equipment used in its provision and use, nevertheless it is a natural extension to talk about prospects for these activities generated by the Agreement.

PEMEX is intending to embark on a significant program of investment to upgrade and refurbish its petroleum facilities. Investment

---

29 *Public Utilities Fortnightly*, July 1, 1991, p.35.

figures of $15 to $20 billion have been bandied about,[30] suggesting scope for large scale foreign technical involvement. In all probability an investment program such as this would provoke some loosening in Mexican trade practices irrespective of NAFTA. But undoubtedly the reduction of tariffs under NAFTA and changes in the rules for Government procurement would provide greater opportunities for the export of Canadian and U.S. petroleum equipment and services to Mexico. This would also be assisted by provisions for freer movement of professionals under the Agreement.

Opportunities will also arise for trade in electrical equipment such as switch gears, motor controls and transformers, given the proposed modernization and expansion of Mexico's electrical infrastructure. Again NAFTA would provide greater scope for these opportunities to be seized—including a lowering of tariffs—than in its absence.

In a broader way, the changes in rules and procedures governing trade between Mexico, Canada and the United States under NAFTA, with somewhat less nationalistic and discriminatory energy policies, cannot but stimulate trade. The transaction cost of conducting trade and investment relations may be reduced.

The significant reduction by Mexico in the list of petrochemicals protected from foreign investment ostensibly provides investment opportunities for Canadian companies. However, the importance of this relaxation is more in terms of its ability to establish market driven trade in North American petrochemicals. Significant direct investment by Canadian companies is unlikely, according to trade sources.[31]

Overall, prospective participation in a large scale revamping of the Mexican petroleum industry could provide a considerable boost to Canadian suppliers, a boost that would in part be attributable to NAFTA. In fact it is this feature of NAFTA that would have the greatest impact on the Canadian energy sector in the medium term, not trade in the energy commodities themselves.

---

30 See *Alberta Report*, March 11, 1991, p.32 and *Petroleum Economist*, January, 1992, p.6. Also see the NAFTA "Overview," p.viii.

31 See the *Globe & Mail*, August 14, 1992, p.B-3.

However, it is important not to lose sight of the fact that while NAFTA should stimulate Canadian trade with Mexico, increasing requirements by Mexico for technical assistance, equipment and the like would arise even in NAFTA's absence. Canada has already advanced lines of credit to PEMEX for $500 million which will encourage it to buy Canadian goods and services. And a memorandum of understanding on a framework for trade and investment consultation was signed prior to emergence of NAFTA.[32]

Moreover, relaxation of Mexico's foreign investment regulations preceded negotiation of NAFTA. New regulation in 1989 constituted an "expansive liberalization of Mexico's generally restrictive foreign investment laws."[33] And in August of 1989 the Government issued a Petrochemical Resolution declassifying some petrochemicals and making them more amenable to foreign investment. In January 1990 a "By-Product Decree" was issued, removing administrative obstacles for investors in certain refined products. All these developments are not contingent on NAFTA and demonstrate that Mexico's foreign investment laws have been evolving to allow limited foreign investment in secondary (including petrochemicals) and tertiary petroleum activities, although primary activities would remain under the exclusive domain of PEMEX.[34]

A wider issue is the relationship between NAFTA and PEMEX's prospective large scale investment program. Without significant, sustained increases in world oil prices or lower tax levies, it is not clear how PEMEX and the Mexican government will be able to finance such an ambitious scheme. This points to what can be regarded as a major deficiency of NAFTA: continued discouragement of foreign equity investment in the Mexican energy sector removes a potential source of funds for PEMEX to pursue its modernization and development projects. A corollary is that those in the United States and Canada antici-

---

32 See External Affairs and International Trade Canada [1992, p.3]. In March 1990 Canada signed 10 joint co-operation agreements with Mexico, of which that dealing with trade and investment consultation was one.

33 Kimball [1990, p.413].

34 *Ibid*, p. 414.

pating some kind of bonanza in the provision of services and equipment to Mexico will find their expectations dampened by PEMEX's financial constraints.

Dispute Mechanisms and Related Matters

The dispute mechanism in the FTA has been maintained in NAFTA and strengthened somewhat—although it is easy to exaggerate the degree to which this has happened. Nevertheless, a continuing shift of economic relationships from the political to the contractual sphere is beneficial. It is generally to the advantage of smaller countries when a larger one is more subject to the rule of law—something that NAFTA (and the FTA) have codified.[35] More stringent obligations on energy regulation should reduce the capacity of U.S. federal and state regulators to interfere in Canadian sales of natural gas to the U.S. Clarification in NAFTA that energy regulations are subject to the discipline of the Agreement not just at the federal level but at lower regulatory tiers is welcome.

The encouragement to observe contracts upgrades the FTA, although whether the impact will be visible remains to be seen. The embellishment was obviously inspired by the on-going imbroglio between Canadian authorities and the California Public Utilities Commission (CPUC). In 1988 the CPUC had supported an extension of long term natural gas export licences for the export of Canadian gas by Alberta and Southern Company (A&S) to California. But subsequently the CPUC saw the contracts as precluding competitive access, allegedly resulting in prices substantially higher than those in the Canadian market. The CPUC then invoked various regulatory measures to upset contractual arrangements between A&S and the main U.S. importer, Pacific Gas Transmission (PGT). In June of this year (1992), Canada's National Energy Board (NEB) took action to counteract what it saw as "detrimental effects" on the Canadian public interest of regulatory decisions by the CPUC. These were seen as undermining existing long-term commercial arrangements under which Canadian producers supply gas to Northern California. The NEB took action to prevent

35 Also, see the *Financial Post*, August 17, 1992, p.S2.

displacement of the long-term gas supply under contract to A&S by short-term (possibly cheaper) supplies.[36]

Not surprisingly, the issue arose of whether such initiatives would offend the FTA by constituting a restriction of exports. The NEB said its actions were consistent with FTA obligations.[37] The merits of that argument need not detain us. What is of abiding interest is this Californian dispute as the possible origin of the new stricture in NAFTA about the intent to honour contracts. I had argued elsewhere[38] that the FTA still left a lot of scope for governments to influence trade. The NEB's amendment to short-term California export licence conditions is a good example of this kind of activity.

In an earlier paper I suggested that until various challenges to interpretation of the FTA were dealt with either through dispute mechanisms or through the courts, the full implications or *modus operandi* of the FTA will not become clear.[39] This comment applies equally to NAFTA.

Concluding Remarks

NAFTA is intended to be a trade agreement to create a more integrated North American market—in fact one economic zone, to use the language of the NAFTA "Overview." While NAFTA may achieve this in terms of energy flows between Canada and the United States, it does not in terms of energy flows between Mexico and the other two Parties. This lack of symmetry can be viewed as a flaw. But the Agreement might also be seen as providing a lever to prise open the Mexican energy sector over time in a way that would lead to greater and more efficient integration of North American energy flows—the essential rationale for free trade. Such a process likely would be a slow osmosis. Indeed, the "Description" of the Agreement refers to enhancing the role of energy

---

36 It rescinded existing orders and issued new short term orders; see National Energy Board [1992, p.42].

37 *Ibid.*

38 Watkins and Jones [1991, p.13].

39 Watkins [1991, p.82].

through "sustained and gradual liberalization."[40] It would be unlikely for Mexico to abruptly cast aside decades of control and state involvement. It is salutary to recall that negotiation of the energy provisions of the FTA were greatly eased by commitments to de-regulation on both sides of the Canada-U.S. border made in advance of the agreement. No such prelude for Mexico preceded NAFTA.

More success can be claimed at this time for the much greater access that suppliers of energy equipment and services to Mexico enjoy under NAFTA. To be sure, some improved access would in all probability have emerged irrespective of the Agreement. However, there is no doubt that NAFTA would reinforce such trends.

The maintenance of restrictions on foreign investment in Mexico's primary energy activities may well thwart PEMEX's ambitious investment plans. The absence in NAFTA of measures to alleviate prospective capital shortages facing PEMEX is a deficiency of the Agreement, and will also slow down efficient integration of Mexican energy resources in North American markets.

The "Description" of the Agreement refers to NAFTA's energy provisions incorporating and building on GATT disciplines "regarding quantitative restrictions on imports and exports." This is clearly an overstatement, given Mexico's exclusion from many of the provisions governing U.S. and Canadian energy flows.[41]

NAFTA is unique in representing an Agreement subjecting the economy of a developing country to the rigours of competition with two fully industrialised countries. On a broader stage it may be a harbinger for corresponding Agreements with other countries in Latin America. Some have already evinced an interest in joining NAFTA.[42] The conclusion of similar trade arrangements to NAFTA with other countries in Latin America could lead to a more cohesive North and South American

---

40 NAFTA, "Description," p.5.

41 NAFTA, "Description," p.5.

42 See the NAFTA "Overview," p. v. Note that the NAFTA agreement does not require re-negotiation of Canada's terms of access to U.S. Mexican markets each time a new member joins.

presence in world oil markets. It is not frivolous to suggest that such developments might affect the strategic balance of world oil.

The title to this paper indicates a realm of unfinished business under NAFTA. This is so. But NAFTA as currently written—if consummated—would remain an important milestone. It would also confirm and modestly strengthen the energy provisions prevailing under the FTA between Canada and the U.S. This is not enough to generate euphoria, but a sense of quiet satisfaction would be justified.

References

Baker and Associates [1991],"Prospects for Increased Gas Trade with Mexico," Testimony for the California Energy Commission, 1991 Fuels Report Hearing, Berkeley, California, June 6.

External Affairs Canada [1987], "The Canada-United States Free Trade Agreement (FTA)," December.

External Affairs and International Trade Canada [1992], "The NAFTA Partnership," August.

Foss, M.M. and W.A. Johnson [1991], "The Economics of Natural Gas in Mexico," Proceedings, International Association for Energy Economics 13th Annual North American Conference, Chicago, Illinois, November 18-20.

Government of Canada [1992], "NAFTA: Overview and Description" (NAFTA "Overview"; NAFTA, "Description").

Kimball, Dale. A. Jr. [1990], "Recent Development: Secondary and Tertiary Petroleum Operations in Mexico: New Foreign Investment Opportunities," *Texas International Law Journal*, Volume 25.

National Energy Board [1991], *1990 Annual Report*, March.

—— [1992], *Reasons for Decision*, Canadian Petroleum Association Application for Review of Decision re: Alberta and Southern Gas Co. Ltd. (GH-5-88), GH-R-1-91, June.

Watkins, G.C. [1991], "The United States-Canada Free Trade Agreement: Implications for Oil and Gas," *Proceedings of the Thirteenth World Petroleum Congress*, John Wiley & Sons, New York.

—— and S.M. Jones [1991], "Free Trade in Energy Among the U.S., Canada and Mexico: State-of-Play and Prospects," Centre for International Studies/Fraser Institute Conference, Toronto, November 18 & 19.

—— and L. Waverman [1985], "Canadian Gas Export Pricing Behaviour," *Canadian Public Policy*, XI: Supplement.

NAFTA Rules of Origin and Automotive Content Requirements

Peter Morici
University of Maine

Introduction

RULES OF ORIGIN ARE ESSENTIAL to any arrangement extending preferential tariff treatment. When guided by laissez faire principles, their central purpose is to ensure that only "genuine" products of countries entitled to differential treatment receive it, and that transhipment and light processing[1] are not used by foreign suppliers to circumvent higher duties. However, defining genuine products is never easy nor free of the intrusion of other policy objectives. Parties to trade agreements often manipulate rules of origin to discourage the imports of components they would prefer were obtained domestically. That is, rules of origin often support interventionist industrial policy objectives.

---

1 For example, simple assembly, repackaging or dilution with water.

In the NAFTA negotiations, rules of origin attracted considerable attention because of concerns that Japanese and European firms would establish assembly operations in Mexico as a back door to the U.S. and Canadian markets. In defining NAFTA's rules, negotiators were encouraged to err on the strict side. Regarding industries vulnerable to international competition, e.g., milk, sugar, peanuts, fruits, vegetables, textiles and apparel, automotive products, and electronic components, they endured considerable pressures to impose rules affording protection to industries that could be aided more efficiently through more direct policy instruments.

In several areas, political calculus won out over economic logic. Although NAFTA rules of origin embody encouraging improvements over the Canada-U.S. Free Trade Agreement (FTA), in places, they reflect the contemporary American protectionist drift.

This paper evaluates the principal elements of NAFTA rules of origin and is divided into five parts. The first part briefly reviews criteria for evaluating rules of origin from the perspectives of effective implementation and as instruments of industrial policy. It then discusses the four principal approaches to creating rules of origin and their strengths and weaknesses. The second part describes NAFTA's general (i.e. nonautomotive) rules of origin, and the third part evaluates these rules. The fourth part assesses regional content requirements for the automotive industry. The fifth part contains some conclusions.

Evaluating Rules of Origin

Generally, rules of origin seek to assign origin to the country domiciling the last *significant* economic activity. To be significant, the most recent activity need not contribute the most value—it must only impart enough value to establish that the country has a genuine economic stake in the product.

Criteria

In 1987, the International Trade Commission suggested four characteristics that focus on effective and consistent application, which closely adhere to laissez faire principles. Rules should be:[2]

Uniform. Rules should be structured to ensure consistent application.

Simple. Rules should be clear, and comprehensive to minimize subjective judgements.

Predictable. Businesses should be able to anticipate how shipments will be treated.

Administrable. Rules should be easily verifiable, uncomplicated and not impose burdensome record keeping requirements.

In 1992, recognizing the industrial policy motivations behind some rules of origin, the present author suggested two additional criteria.[3]

Transparent. Deviation from the significant economic activity standard should be obvious, facilitating public scrutiny.

Efficient. Specific industries should be promoted in the least distorting way.

Approaches

Generally, advanced industrial countries apply some combination of four approaches when implementing MFN tariffs, free trade agreements and differential treatment for developing countries, e.g., General Preferential Tariffs (GPT).

Substantial Transformation

When implementing Most Favoured Nation (MFN) tariffs, quantitative restrictions and government procurement regulations, the United States

---

2 United States International Trade Commission, *Standardization of Rules of Origin*, USITC Publication No. 1976 (Washington: D.C., May 1987), pp. 12-13.

3 See Peter Morici, "Rules of Origin for a North American Trade Accord," (Vancouver: The Fraser Institute, 1992), p. 5.

uses a substantial transformation test,[4] and similar approaches are applied for MFN by the EC and Mexico. U.S. practice assigns origin if a process results in a new article with a distinctive name, character or use.[5] Although this test captures the essence of significant economic activity and does not impose particularly burdensome record keeping requirements, the wide discretion afforded customs officials by words such as "distinctive character" can make application of this rule arbitrary and inconsistent.[6] In U.S. application, this concept has been prone to costly litigation; wherever applied, it is susceptible to abuse by officials with opaque trade and industrial policy agendas.

Value Added Tests

The trend in recent years has been to rely on more objective, value based and process based tests. For the GPT (1975) and Caribbean Basin Initiative (CBI—1982), the United States requires both substantial transformation and a value added test—at least 35 percent of the value of materials plus direct cost of processing must be contributed by the exporting nation to qualify for preferential treatment. Canada employs value added tests for preferential arrangements, e.g., British Preferential, MFN and GPT. In FTA, a 50 percent materials plus direct cost of processing test was chosen as a back up to a change in tariff classification test (CTC) and is the primary rule for automotive products.

For example, under CBI rules a small engine assembled in the Dominican Republic from parts imported from the EC would qualify for duty free entry into the United States if the domestic materials, labour costs and other direct costs (e.g., depreciation on equipment and electricity) are at least 35 percent of the total of imported materials, domestic materials, labour costs, and other direct costs.

---

4 For the Multifiber Agreement, the United States supplements its substantial transformation rules with a list of processes that will confer origin, giving rise to a system called substantial transformation plus (ST+).

5 United States International Trade Commission, *Standardization of Rules of Origin*, p. 1, especially footnote 2.

6 See Peter Morici, "Rules of Origin for a North American Trade Accord," p. 6.

Also the CBI permits accumulation among "beneficiary countries." For example, if the total cost of a small engine assembled in the Dominican Republic contains 20 percent domestic materials and direct cost of processing *plus* imported components from another CBI country contributing another 15 percent to the total cost, the small engine qualifies for duty free entry into the United States.

Value added tests are appealing, because they appear to be uniform, simple, predictable, and administrable; however, they can be fraught with difficulties.

First, applying "a single value added threshold," for example 50 percent, is an arbitrary standard for significant economic activity; it may be too high for some products and too low for others. This problem may be finessed by varying thresholds by products; however, this tactic opens the door to industry lobbying and inefficient industrial policy making. The efficiency gains achieved by specifying reasonable and appropriate thresholds for most individual products could be overwhelmed by the inefficiencies imposed by politically-inspired, excessively high thresholds for the products threatened by import competition and industries using them as components. Even when political expediency requires protection, rules of origin are usually not the least distorting way of achieving this end.

For example, to protect U.S. lawn mower manufacturers from offshore competition, the drafters of the FTA could have required a 75 percent materials and direct cost of processing test for lawn mowers. Since small engines account for more than 25 percent of the cost of lawn mowers, this would have discouraged Canadian (U.S.) manufacturers from seeking substantial sales in the U.S. (Canadian) market by obtaining small engines in low-wage, developing countries. Major suppliers of small engines would be discouraged from moving assembly offshore.

Such a strategy would impose distortions in markets for both small engines and lawn mowers by imposing a hidden tariff on small engines and raising the costs and prices of small engines and lawn mowers. Production and consumption decisions would be directly distorted in two markets, *ceteris paribus*.[7] Imposing a common or coordinated exter-

7 Here the focus is on first order impacts. Obviously, smaller second order consequences would be felt in other markets such as suppliers to small

nal tariff on lawn mowers would only impose distortions in the market for lawn mowers; therefore, it would impose fewer efficiency losses. A subsidy to lawn mower producers would impose the fewest inefficiencies.[8] If free trade is not possible, subsidies are second best, tariffs are third best, and rules of origin that dictate where components are obtained are no more than fourth best.

Second, just selecting a working definition for value added is itself difficult. From the perspective of economic theory, the transaction price is most attractive, because it includes the most comprehensive concept of domestic contribution to value and it is the least messy to apply.[9]

---

engine manufacturers, other suppliers to lawn mower manufacturers, electric lawn mowers, and electric motors.

8 Essentially, a subsidy is superior to a tariff because it aids the domestic industry without penalizing consumers in that industry.

Simply put, a tariff increases both the prices received by producers and paid by consumers, inducing increased production in the domestic lawn mover industry even as consumers purchase fewer lawn mowers. Both sets of actions impose welfare losses on the society as a whole. Additional lawn mowers are made domestically at a cost that is higher than the international price and domestic consumers are deprived of low cost imports.

A subsidy to the lawn mower industry also raises the effective price domestic producers receive, the number of lawn mowers they make and imposes production efficiency losses similar to a tariff; however, a subsidy would leave consumers free to purchase lawn mowers at international prices and their consumption decisions would remain unaffected.

This is merely a restatement of a fundamental theorem of modern international economics: free trade is best, subsidies are second best, tariffs third best, and various types of quantitative restrictions fourth best. Among other things, quantitative restrictions tend to be fourth best because of their rigid application.

Depending on their structure and objectives, aggressive rules of origin tend to be fourth best, because they raise the prices faced by both producers and consumers in multiple markets (in this case small engines and lawn mowers), and they tend to be as rigidly imposed as quantitative restrictions.

9 It is the least messy concept because, unlike cost based concepts (e.g. the FTA materials and direct cost of processing or the NAFTA net cost method) it avoids issues of valuation of local inputs and the allocation of overhead.

However, such transaction prices often do not represent true market values, because they involve, for example, intracompany transfers of goods. This is an important reason why a cost based approach to measuring value added, including materials, labour costs and other direct processing costs, is frequently preferred.

Conceptually, to best approximate market value, labour costs, returns to capital and intellectual property, rent for land, and a share of firm wide managerial, R&D, advertising, and other overhead costs should be included; however, difficult issues arise. For example, capital cost allowances and depreciation schedules, established by accounting and tax rules, often do not adequately reflect the contribution of plant and equipment to the market value.[10] Royalties for foreign intellectual property can be manipulated to the advantage of exporters, creating transfer pricing problems similar to the ones encountered in international taxation. Imputed rents should be applied when land is owned by the manufacturer but such shadow pricing is difficult and imprecise. And consider, for example, the problems of allocating Ford's spending on R&D for engine and transmission design, or its overhead expenses for central administration and advertising.

To minimize, though not eliminate these complications, value added may be defined over a narrower base than may be justified on grounds of economic theory. This was the tack chosen in FTA by selecting "materials and direct cost of processing" and in strictly limiting the list of allowable costs to exclude most overhead costs.

Third, finished products can meet, for example, a 50 percent content test when they have much less than 50 percent value added originating in the free trade area, if products are assembled from components that in turn are partially made with imported components. For example, small engines assembled from imported kits may have 50 percent domestic materials and direct cost of processing. When these engines are combined with other wholly imported parts to make lawn mowers,

---

10 At best, these only roughly approximate the economic lives of buildings and equipment, which are determined as much by changes in technology as by the age of equipment; they do not adequately consider the effects of inflation or, as importantly, changes in relative prices for final goods, on asset values.

their entire value counts as domestic materials. From a customs perspective, the value of these small engines plus the direct cost of assembling the lawn mower may equal or exceed 50 percent but the value added originating in the domestic economy may be much less.

This is the so-called roll up problem that has been so troublesome in the automotive sector under FTA. It may be countered by tracing the value of imported components through the stages of production but this imposes burdensome record keeping, especially for complex products involving many layers of suppliers like automobiles and telecommunications systems. Small producers, lacking the leverage with vendors that the Big Three and major Asian and European automakers enjoy, would find such tracing requirements quite difficult to fulfil.

Fourth, value added tests can fall prey to the kinds of valuation problems common in dumping cases. For example, when transaction prices for components or the final good in question do not reflect market values, owing to intracompany transfers or purchases from captive suppliers, finding proxies and assigning values for inputs and outputs offers opportunities for abuse by both private firms and government officials enforcing the rules.

Fifth, for many manufacturing processes, value added requirements may prove more burdensome for low wage members of a free trade area. Moreover, with NAFTA value added requirements set fairly high, NAFTA rules may actually place Mexico at a competitive disadvantage *vis-à-vis* countries eligible for CBI treatment. Both of these issues are discussed below in the section evaluating NAFTA rules of origin.

Process Tests

Alternatively, origin may be assigned by a nomenclature that distinguishes between components and final products on the basis of significant steps in production processes. In 1987, the International Trade Commission suggested such a nomenclature be developed to standardize and add more certainty and clarity to the administration of rules of origin.[11] The continual evolution of products and processes poses obvious problems.

---

11 United States International Trade Commission, *Standardization of Rules of Origin*, pp. 20-23.

Change in Tariff Classification Tests

Approximations of process tests are CTC rules that serve as primary tests for FTA, NAFTA and EC preferential arrangements. These are defined in terms of the Harmonized Tariff Schedule (HTS) employed by most GATT countries.

The HTS is divided into sections numbered in Roman Numerals from I to XXI. Within these are ninety-seven chapters, e.g., Section I, Live Animals and Animal Products contains Chapters 1 to 5 and Section XXI, Works of Art, Collectors' Pieces and Antiques contains Chapter 97. Chapters establish two digit classifications, e.g., all classifications within Chapter 11 begin with the prefix 11. In turn, these are divided into four digit headings (1110) and six digit subheadings (1110.10). Countries using the HTS may divide these further into eight digit tariff lines.

Qualifying FTA CTCs are specified for each section of the HTS. For some products, changes at the chapter level are required, while for others, changes at the heading or subheading level will suffice.

CTC tests may have several attributes. For countries applying the Harmonized Tariff System (HTS), they are uniform, simple, predictable, easily administered, and transparent. Large required CTCs motivated by policy goals are easily identified. For example, the FTA disallows the transformation of fruits and vegetables (Chapters 7 and 8) into frozen or canned goods (Chapter 20). Clearly, canning is a significant economic activity. This tactic protects farmers by penalizing canners but at least it is transparent.

CTC tests may have shortcomings too. First, HTS was not constructed for this purpose and does not systematically sort products according to stages of production. In some cases, substantial transformation may most closely coincide with a CTC at the chapter level, while in other cases it may coincide with a change in headings, subheadings or tariff lines. For some products, HTS does not distinguish between final products and parts. For example, HTS assigns separate headings to bicycles (HTS 8712) and parts (8714) but not to baby carriages and parts (8715). HTS may not distinguish between complicated assembly operations and assembly that adds little value.

FTA handled these problems by varying the scale of tariff classifications that must be traversed and, for some goods, by applying a supplementary value added test noted above. In addition, where the

HTS does not provide separate classifications for products and their components, a 50 percent U.S.-Canadian materials and direct cost of processing test is applied to assembly operations. Also, for some products, both a CTC and 50 percent U.S.-Canadian materials and direct cost of processing is required.

EC requires a four digit CTC, and for some goods, this test is supplemented by lists of processes that can confer origin without a CTC (positive tests) and processes that cannot confer origin (negative tests).

These approaches are open to all kinds of inefficient industrial policy making. NAFTA value added requirements for plastics (discussed below), and EC negative process tests for footwear are examples of such abuses. Under EC rules, origin status cannot be accorded a shoe manufactured with an imported upper even though this process constitutes a CTC at the four digit level (6406.10 to 6401-6405)[12] and is clearly a significant manufacturing process.

Second, HTS specifies a nomenclature to the six digit level. Tariff schedules often further disaggregate product categories to the eight and ten digit levels, and distinctions among categories at these levels can be important in defining CTC requirements. Inconsistencies at eight digit levels between the U.S., Canadian and Mexican tariff schedules required attention in NAFTA.

Third, CTC tests require customs officials to make two sets of classifications, one for imported products and another for third country components. They may rely on classification decisions made by the source country; however, lacking uniform customs regulations this can lead to disputes.

NAFTA General Rules of Origin

Owing to the pressures on negotiators noted in the introduction, NAFTA aspires to quite strict standards for rules of origin. The framers sought "to ensure that NAFTA benefits are accorded only to goods produced in the North American region, not goods made wholly or in

12 As noted below, the NAFTA also disallows CTCs from HTS 6606.10 to 6401-6405.

large part in other countries."[13] When regional content tests are required, for example, the standards the United States and Canada impose on imports from Mexico are tougher than the standards the United States imposes on Mexican GPT imports or CBI imports.

Like FTA, the basic NAFTA rules afford North American status to goods containing nonregional materials if they are sufficiently transformed to achieve a CTC, and generally, these criteria are supplemented by value added tests.

CTC Criteria

Required CTCs vary from two to eight digits. Where differences in nomenclature pose problems, the rules define correspondences between the three nation's tariff schedules at the eight-digit level. For example, the manufacture of paper, paper board and similar products (HTS 48) from imported wood pulp (HTS 47) confers origin. The manufacture of envelopes, letter cards, postcards, assorted stationary sets, etc. (HTS 48.17) from paper and paperboard of the kinds used for writing and printing (HTS 48.10) confers origin.

Value Added Criteria

Where finished products and components are named in the same tariff classification, meeting one of two regional value content (RVC) tests will suffice to achieve North American status. The assembly of baby carriages with imported parts (HTS 8715) is an example.

For some products both the CTC and RVC tests must be met to qualify for duty free status, for example, the assembly of bicycle parts into a bicycle (CTC from HTS 8714 to 8712) and the assembly of trailer parts such as wheels, axles and major body components into a camping trailer (HTS 8716.90 to 8716.10).

Usually, exporters may choose between satisfying the 60 percent of "transaction value" test or the 50 percent of "net cost" test. The former concept is based on the f.o.b. price paid or payable for the good; the

---

13 Governments of Canada, the United Mexican States and the United States of America, *Description of the Proposed North American Free Trade Agreement* (August 12, 1992), p. 2.

value of nonoriginating components is subtracted from the transactions value to compute RVC.

The net cost concept employs a narrower definition of value added. Excluded from allowable costs are royalties, sales promotion, packaging and shipping; a cap will be placed on allowable interest expenses.[14]

The transaction value and the narrower net cost concepts are both broader concepts of value added than the FTA materials and direct cost of processing concept. Net cost is broader than its FTA analog, because it encompasses more of the general costs of doing business and more interest expenses.[15]

The net cost method must be applied if the transaction value is not acceptable under the GATT Customs Valuation Code, or if the good is sold by the producer to a related person and the producer sells 85 percent of identical or similar goods to one or several related persons over a six month period preceding the sale. The purpose of these conditions is to ensure that the transaction value, when it is applied, represents a market value and not a manipulated price.

For automotive products, the net cost method is mandatory (the transaction value may not be used), and depending on the product, 60 or 62.5 percent is required. For footwear, the net cost method is also mandatory, and 55 percent is required.

For many secondary chemical products (HTS 34, 35 and 36), either the transaction value or net cost requirement must be met. When the transaction value is used, a 65 percent threshold applies. For insecticides, fungicides, herbicides and disinfectants (HTS 3808), the transactions and net cost standards are 80 and 70 percent if the product contains more than one active ingredient.

Special Provisions

A *de minimis* rule prevents goods containing less than seven percent imported materials from losing eligibility because they otherwise fail to

---

14 This will be spelled out in the yet to be drafted Uniform Regulations.

15 A notable exception to this statement is royalty payments, which are allowable under the FTA "materials and direct cost of processing" definition but not under the NAFTA "net cost" definition.

meet a specific rule of origin, e.g., achieving a required CTC. Excluded from this provision are several primary agricultural products whose markets are generally protected by very strict rules of origin for downstream products. Examples include various uses of milk, sugar, lard, pig and poultry fat, ingredients for alcoholic beverages, coffee, tea, and spices. Also excluded are materials used in gas and electric stoves and ranges, and trash compactors.

An *accumulation* provision permits the exporter of a good to include the activities of other North American firms involved in the production of the good to demonstrate that the good meets the necessary CTC and RVC requirements.

Where a firm uses *fungible materials* from North American and non-North American sources to make a good, the firm need not account for originating and nonoriginating materials in each item shipped as the Uniform Regulations will provide rules for averaging.

Uniform Regulations

NAFTA contains a chapter on customs valuation which was absent from FTA. In it the three countries agree to establish Uniform Regulations regarding the interpretation, application and administration of rules of origin, and to embody these regulations in domestic law. For example, when using the net cost method businesses may "reasonably allocate" certain overhead expenses and general costs of doing business according to provisions to be set out in the Uniform Regulations.

The customs valuation chapter also provides for the creation of a Certificate of Origin that the exporting country will issue producers or exporters, and transparent procedures for the importing country to review these certificates if it suspects a designation of North American origin is incorrect. This chapter establishes procedures for producers and exporters to obtain advanced rulings, as well as their right to appeal customs decisions before domestic authorities. A trilateral working group will focus on issues such as uniform interpretation of CTC schedules and valuation, as well as making modifications to the rules.

Evaluating the General Rules

As noted in the first part of this paper, evaluating rules of origin has two sides: effective and consistent implementation, and the use of rules as instruments of industrial policy.

Effective Implementation

Overall, the general (nonautomotive) rules of origin should prove to be at least as uniform, simple, predictable, and administrable as the FTA rules. The rules exhibit the qualities anticipated from a system founded on CTCs and backed up by value added tests. They lay out required CTCs in painstaking detail. This is why the rules chapter numbers nearly 200 pages. Where necessary, they provide precise translations among the three countries' tariff nomenclatures at the eight digit level. The Uniform Regulations and working group established to achieve consistency in the implementation of rules should limit problems and disputes emerging from exporting country assignments of origin to final products and components, or that may arise concerning valuation. These are important improvements over FTA rules, as are the broader definitions chosen for measuring regional content.

Notwithstanding exceptions to the 50/60 rule for automobiles, footwear and many secondary chemicals, NAFTA RVC requirements impose most of the benefits and costs of a single value added threshold, albeit with two choices for measuring it.

Regarding the Uniform Regulations one caveat is in order.. In the FTA, uniform application has been absent. Revenue Canada issued its guidelines, the U.S. Customs Administration issued its rulings, and U.S. unilateralism has been perceived to be a big problem by Canadians. Under the NAFTA, what happens after the Uniform Regulations are written?

If one party applies these unilaterally to other parties dissatisfaction, will the latter be able to obtain effective redress through the working group process? If not, dispute settlement, as provided for by NAFTA Chapter 20 (the analog to FTA Chapter 18), could prove a long, circuitous route. Certainly, this is what was indicated by the FTA dispute over U.S. customs treatment of nonmortgage interest by Honda. With mutually agreed upon standards in the NAFTA chapter on customs valuation and the soon to be drafted Uniform Regulations in hand, the three countries should seriously consider establishing a speedy and binding dispute settlement regime.

The provisions for *de minimis*, accumulation among firms, and fungible materials are welcome innovations. They will ease the fulfilment of the rules of origin without diminishing their effectiveness; hence, they will improve efficiency.

With the exception of automobiles (discussed below), NAFTA rules do not address the roll up problem. On balance, this is probably a plus, because of the administrative burdens that tracing the contents of components would impose on many smaller and medium sized firms.

NAFTA Rules as Instruments of Industrial Policy

In specifying required CTCs and RVC requirements, NAFTA imposes some fairly inefficient, even if transparent, industrial policies.

Like FTA rules, NAFTA CTC rules disallow the transformation of fresh fruits and vegetables into frozen or canned goods, protecting farmers at the expense of food processors. Also, NAFTA rules limit or disallow CTCs, even at the chapter level, for significant amounts of imported sugar, coffee, milk, or peanuts used in processed foods.

As noted, NAFTA imposes a 55 percent net cost test on the manufacture of shoes made with imported soles, heels and other components (CTC from HTS 6406.20-6406.99 to 6401-6405), and NAFTA rules will not award duty free status to shoes made with imported uppers (CTC from HTS 6406.10 to 6401-6405). This tactic will discourage imports of shoe components from offshore for assembly in Mexico and reexport to the United States and Canada. Whether such protection has merit is one issue; however, using rules of origin to do so will likely impose more distortions and create greater inefficiencies than assisting the shoe industry through subsidies or common or coordinated tariffs.

In another example, NAFTA, like the FTA, imposes both CTC requirements and a 50/60 RVC test 39 (Plastics and Articles Thereof). This chapter includes separate tariff headings for: primary plastics, e.g., polymers; intermediate products used to make other plastic products and consumed by nonrelated industries, e.g., tubes, boxes and plates; and final products, e.g., floor coverings and plastic document binders.

Clearly, significant economic activities are involved in the transformation of polymers into sheets and tubes or floor coverings, and value added tests to supplement changes in headings is unnecessary in these cases. Perhaps for some less obvious situations, the 50/60 RVC test may be appropriate, but generally it appears to be overkill.

Generally, these value added requirements may be expected to protect North American primary plastics at the expense of secondary plastics, or to protect both industries at the expense of final products. They impose multiple distortions with difficult to calibrate consequences. Used in this way, rules of origin are inefficient and crude instruments of industrial policy.

For textiles/apparel, NAFTA imposes a much stricter regime than the FTA. For cotton and some manmade fibres, required CTCs create a fibre forward regime, e.g., garments must be made from North American cloth that was made from North American thread, which in turn was made from North American fibres. For most products, including wool, the rule is thread forward.[16] For fibres in short supply such as silk and flax (linen), garments made from imported fabric may qualify for duty free treatment.

The textiles/apparel provisions exemplify rules of origin at their worst. They impose cascading distortions of unknown proportions as their effects on costs and prices ascend through the production chain from fibres to fabrics to finished garments. This scheme protects fibres, yarns and thread, and textiles more than apparel, with many crosscutting effects. For example, since apparel is such a labour intensive industry, many segments of the U.S. industry may benefit by denying duty free status to Mexican garments made from offshore fabrics; however, these U.S. manufacturers will be constrained to purchase more expensive North American textiles for exports to Mexico. Overall there are more efficient ways to assist these industries, e.g., subsidies or a common/coordinated import regime for textiles and apparel. However, as

---

16 Tariff quotas will permit duty-free trade up to specific limits in garments that are made from cloth that does not satisfy these rules—these may either be garments made from imported cloth, or North American cloth made from imported thread or fibres.

is the case for the industries discussed above, such approaches impose political costs that the three governments are not willing to endure.

Overall, although NAFTA rules of origin closely follow FTA rules, they appear to be at least as strict and in many places stricter. Even putting aside the textile/apparel and automotive regimes, NAFTA CTC rules are more demanding in some places and mandatory value added tests are more frequent in NAFTA than FTA. Also, after tariffs reach zero, imports from Mexico will no longer be able to qualify for zero tariff treatment, where applicable, under GPT. This effectively raises value added requirements for Mexican made goods that formerly qualified under GPT.[17]

Consequences of Strict Rules

Although NAFTA rules of origin may not be characterized as draconian,[18] the trend toward more restrictive rules is disappointing. Adding Mexico to the Canada-U.S. free trade area increases the range of human and physical resources available cheaply within the free trade area; in turn, this increases the range of products that may be made and "significant economic activities" that may be undertaken on a competitive basis inside the free trade area.

With the addition of Mexico, fewer market incentives should be present merely to ship, for example, television or bicycle component kits to Mexico for assembly and reexport, because having deregulated its economy and offered literate workers at low wages, free trade makes Mexico as good a place as any to manufacture most of the labour intensive components used in televisions and bicycles. And, as the maquiladora experience indicates, trilateral free trade should make the United States and Canada more attractive locations for obtaining more sophisticated components that are not economical to make in Mexico.

---

17 This is not formally stated in the NAFTA but the Bush Administration announced U.S. plans to cancel GPT status for Mexico—see *International Trade Reporter*, Vol. 9 (August 19, 1992), p. 1431. Interviews with Mexican officials confirm that they anticipate this action.

18 Textiles and apparel provide a major exception.

Furthermore, overly strict rules of origin do not provide a powerful incentive when tariffs are low or quantitative restrictions are not imposed. Overly burdensome requirements may have perverse effects, e.g., cause manufacturers to increase instead of decrease their use of imported components or be ignored all together.

For example, the 50/60 percent NAFTA RVC requirements imposed on baby carriages could cause assemblers in Mexico to purchase mostly imported parts and absorb the 4.4 and 12.5 percent U.S. and Canadian duties *if* the additional cost of U.S. and Canadian parts is not worth the tariff savings. In contrast, a 35 percent value added standard, such as the United States applies for GPT and CBI, might be more often observed and better encourage Mexican assemblers to source U.S. and Canadian parts. With average U.S. and Canadian tariffs on dutiable Mexican imports at only about 6 and 11 percent, this is more than an academic concern.

High RVC requirements place a heavier burden on firms in Mexico, owing to its low wages, than on firms in the United States and Canada. For example, the high value added tests applied by NAFTA to the assembly of motorcycles, bicycles, wheelchairs, and baby carriages are potentially much less onerous for Canadian firms than Mexican firms. Identical processes, employing an assortment of moderately skilled labour and management, could result in products that qualify for duty free entry into the United States when made in Canada but not when made in Mexico.

One consequence of NAFTA offering exporters the option of applying the transaction value method is to give Mexico a break in this regard. For example, when a Mexican product only competes with a Canadian product in the U.S. market and enjoys lower labour costs, the Mexican producer should be able to price up to the Canadian competition and lower wages in Mexico would become irrelevant in establishing the Mexican share of North American content, *ceteris paribus.*[19] However, if the Mexican product competes with a CBI product and a Canadian product, then the Mexican producer must price to compete with the

---

19 The labour cost differences between the Canadian and Mexican made product will accrue to the producer in the form of higher profits.

lowest cost competitor. It could work out that the CBI product could meet its 35 percent threshold while the Mexican product failed to meet its 60 percent threshold.

It would seem odd to permit products resulting from identical manufacturing activities to qualify for duty free entry into the United States when undertaken in Canada or the Dominican Republic but not when undertaken in Mexico. Yet, as the rules of origin are structured, that is exactly what could happen.

All of these considerations would seem to favour more lenient, as opposed to stricter, rules of origin for NAFTA than are embodied in FTA. NAFTA rules require easier, not more difficult, CTCs, lower value added thresholds, and fewer mandatory value added tests. It would be reasonable to lower transaction value threshold to 50 percent or less and the net cost test to 35 or 40 percent.

North American Content Requirements for Automobiles

All three national governments have sought to maintain a large presence in the automobile industry. The central role trade management has played in these industrial policies[20] is reflected in the structures and distinctive characteristics of three national automobile industries.

Broad Outlines of Pre-NAFTA Regimes[21]

Since 1981, Japanese producers have restrained exports into the U.S. and Canadian markets under formal and informal voluntary restraint agreements.

---

20 Notable among recent or present policies are U.S. and Canadian voluntary restraint agreements with Japanese manufacturers, U.S. efforts to increase purchases of components by Japanese manufacturers, Canadian safeguards in the Automotive Agreement of 1965, Canadian duty draw back and remissions benefits tied to exports and production, the maquiladora program, and Mexico's domestic content and export requirements and severe import management regimes.

21 For more detailed accounts see the chapter by Jon Johnson elsewhere in this

By 1998, duties will be eliminated on all bilaterally traded automotive products meeting a 50 percent materials and direct cost of processing test. Canada may continue to offer GM, Ford, Chrysler and Volvo[22] the option instead of meeting the stricter 1965 Automotive Agreement performance requirements[23] to qualify for the additional privilege of importing products from third countries duty free. Essentially, firms must assemble one vehicle in Canada for each one sold there and achieve value added in Canada equal to 60 percent of fleet sales. Other U.S. based firms (e.g., Japanese transplants) enjoy similar benefits under duty remission agreements but Canada has agreed to phase these out.

In Mexico, two automotive industries have emerged—the maquiladora sector, and a highly protected and regulated indigenous industry composed of domestic parts suppliers and vehicle assembly by the Big Three, Nissan, and Volkswagen. The 1989 Automotive Decree required individual vehicle producers to match each dollar of imports with 2.5 dollars of exports in 1991, declining to 1.75 dollars in 1994. Imports of finished vehicles were limited to 15 percent of domestic sales in 1991 and 20 percent in 1993. Vehicle assemblers must achieve 36 percent domestic content (parts and labour) for vehicles and 30 percent for parts. Generally, qualifying parts must be produced in non-maquiladora plants, where foreign ownership is limited to 40 percent with some exceptions.

Objectives in Negotiations

While voluntary restraint agreements and Canadian duty remission incentives have encouraged Japanese and other foreign producers to locate assembly facilities in North America, the U.S. parts deficit with Japan has ballooned. Most Japanese parts purchases in North America

---

volume, and Peter Morici, *Rules of Origin for a North American Trade Accord*, pp. 11-30.

22 Also qualifying for similar duty free treatment are CAMI, GM's joint venture with Suzuki, and remnants of American Motors operated by Chrysler. These companies benefit from duty remission agreements which will not be phased out like benefits for transplants.

23 These are commonly called the Canadian "safeguards."

tend to be low technology items, instead of engines, transmissions, or electronic control components. Related to this issue, the U.S. industry has become convinced that Japanese transplants have either abused or too greatly profited from "roll up" in meeting FTA rules of origin. Entering NAFTA negotiations, General Motors proposed a 60 percent North American content requirement, Chrysler and Ford endorsed a 70 percent requirement, and the U.S. Motor Vehicle and Equipment Manufacturers Association supported a 75 percent rule.

In Canada, the Automotive Agreement safeguards and duty remission incentives have fostered a competitively strong vehicle assembly sector but a weaker parts sector. Coupled with the fact that the Big Three and Volvo account for 90 percent of Canadian vehicle production and already have a strong incentive to achieve 60 percent Canadian value added, high North American content requirements would do more to benefit U.S./Mexican parts producers than Canadian suppliers. Hence, Canada had little incentive to support high content requirements that might also discourage Asian and European investment in Canadian assembly operations.

Outside the maquiladora sector, Mexico's auto decrees encouraged the development of a Mexican parts sector and a foreign-owned vehicle assembly sector. The former is fragmented and backward,[24] and the latter is much in need of rationalization. In NAFTA, facing a major overhaul of its automotive regime, Mexico had some interest in high North American content requirements and phased elimination of its domestic sourcing requirements to assist the modernization, as opposed to the elimination, of its parts sector, and to give foreign assemblers some time to reconfigure. This said, over the longer term, Mexico, like Canada, should be more interested in attracting *globally competitive* production than in maximizing the regional content of vehicles sold in North America.

---

24 The notable exceptions are foreign owned engine plants having large exports.

NAFTA's Automobile Regime

NAFTA will impose a 62.5 percent of net cost requirement for passenger automobiles, light trucks and their engines and transmissions; for other vehicles and parts, the threshold will be 60 percent.[25] Canada may still offer the Big Three and Volvo the option of complying with Automotive Agreement rules if they wish to retain duty free access for third country products. To eliminate "roll up," in computing the regional content, the value of components obtained from outside North America must be traced through the production chain.[26]

Mexico's Auto Decree policies, including import restraints, performance requirements and investment restrictions, will be phased out by January 1, 2004. For vehicle assemblers, trade balancing requirements will be liberalized immediately through adjustments in the formulae used to compute compliance. Domestic content requirements (parts and labour) will fall from 34 percent in 1994-1998 to 29 percent in 2003 and disappear in 2004. Maquiladora plants will be able to qualify suppliers to meet these requirements, and the 40 percent ceiling on foreign investment in the non-maquiladora parts plants will be phased out for U.S. and Canadian investors.

Evaluating the Automotive Rules

Essentially, the United States and Canada/Mexico split their differences. The 62.5/60 rule represents some tightening of regional content requirements. However, this is not a sizeable concession to the automotive industry, because the net cost concept is broader than its FTA analog. The real concessions to the U.S. industry will likely prove to be the tracing requirements designed to eliminate roll up. Given the num-

25 The net cost requirements will be 50 percent initially, then rise to 56 and 62.5 percent (55 and 60 percent) for cars, light trucks, and engines and transmissions (other vehicles and parts) in the 1998 and 2002 model years.

26 For cars, the rules require producers to trace imported materials entering under a wide range of specified tariff provisions. For trucks and buses, producers must only determine the origin of a specified list of engine and transmission components, i.e., block, head, fuel injector pump. For more details see Jon Johnson's chapter elsewhere in this book.

ber of stages in the transformation of basic components into automobiles, the use of non-North American parts by transplants should be substantially reduced.

The continuation of Canada's Automotive Agreement incentives for the Big Three and Volvo to assemble cars and source some parts in Canada has not in the past proven troublesome for North American producers and will not likely create new problems. It is a political plus for Ottawa and does not cost the Americans or Mexicans much.

Nevertheless, the rules of origin are not likely to appreciably affect the health of the Big Three and their suppliers. The rules will cause some offshore firms doing business in Mexico to make a larger commitment to Mexico. Volkswagen, for instance, is moving in this direction. And these rules may prevent an acceleration in the erosion of North American industry's market share through the establishment of additional transplants in Mexico. However, by themselves, they don't offer a tonic for an ailing industry. If the automotive industry merits additional government assistance, a more comprehensive industrial policy will be needed.[27]

Overall, the rules of origin for automobiles are clear and precise so as to avoid the kinds of disputes that have emerged from interpretations of FTA rules. Seen in terms of the effective implementation criteria suggested by the International Trade Commission, they should prove uniform, simple and predictable. However, they will be burdensome to administer; the tracing requirements will impose burdensome record keeping requirements, especially for small and medium sized suppliers of components for cars.

As instruments of industrial policy, NAFTA regional content rules are fairly innocuous. Lower regional content requirements would probably better serve laissez faire principles; however, NAFTA rules are not draconian either, and there was a real danger that this could have happened. Given the political tone of the negotiations, the embattled state of North American industry, and the legacy of content and performance requirements under the Automotive Agreement, FTA and Mex-

---

27 See Peter Morici, *Rules of Origin for a North American Trade Accord*, pp. 22-30.

ican Decrees, NAFTA negotiators deserve high marks for not caving in on this one.

Conclusions

Like all rules of origin, NAFTA's rules reflect both the pull of economic rationalism and the drag of political pragmatism. Generally, they are strictly structured to ensure that only genuine products of Canada, Mexico and the United States receive duty free treatment. They are clear and precise. Overall, they should prove simple, uniform and predictable. With the exception of the tracing provisions for automotive components they should prove administrable. In several specific industries NAFTA's rules also reflect pressures on trade officials to protect and promote North American producers besieged by fundamental competitiveness problems.

Considering the 1991-1992 environment for NAFTA negotiations—gridlock in the GATT, sweeping structural change in Mexico, high unemployment and politically embattled national leaders in Canada and the United States—negotiators could have done a lot worse. Since the NAFTA envisions continuous review of the rules of origin, and by January 1992 an assessment of the textiles/apparel regime, the focus should be on how to improve them.

As integration of Mexico into the broader U.S.-Canada economy continues and the macroeconomic environment improves, trade officials should consider relaxing rules of origin. High on the list of priorities should be shorter required CTCs, lowering transaction value threshold to 50 percent or less and net cost threshold to 35 or 40 percent, and eliminating value added tests where they are unnecessary or patently protectionist. In areas such as textiles/apparel, footwear and plastics, the framers seem to be using NAFTA rules of origin to achieve outcomes that could be more efficiently achieved through more direct methods of trade and industrial policy. These flaws ought to be corrected.

Also, to ensure that the principles and protection for exporters laid out in the rules of origin and Uniform Regulations are respected, a binding dispute settlement mechanism should be considered.

With regard to automobiles, considering the history of trade and industrial policies in that sector, negotiators did remarkably well. The dismantling over ten years of the principal elements of Mexico's nationalist industrial policies is a major achievement, and NAFTA's regional content requirements should not appreciably exacerbate the problems imposed by other measures already in place. Real help for what ails the North American automobile industry, if it merits help, will require other industrial policies. It will likely be the task of future trade officials to resist cries for tougher, more damaging, regional content requirements.

Dispute Settlement in NAFTA and the FTA

Gilbert R. Winham
Dalhousie University[1]

Introduction

DISPUTE SETTLEMENT HAS BEEN a longstanding goal of Canada in international trade. As a middle power dealing with large players like the United States or the European Community (EC), Canadian governments have promoted clearly-enforced trade rules as being in Canada's national interest as well as in the interest of the broader trade system. Canada's concern over trade rules and dispute settlement quickened after the conclusion of the Tokyo Round negotiation in 1979,

---

1 I gratefully acknowledge research assistance on this chapter from Heather Grant of McGovern, Roine, Ottawa; and Katherine Trueman, M.A. Candidate, Dalhousie University. I also thank several who criticised the first draft, namely, Jonathan T. Fried, EAITC; Steven Globerman, The Fraser Institute; Heather Grant, McGovern, Roine; Michael Hart, EAITC; and Jeffrey S. Thomas, Ladner Downs, Vancouver. I alone am responsible for the final draft. Finally, I gratefully acknowledge research support from the SSHRC.

as the United States gradually enhanced its unfair trade remedy procedures especially dealing with anti-dumping and countervailing duties. Both the private sector and governments in Canada became alarmed that trade remedy actions against products like timber, fish and pork threatened Canada's existing trade to the United States, and this alarm quickly translated into a concern for the "security of access" to U.S. markets. Effective and binding dispute settlement was seen as the most effective means for dealing with security of access, hence dispute settlement became a political *sine qua non* for Canada in the negotiations for a Canada-U.S. Free Trade Agreement (FTA).[2]

Developing a more formal dispute settlement system has only recently become a major concern in international trade policy. This can be seen in the General Agreement on Tariffs and Trade (GATT), where the incidence of GATT dispute settlement panels increased sharply during the 1980s.[3] In regional trade agreements, the increasing importance of dispute settlement can be seen by comparing the Australia-New Zealand Closer Economic Relations Trade Agreement of 1983 with the Canada-US FTA concluded in 1987. In the earlier agreement, dispute settlement was clearly an afterthought. In the FTA, the parties established a more formal mechanism for general dispute settlement than that existing in the GATT, and they created a wholly unique dispute settlement mechanism for dealing with antidumping and countervailing duties. The latter undertaking was one of the most contentious issues in the FTA negotiation.

Arguably, dispute settlement procedures in the FTA have worked very well. Professional opinion has been supportive, as evidenced by the remarks of Professor Andreas Lowenfeld in a major evaluation of binational dispute settlement practice: "All things considered, the

---

2 For further discussion, see Michael Hart "A Lower Temperature: The Dispute Settlement Experience under the Canada-United States Free Trade Agreement," *American Review of Canadian Studies*: (Summer/Autumn, 1991) 193-205.

3 Robert E. Hudec, "The Judicialization of GATT Dispute Settlement" in Michael M. Hart and Debra P. Steger, eds., *In Whose Interest? Due Process and Transparency in International Trade*, Ottawa: Centre for Trade Policy and Law, 1992, p. 9-44.

unique binational dispute settlement mechanisms created by the Canada-United States Free Trade Agreement have worked extraordinarily well."[4] Lowenfeld has praised the opinions of panellists as "thorough," "articulate," and "on the whole persuasive," and has been unable to detect either a bias toward protectionism or unrestrained trade, or a "Canadian" or "American" approach in panel decisions.[5] At the political level, statements of government leaders about FTA dispute settlement have generally been positive, although there has been occasional criticism especially from the U.S. Congress. The fact that the United States and Canada both negotiated an essentially similar dispute settlement mechanism in the North American Free Trade Agreement (NAFTA) as the FTA demonstrates that the latter mechanism met with political approval.

Dispute settlement could be described under three headings in the FTA:[6] namely, (i) a general dispute settlement mechanism under Chapter 18; (ii) various sector-specific provisions for arbitration and/or dispute resolution, especially regarding safeguard measures; and (iii), a dispute settlement mechanism for anti-dumping and countervailing-duty actions under Chapter 19. Dispute settlement procedures in the NAFTA can be aggregated under similar headings to the FTA. Except where otherwise provided, once NAFTA enters into force the FTA will be suspended because it will have been subsumed into the NAFTA. The

---

4 Andreas Lowenfeld, "Binational Dispute Settlement under Chapters 18 and 19 of the Canada-United States Free Trade Agreement: An Interim Appraisal," Administrative Conference of the United States, December, 1990, p. 78.

5 *Ibid*, p. 78. Stewart Baker has noted that "... panel review thus far has been much more intense and demanding than review by U.S. courts." See Stewart Abercrombie Baker "Antidumping and Countervailing Duties Law," *North American Free Trade Agreement: A Segment in Law and Practice under the GATT and Other Trading Arrangements*, Oceana Publications, 1992, p. 22.

6 William J. Davey, "Dispute Settlement under the Canada-U.S. Free Trade Agreement" in Marc Gold and David Leyton-Brown, *Trade-offs on Free Trade: The Canada-U.S. Free Trade Agreement*, Toronto: Carswell, 1988, p. 173-181.

purpose of this chapter is to compare the dispute settlement provisions of NAFTA with those of the FTA, noting principal differences and especially those areas where improvements have been made to the dispute settlement mechanism.[7]

General Dispute Settlement

FTA

Chapter 18 of the FTA creates an institutional structure to manage the agreement, and to resolve disputes over different interpretations of the rights and obligations of the parties. The basic model for dispute settlement in the FTA is the GATT panel process, which evolved largely through customary usage. Like the GATT, Chapter 18 obliges the parties to provide information that affects the operation of the Agreement, and to consult on any measure at the request of the other party. In the event consultations fail, a dispute will be referred to a Canada-United States Trade Commission which is a political body analogous to the GATT Council. The principal representative to the Commission is the trade minister (or equivalent) in each party, although in practice Commission functions are discharged by task-oriented groups of government officials. The Commission is obliged to meet at least once a year to review the functioning of the Agreement.

In the event the Commission cannot resolve a dispute, the FTA provides for binding arbitration on Safeguard measures or on any other issues on which the parties agree; and it provides for the establishment of ad hoc panels specifically to deal with particular disputes. The panel process functions like that of the GATT, and it is the staple of FTA dispute settlement. Both parties maintain a roster of individuals qualified to serve as panellists, from which a panel of five members is selected to hear individual cases. Panels make a recommendation to the Commission on whether a disputed measure causes nullification or impairment of a party's rights under the Agreement, and what action should be taken to resolve the issue. The Commission is then expected to take

---

7 In NAFTA, the equivalent of FTA Chapter 18 is Chapter 20. Chapter 19 of the FTA and Chapter 19 of NAFTA have identical subject material.

political action on the dispute, which should normally conform to the panel's recommendation. The FTA obliges parties to resolve disputes wherever possible by removing any measure found not to be conforming to a party's obligations under the Agreement. In the event of non-compliance by a party, the injured party has a right to retaliate, or specifically to suspend benefits of equivalent effect under the Agreement until the dispute has been resolved.

Three panels have been completed under Chapter 18, and several others are in progress. One completed case produced a unanimous decision in favour of Canada's interpretation of FTA Article 304 concerning non-mortgage interest deductibility under the automotive rules of origin. The two other completed cases arose in the fishing industry.[8] The first case—*Salmon and Herring*—produced a unanimous although obviously conflicted report that reduced Canada's landing regulations from 100 per cent of fish caught to 80 per cent. The parties later negotiated a settlement. In the second case—*Lobsters*—the Panel by a 3-2 majority upheld a U.S. regulation which prevented the importation of short lobsters from Canada. The parties subsequently negotiated an agreement that was then repudiated by Canada, and the regulation remains in force.

The two fishing cases turned more on an interpretation of GATT rules rather than on any new rules assumed under the FTA, thereby emphasizing the more general point that the FTA should be viewed as an addition to, and not a replacement of the parties' contractual obligations under the GATT. Neither panel achieved a complete consensus on the issues. In *Salmon and Herring*, the grounds on which the panellists agreed differed along technical and legal lines, but in *Lobsters* the formal 3-2 split decision was widely alleged to be along national lines and it raised a question about the impartiality of the panel and even of the process itself. Despite the difficulties in achieving consensus, the panels clarified the legal issues in question, and helped to structure a political settlement.

---

8 The two cases are: *Canada's Landing Requirements for Pacific Coast Salmon and Herring*, CDA-89-1807-01 (October 16, 1989); and *Lobsters from Canada*, USA-89-1807-01 (December 12, 1989).

NAFTA

Chapter 20 of the NAFTA carried on the basic institutional arrangements and dispute settlement procedures established in Chapter 18 of the FTA. The changes in NAFTA constitute essentially incremental improvements in dispute settlement procedures, a somewhat enhanced institutional relationship between the parties, and a greater commitment to reach agreement at the working level as opposed to seeking litigation under formal dispute settlement procedures.

The NAFTA establishes a Free Trade Commission comprised of cabinet-level representatives or their designates. The Commission acts on the basis of consensus, unless otherwise agreed, and it is responsible for overall political oversight and implementation of the Agreement. As in the FTA, the Commission can establish standing committees, working groups or expert groups and it can delegate responsibilities for information gathering and dispute settlement to such groups. The NAFTA specifically establishes about twenty sectoral Working Groups which are identified in Annex 2001.2, and which—under the supervision of the Commission—are intended to assume greater managerial responsibility to pursue dispute avoidance in lieu of more formal dispute settlement procedures. The objective of political oversight of sectoral Working Groups is to create a greater obligation by the parties to seek agreement on a daily basis, and in practice to avoid technical disagreements like the recent Honda customs case from becoming a full-blown political dispute.[9]

---

9 The Honda case involved a ruling by the U.S. Customs Service on March 2, 1992 that Canadian exports of Honda Civics during 1989/90 failed to qualify as North American products under FTA content rules, resulting in U.S. duties being applied to the products. U.S. Customs held that the Canadian manufacturer had used engines made in the United States that contained too many foreign parts to qualify as North American. However, Revenue Canada had previously approved the engines on import into Canada as meeting rule-of-origin requirements. For further information, see "Customs Rules that Canadian Honda Civics Failed to Meet Content Standards under FTA," *International Trade Reporter*, Vol. 9:10, March 4, 1992, 384.

The main institutional change created by the NAFTA is to upgrade the role and importance of the Secretariat. Under the FTA, a Binational Secretariat was established—with an office in Ottawa and Washington—which essentially performed a court registrar's function in support of Chapter 18 and 19 panels. The importance of the secretariat function was formally recognized in the NAFTA. In Article 2002, provision is made for a Secretariat that will provide assistance to the Commission, as well as provide logistical support to all dispute settlement panels, working groups and other standing committees and *ad hoc* committees established under the NAFTA. It appears from Article 2002 that the parties anticipate the NAFTA will take on a larger institutional presence than did the FTA. An expanded secretariat function may also have been considered necessary in the event other nations should accede to the NAFTA.

Dispute settlement in the NAFTA follows the FTA model, with appropriate allowances being made for multiple parties, and with innovative alternatives being provided to the normal panel process. Dispute settlement in the NAFTA proceeds in three stages. In the first stage, any party can request consultations with any other party, while a third party that feels it has an interest at stake is entitled to participate. If the matter has not been resolved in 45 days, parties can proceed to the second stage by formally requesting a meeting of the Commission. The Commission is empowered to extend a wide range of Good Offices, Conciliation or Mediatorial services, including calling on technical advisors or on the Commission's Advisory Committee on Private Commercial Disputes. The intent of the second stage is clearly to resolve matters through government-to-government negotiation, or to employ methods of alternative dispute resolution (ADR) in order to avoid expensive and time-consuming litigation. If at the end of 30 days the matter has not been settled, the parties may proceed to the third stage, namely to request the establishment of an Arbitral Panel under Article 2008. Such a panel is the equivalent of a Chapter 18 panel under the FTA.

Chapter 20 of NAFTA adopted the main provisions of FTA Chapter 18, with the exception of panel selection as discussed below. Panels are expected to present an initial report to the Commission within 90 days after the panel is selected, and parties are given an opportunity to respond. The panel is then expected to present a final report, following which the parties "... shall agree on the resolution of the dispute, which normally shall conform with the determinations and recommendations of the panel. ..."[10] As with the GATT and the FTA, implementation of a panel ruling in NAFTA normally consists of removing a measure that does not conform to the Agreement, and the sanction for non-implementation is to withdraw equivalent benefits from the offending party.

Dispute settlement procedures operate under similar time limits in NAFTA as those in the FTA. In the NAFTA, panels may, but are not required to, solicit reports from scientific review boards on issues concerning environmental, health, safety or other scientific matters. This measure was obviously designed to meet criticism from the environmental lobby, but it apparently fell short of the demands of the lobby.[11] Another difference related to trilateral membership of NAFTA is that parties not involved in a dispute are allowed intervenor status, with rights to attend all hearings, make written and oral submissions, and to receive submissions of the disputing parties. Intervenor parties may not, however, have the right to receive and comment on the initial report of the Panel, which under Article 2016:2 is to be presented to the "disputing parties."

The procedures for selecting panellists are improved in the NAFTA. Under Chapter 18 of the FTA, parties maintain separate rosters of experts. In order to form a panel, each party selects two individuals from their own roster (with rights of peremptory challenge by the other side), and then the fifth panellist is chosen by the Commission. Under Chapter 20 of the NAFTA, parties will establish by consensus a common roster of 30 individuals experienced in law, international trade, and dispute settlement. In order to form a panel, the disputing parties will first agree on a chair for the panel or, in the event of disagreement, a disputing party chosen by lot will select as chair an individual who is not a citizen of that party.[12] The disputing parties are then each obliged to select two

---

10 Article 2018:1.

11 See "Draft Dispute Settlement Text Leaves NAFTA-FTA Priority Unresolved," Special Report, *Inside U.S. Trade*, July 31, 1992.

12 Despite the language of the FTA, the practice followed in Chapter 18 panels

panellists who are citizens of the other disputing party. Appropriate alterations to this pattern are made where there are more than two disputants, but the principle of selection of the other party's nationals remains the same. This principle is drawn from state-of-the-art practice in mediation and dispute settlement. The NAFTA parties apparently expect the common roster and selection procedures will result in higher quality roster members and the best candidates being selected as panellists. If Chapter 18 is open to any criticism, it is that the panels may not have had sufficient expertise to rule on the issues that were put before them. This problem was compounded by the lack of institutional knowledge and support for Chapter 18 panels such as that provided to GATT panels by the GATT Secretariat. The NAFTA roster/panel selection process is an attempt to address these deficiencies.[13]

With regard to non-NAFTA forums for dispute settlement, Article 2005 deals with the option of the parties to take a dispute to the GATT in lieu of a NAFTA panel. As in the FTA, where a dispute arises both under GATT and NAFTA, either forum may be chosen by the complaining party for the resolution of the dispute. Once chosen, the dispute shall be resolved in that forum to the exclusion of any other. However, there is a new limitation introduced in the NAFTA. If a complaining party wants to take a dispute to a GATT panel, it must notify third parties of its intentions. If a third party wishes to have the dispute resolved under NAFTA, the disputing parties are obliged to consult and reach an agreement as to a forum. If no agreement is reached, the NAFTA mechanism will supersede. Therefore, a party's choice of forum is more limited under NAFTA than the FTA.[14]

---

has been for the Commission to decide initially which party had the right to select the chair, and then to accept three names (including the chair) from that party at the same time as the other party submits two names.

13 The observation about Chapter 18 panels has been prompted by personal communication from Jeffrey S. Thomas, Ladner Downs, Vancouver.

14 In an interpretative note, the parties agreed that the obligation to use NAFTA dispute settlement is itself subject to dispute settlement, in an effort to avoid preventing a party from invoking its rights to GATT dispute settlement. However, in the case of some environmental, health or conservation issues, parties can be forced to use NAFTA in lieu of the

A further provision for non-NAFTA forums between private parties (i.e., such as private companies) is contained in Article 2022. The NAFTA parties are obliged to encourage the use of private methods of alternative dispute resolution (ADR) and are to provide appropriate procedures to that end. The latter obligation can be discharged by being a party to the UN Convention on Arbitral Awards or the Inter-American Convention on International Commercial Arbitration.

Sector-specific Provisions for Arbitration and/or Dispute Settlement

The FTA provided for a number of opportunities for consultations outside the general dispute settlement mechanism established in Chapter 18. These included, for example, provisions in Article 1004 for a Select Panel on Automotive Products to propose public policy measures to the parties, and the provisions in Article 1704 for direct consultations on financial services between the Canadian Department of Finance and the U.S. Department of the Treasury. The FTA also provided for "binding arbitration" in Article 1806, which was to apply to all disputes regarding safeguards (i.e., Emergency Actions in Chapter 11), or to all other disputes where the parties agreed to resort to arbitration.[15] The provision of "binding arbitration" on safeguards was a product of the negotiating history of the FTA. During the negotiation, the United States took a highly-visible safeguard action on Canadian shakes and shingles, and the resultant political fall-out led the Canadian Government to demand that such actions be subject to binding dispute resolution.

The NAFTA removes the distinction between binding and other forms of arbitration under Chapter 20, and simply uses the term "arbitral panel" for the panels to be established under that chapter. The

---

GATT.

15 Safeguards or emergency actions are a common feature of trade agreements that permit parties to impose temporary restrictions such as tariffs or quotas that would otherwise be inconsistent with the agreement. The normal condition for this action is that surges in imports are causing serious injury to domestic producers.

reason the distinction is dropped is that the obligation to comply with a panel's finding is identical whether or not it is described as "binding" arbitration; and the sanction for non-compliance is also identical in either case, namely, retaliation through withdrawal of compensating benefit. It is likely that the reference to binding arbitration in the FTA is best understood as an artifact of the politics of that negotiation. Even the use of Chapter 20 dispute settlement is withdrawn entirely by NAFTA Article 804 in the case of proposed emergency actions, but the trade-off is a fuller process of consultations during the imposition of the emergency action itself. This is consistent with the NAFTA philosophy of resolving disputes at the ground level before they become difficult.

The substantive chapters of NAFTA provide ample opportunity for consultation and dispute settlement other than that provided formally in Chapters 19 and 20. Like the FTA, the chapter on Financial Services has a distinct process for dispute resolution, and it goes further than the FTA in providing for a separate roster of experts. The Standards chapter provides for direct party-to-party consultation. Some of the incentive to place dispute settlement mechanisms in substantive chapters resulted from previous difficulties with the FTA. For example, following the experience with the customs dispute over Honda autos, the chapter on Customs Procedures was designed to permit traders to receive advance rulings on customs determinations prior to shipping goods, and to provide for review and appeal of origin determinations and advance rulings. The chapter also sets up a Working Group to monitor the overall application of customs formalities, and a Customs Subgroup to ensure the uniform interpretation of NAFTA requirements. These provisions have an important dispute avoidance dimension as well as providing a better basis for dispute settlement if necessary.

Finally, the chapter on Investment contains a lengthy sub-chapter outlining procedures for dispute settlement and arbitration between a party and an investor of another party. The NAFTA gives investors in other parties the right to convoke an arbitral tribunal in the event that a host government (including provincial governments) breaches an obligation of the investment chapter. Such obligations include national treatment, disciplines against certain performance requirements, and the right to a minimum standard of treatment. The sub-chapter is designed to cover a full range of potential investment disputes, and especially matters of expropriation and compensation that have arisen between North American partners in the past. An annex to the chapter provides that decisions of Investment Canada regarding foreign acquisitions are excluded from being subject to dispute settlement. A similar exclusion is additionally provided to Mexico on matters of acquisitions.

Dispute Settlement for Antidumping and Countervailing Duties

FTA

Chapter 19 of the FTA created a wholly unique mechanism for resolving disputes over antidumping and countervailing duties. The hallmark of this mechanism is international (or more precisely, binational) judicial review of the actions of domestic agencies. Chapter 19 is an important step toward accepting a role for international legal procedures in the application of unfair trade remedies, which have often created strained relations between trading partners. Chapter 19 is a step away from the notion that national trade policy can be applied by domestic agencies without concern for the interests of trading partners.

Chapter 19 can be summarized in three parts. First, each party agreed to retain its own antidumping and countervailing duty practices, which are fairly similar to each other's. The parties agreed that amendments to either country's antidumping or countervailing duty laws would be subject to constraints of notification and consultation, and that such amendments would be consistent with relevant provisions of the GATT and other multilateral accords, and the FTA itself. Additionally, the parties agreed—if requested by the other party—to refer proposed legislative changes to a binational panel for an advisory opinion on the consistency of the change with existing obligations under international law.

Second, the parties established binational panels to replace judicial review by domestic courts of final antidumping or countervailing duty determinations by national agencies. Each party agreed to make available binational panels to persons who would otherwise have been entitled to judicial review under domestic law. The panel's mandate is to consider the administrative record of the case appealed, and decide generally whether the final determination is supported by evidence and is in accordance with domestic law.

Third, the provisions of Chapter 19 were to be maintained for seven years. The parties agreed to continue negotiating on dumping and subsidy issues during that period, with the aim being to establish jointly-accepted rules on dumping and subsidy practices that would eliminate the resort to antidumping and countervailing duties. A Working Group was created to pursue this task, but both countries agreed instead to negotiate issues of antidumping and countervailing duties in the multilateral GATT Uruguay Round in lieu of bilateral talks. Should new Dumping or Subsidy codes be completed in the multilateral negotiation, they would be applicable in regional free trade agreements.

The panels under Chapter 19 are composed of five members chosen from a roster of trade experts, primarily lawyers, established in each country. Two panellists are selected by each country while the fifth member is chosen jointly, or by lot, where there is no agreement on the final member. In practice, the fifth member's nationality has alternated between the two countries from one panel to the next.

The standard of review to be applied by the panel is the standard applicable in the country where the antidumping or countervailing duty was initiated. In Canada, the test is whether the agency (a) failed to observe a principle of natural justice or otherwise acted beyond or refused to exercise its jurisdiction; (b) erred in law in making its decision or order, whether or not the error appears on the face of the record; or (c) based its decision or order on an erroneous finding of fact that was made in a perverse or capricious manner or without regard to the material before it. In the United States the test is whether the agency's decision is unsupported by substantial evidence on the record, or is otherwise not in accordance with law.

It is important to note that the panels are not authorized to create substantive law but must act consistently with the laws of the importing country. Consequently, determinations of dumping and subsidization can be different in each country but will still be upheld as long as the administrative agency made its determination in accordance with domestic law.

Review of a panel's decision is very limited. There is no appeal mechanism in the FTA to challenge a panel's findings on the grounds of legal or factual error. Only where there are allegations of gross misconduct, bias, serious conflict of interest or other material violation of the rules of conduct by a panellist, or there is a serious departure from a fundamental rule of procedure by the panel, or if the action by the panel is manifestly in excess of its powers, authority or jurisdiction; and any of the actions outlined above materially affected the panel's decision or threatened the integrity of the review process, can extraordinary challenge procedures be invoked.

Through November 1992, thirty Chapter 19 cases had been initiated, plus one Extraordinary Challenge.[16] Of these cases, 24 were directed against U.S. agencies (i.e., the Department of Commerce (DOC) or the International Trade Commission (ITC)), and six were directed against Canadian agencies (i.e., Revenue Canada or the Canadian International Trade Tribunal (CITT)); see Table 1. Since cases are usually brought

Table 1: Status of 30 Chapter Nineteen Cases*

Status	Action Brought Against	
	U.S. Agencies	Canadian Agencies
Active**	9 (9C/3A)***	3 (3A/0C)
Completed	15 (15C/4A)	3 (3A/1C)

* Source: *Status Report of Cases*, November, 1992.

** It should be noted that some cases listed as active may have been decided by panel but are awaiting a remand determination by the agency (i.e., "action not inconsistent with the panel's decision." See footnote 16).

*** Indicates number of cases appealed by Canadian or American parties (producers, exporters, and/or governments); i.e., 9 Canadian appellants/3 American appellants. Cases can be appealed simultaneously by Canadian and American appellants.

---

16 *FTA Dispute Settlement (Chapters 18 and 19): Status Report for November 1992, Canada-U.S. FTA Binational Secretariat*, Canadian Section, 13 November 1992.

against U.S. agencies by Canadian parties, and cases against Canadian agencies by U.S. parties, it is apparent that Canadians have been the major users of Chapter 19 procedures, and the main respondents have been U.S. agencies.

Of the 18 completed cases, eight were terminated by the parties, five affirmed the agency's determination in question, and five remanded the determination to the agency in whole or in part; see Table 2. A remand means that the determination was returned to the agency for "action not inconsistent with the panel's decision."[17]

Table 2: Disposition of 18 Completed Chapter Nineteen Cases*

Country	Affirmed	Remanded	Affirmed/ Remanded**	Terminated
U.S. (n=15)	4	1	3	7
Canada (n=3)	1	0	1	1

* Source: *Ibid.*, Figures represent one disposition per case; however cases may receive more than one disposition (i.e., panel decision and agency determinations on remand).

** Indicates case affirmed in part and remanded in part.

In the two non-terminated Canadian cases, the actions of the agency were affirmed in one panel and remanded in the other. For the eight non-terminated U.S. cases, four were remanded and four were affirmed.[18] Overall, the degree of consensus in panel reports has been high; of the ten non-terminated decisions on both sides, seven were by

17 FTA, Art. 1904 (8).

18 Because cases can be remanded in whole or in part, a "remand" may be a relatively insignificant action.

unanimous decision and three sustained a dissent on the part of one panellist. This level of consensus has increased the confidence of the FTA parties in the binational panel process.

NAFTA

The dispute settlement provisions for cases involving antidumping and countervailing duties under Chapter 19 of NAFTA are essentially the same as those under the FTA. First, NAFTA provides as did the FTA for the retention of domestic antidumping and countervailing law, although changes will be made in Mexican law as outlined below. Second, both agreements establish a process of judicial review by *ad hoc* binational panels of the determinations of domestic agencies. The Chapter 19 panel process in NAFTA is binational and is established between the disputing parties: selection of panellists is similar to that of the FTA,[19] and no intervenor status is granted to third parties as under Chapter 20 of NAFTA. Third, both agreements impose similar notice and consultation requirements on parties where they intend to amend their unfair trade remedy legislation, as well as provide a complaining party with recourse to a binational panel for a declaratory determination as to the consistency of the amendment with the objectives of the Agreement and the GATT.

There were four important changes to Chapter 19 introduced by the NAFTA. First, the NAFTA has no sunset provision limiting the continuation of the Chapter 19 binational process, and it drops the working party established in the FTA to develop different rules for subsidies and antidumping procedures. It will be recalled that the Chapter 19 mechanism was established as a temporary measure in the FTA, and the parties allowed themselves a total of seven years to revamp antidumping and countervailing duty practices in bilateral relations. Arguably, according to FTA Article 1906 the Chapter 19 mechanism itself could have been suspended after seven years, although obviously any attempt by a party to do so would likely have created a crisis for the overall

---

19 Annex 1901.2(1) of NAFTA adds a statement that national rosters of prospective Chapter 19 panellists shall include "sitting or retired judges to the fullest extent practicable," whereas the FTA was silent on this point.

Agreement.[20] The NAFTA has resolved this uncertainty, and by not incorporating a sunset clause into the Agreement has ensured that the Chapter 19 mechanism is as permanent as the trade agreement itself. The NAFTA does, however, oblige parties to consult generally on more effective rules on subsidies and unfair transborder pricing, but there is no time limit or provision for terminating the binational panel process if agreement is not reached.

Second, the NAFTA adds a section (Article 1907:3) that outlines desirable qualities for the administration of antidumping and countervailing duty laws.[21] This change (as well as the two following changes) were added to NAFTA to ensure that Mexico's trade remedy system is sufficiently similar to that of Canada and the United States to make a Chapter 19 mechanism suitable; and if not, to ensure that adequate remedial provisions are incorporated into the Agreement to protect the other parties. The rationale underlying these changes is that Chapter 19 presupposes a binational panel will apply the domestic law of the party whose agency's determination is being challenged. Where a party's administrative procedures, statutes, or standard of judicial review do not match, or at least come close to, those found in the other parties' unfair trade remedy systems, interested nationals of those other parties may not receive a standard of due process equivalent to that extended by their governments to foreign exporters.

Third, the NAFTA adds a section (Annex 1904.15(d) Schedule B) that outlines a series of twenty obligatory amendments to Mexico's unfair trade remedy legislation. These amendments essentially will

---

20 Article 1906 is titled "Duration" and reads as follows: "The provisions of this Chapter shall be in effect for five years pending the development of a substitute system of rules in both countries for antidumping and countervailing duties as applied to their bilateral trade. If no such system of rules is agreed and implemented at the end of five years, the provisions of this Chapter shall be extended for a further two years. Failure to agree to implement a new regime at the end of the two-year extension shall allow either Party to terminate the Agreement on six-month notice."

21 For example, "publish notice of initiation of investigations;" "provide disclosure of relevant information . . . [including] . . . an explanation of the calculation or the methodology used to determine the margin of dumping or the amount of subsidy;" and so forth.

require Mexico to adopt an unfair trade remedy regime similar to that of Canada and the United States. The proposed amendments are mainly procedural, and are intended to address the low standards of due process that are characteristic of Mexico's unfair trade remedy legislation.[22] For example, there are requirements that Mexican legislation shall provide explicit timetables for administrative proceedings, participation by interested parties, and timely access to all non-confidential information. The Mexican law that allows for the imposition of duties only five days after receipt of a petition must be changed, and, as well Mexico's recognition of parties having standing to request judicial review must be expanded to include foreign producers and exporters who were formerly excluded from seeking judicial review of an agency's determination. Perhaps most importantly, Mexico will be required to compile a comprehensive administrative record of the proceedings of the investigating agency and a detailed statement of legal reasoning underlying the agency determination, which is the basis for judicial review by a binational panel.

Fourth, under the title of "Safeguarding the Panel Review System," the NAFTA adds a section (Article 1905) that provides remedies if a party does not comply with its obligations under Chapter 19. If the application of a party's domestic law prevents a binational panel from carrying out its functions, the NAFTA provides recourse to consultation and then to a Special Committee of three individuals selected from the same roster used for the purpose of establishing Extraordinary Challenge Committees.[23] If the Committee finds that a party has not complied with Chapter 19 the complaining party can suspend binational panel review or equivalent "appropriate" benefits with respect to that party. Article 1905 further provides that binational panel reviews between the disputing parties will be stayed, and will revert to domestic courts if necessary; and it gives the party complained against rights to

---

22 It is probable that Mexico provides greater due process in practice than that required by Mexican law.

23 Extraordinary Challenge Committees were provided for in the FTA to permit an appeal from a binational panel decision on grounds, *inter alia,* of misconduct or abuse of power. The NAFTA has a similar provision.

retaliate in kind to a suspension of binational panel review by the complaining party. In the event the party initially complained against removes the cause for complaint, provision is made to reconvene a Special Committee to assess the situation, and then to terminate counter-measures if appropriate. To sum up, it appears that given the successful history of Chapter 19 in the FTA it is unlikely a Special Committee would arise between Canada and the United States, but it may form a useful sanction to ensure that Mexico (or any other country acceding to the NAFTA) adopts the domestic practices necessary to implement Article 19. However, it is unlikely that the extension of Chapter 19 to Mexico could survive any substantial use of Article 1905, since that article essentially signals a breakdown of the undertakings of Chapter 19 itself.

Conclusion

The NAFTA provisions for institutional arrangements and dispute settlement (Chapter 20) and review of antidumping and countervailing duty matters (Chapter 19) will supersede the equivalent chapters in the FTA. Chapter 20 is an incremental improvement and technical extension of dispute settlement provisions in the FTA, which in turn represented a similar improvement over dispute settlement methods in the GATT. Chapter 20 was not particularly controversial in the NAFTA negotiation, as evidenced by the early completion of the chapter. If this chapter has a philosophy, that philosophy is to push dispute settlement down to the level of working groups and other technical international committees, in an effort to resolve problems before they reach serious proportions. The history of Chapter 18 dispute settlement in the FTA has not been a particularly successful one, and there is a desire to head off the formal mechanism of binational panels if this can be achieved.

Chapter 19 is another matter. Chapter 19 in the FTA was a surrogate for the bilateral code on subsidies and pricing practices that the parties were unable to conclude. It was legally innovative because it empowered a binational panel (effectively an international court) to review and reverse the antidumping and countervailing duty actions of domestic agencies, whereas such powers had been normally exercised exclusively by domestic courts. Chapter 19 was extremely difficult to negotiate, but once implemented the binational panels worked well and the decisions produced were reasonably consistent with those of domestic courts prior to the FTA.

Chapter 19 was highly contentious in the NAFTA, and it was only settled late in the negotiation. In the United States there was Congressional pressure to downgrade Chapter 19, or to dismantle the mechanism altogether. Alternatively, there were attempts to expand the role of Extraordinary Challenge Committees, which would have reduced the capacity of binational panels to produce a definitive judgment. The United States and Canada were wary of extending the mechanism to the Mexican legal system, and there were efforts to insert elaborate guarantees of due process in the NAFTA, as well as a review mechanism to monitor Mexican compliance. An important issue for the Mexican Government was how far it could tolerate a foreign and essentially intrusive legal procedure in order to gain access to binational scrutiny of Canadian and U.S. antidumping and countervailing actions. For Canada, the issue on Chapter 19 boiled down to the maintenance of the status quo of the FTA.

The NAFTA maintained intact the FTA Chapter 19 mechanism, and it made that mechanism a permanent feature of North American trade relations. This will provide legitimacy to the mechanism, and will reinforce the notion that it is an interesting and important new departure in international law. For Mexico, Chapter 19 will promote a more transparent, rules-based system of unfair trade remedies than existed previously, which will benefit Canadian and American exporters. With its emphasis on due process, Chapter 19 could even become a vehicle for changes in Mexican administrative law, which would be consistent with the Mexican government's goal of using NAFTA as a tool to promote Mexican development.

The Investment Provisions of NAFTA

Alan M. Rugman
Professor of International Business
and Michael Gestrin
Policy Analyst,
University of Toronto[1]

Introduction

THE INVESTMENT PROVISIONS IN CHAPTER 11 of NAFTA represent an improvement over those in Chapter 16 of the Canada-U.S. Free Trade Agreement (FTA).[2] The most important changes concern the

---

1 This commentary is based upon the 7 October 1992 initialled NAFTA text. We are grateful to Alan Nymark, Emmy Verdun, Steven Globerman, and Lorraine Eden for their helpful comments and suggestions on earlier drafts of this paper.

2 The FTA's investment provisions have been discussed previously by Lipsey and York (1988), Safarian (1988, 1991), Steger (1988) and Rugman (1988, 1990), amongst others.

scope of coverage of the new chapter, the level of security offered to investments, and the increased transparency of each signatory's discriminatory measures. Problems which persist include the continued effective exclusion of entire sectors from the agreement and the latent potential, despite the strengthening of the investment chapter, for increased discriminatory behaviour in the use of review procedures.

In the FTA there were four principal components to the investment chapter:

1. Investments between Canada and the U.S. would be subject to "national treatment" (Article 1602). This meant that, from the time the FTA came into effect on 1 January 1989, Canadian federal and provincial laws and regulations would be applied equally to Canadian and U.S. investors in Canada, i.e. U.S. investors in Canada must be treated "no less favourably" than Canadian investors, and vice versa in the United States. With the passage of Exon-Florio in 1988 (U.S. investment screening legislation with potentially far-reaching discretionary scope), the national treatment provision of the FTA ensured that Canadian investors would enjoy more secure access to the United States than investors from any other country.
2. Sensitive sectors in the United States and Canada were excluded from the agreement. Particularly important to Canada were its cultural industries, and to the United States, the transportation sector. Other sectors not covered by the FTA included health, social services, and education. All pre-existing non-conforming measures were also exempted from the provisions of the FTA, i.e. grandfathered (Article 1607).
3. Both countries retained review mechanisms. The Exon-Florio amendment was introduced into the Omnibus Trade and Competitiveness Act of 1988 and gave the President the power to block international transactions under certain conditions. Canada's right to review U.S. acquisitions in Canada was retained, but the threshold for review was increased from $5 million to cover large investments of over $150 million (Annex 1607.3).

4. In the FTA four performance requirements regarding establishment and regulation of conduct were identified and barred from use. These included: i) export requirements, ii) import substitution requirements, iii) domestic sourcing requirements and iv) domestic content requirements (Article 1603).[3] The FTA did not cover performance requirements associated with subsidies.

NAFTA retains and builds upon these four provisions of the FTA. Therefore, it is critical to realize that NAFTA is not just the FTA plus Mexico. The NAFTA investment chapter differs from the FTA investment chapter in fundamental ways. Since NAFTA will likely replace the FTA on 1 January 1994, it is very important to understand these changes.

Changes to the Rules Governing Investment in North America

There are several important changes and new features in the investment provisions of NAFTA, compared to the FTA. We have identified five key areas where the NAFTA investment chapter is different from its FTA predecessor. These areas concern i) the definition of an investment, ii) the security of investments, iii) the application of the MFN (most favoured nation) principle to investments, iv) the replacement of universal grandfathering with explicit negative lists, and v) changes to the rules governing performance requirements. In this section we outline the details and implications of each of these in turn.

Definition of Investment

The definition of an investment, and hence the coverage of the NAFTA investment chapter, has been immensely broadened (pp. 11-24 to 11-25).

---

3 Performance requirements set conditions on the investor for the right of establishment or acquisition. Export requirements usually involve the stipulation that a certain share or quantity of output will be exported. Import substitution requirements and domestic sourcing requirements both commit the investor to replace foreign sourced inputs with local or national inputs. Domestic content requirements involve a commitment on the part of an investor to source locally a certain share of the costs of production.

Under the FTA, the investment chapter only covered foreign direct investment, i.e. investments involving control by the investor of the business enterprise in question. Under NAFTA coverage has expanded to include virtually all investments, i.e. equity and debt securities of an enterprise, a loan to an enterprise, any interest in an enterprise entitling the owner to a share of the income and/or profits of the enterprise, any interest in an enterprise entitling the owner to a share of the assets of the enterprise upon its dissolution, business real estate, and interests arising from the commitment of capital or other resources. It is not possible to place an exact value upon the increased coverage of the NAFTA investment chapter over its FTA predecessor but it is clear that it is wider in its scope by a very large multiple.

Security for Investments

As well as expanding the coverage of the investment chapter to cover more than just direct investments, Chapter 11 also "deepens" the security of investments in North America. Several sections of the Chapter are relevant in this respect.

First of all, the investment chapter is now divided into two subchapters (A and B). Subchapter A deals with the investment provisions. Subchapter B outlines a detailed set of procedures upon which dispute settlement procedures for investments will be based.

Within the context of subchapter B, one of the most significant provisions stipulates that disputes between NAFTA investors and any of the parties to the agreement can go to binding, enforceable international arbitration. This is especially significant for Canadian and U.S. investors in Mexico as it supplies them with an alternative to the occasionally unpredictable Mexican court system. Furthermore, once any two disputants agree to take their case to international arbitration, strict limits are placed upon the ability of the parties involved to subsequently take further action through domestic legal systems.

Unlike the FTA, NAFTA also offers increased security to non-NAFTA investors and their investments in North America. Non-NAFTA investors with investments in one NAFTA country are assured the benefits of Chapter 11 if they decide to expand their operations into the other NAFTA countries as long as they have "substantial business activities in the territory of the Party" where they were originally established. It will only become clear through practice whether the expression "substantial business activities" might be subject to abuse in the courts (Article 1113.2), but this provision nonetheless affords offshore investors recognition and rights which were absent in the FTA.

Another new article calls for Minimum Standards of Treatment (Article 1105). This article seems specifically aimed at securing American and Canadian investments in Mexico, again due to the perceived unpredictability of the Mexican legal system.

Article 1110 deals with expropriation and compensation, which was a contentious issue due to conflicts with the Mexican Constitution. However, full and fair compensation is now accepted by the Mexican government. Both Articles 1105 and 1110 will become even more significant if other countries accede to NAFTA.

Most Favoured Nation Status for Investments

Signatories to the Agreement are assured most favoured nation (MFN) status with respect to investments (Articles 1103, and 1406 in the financial services chapter). The concept of MFN is borrowed from the international trade regime, and Article 1103 states that each party must treat investors and investments of the other Parties no less favourably than it treats any other foreign investors or their investments. In conjunction with the addition of the MFN article, another new article, Article 1104, stipulates that investors are to be granted the more favourable treatment associated with Articles 1102 and 1103 (national treatment and MFN) if such a difference exists.

One of the effects of including the MFN clause is greater flexibility for the signatories to the agreement in formulating their respective "reservations" to the key investment provisions. For example, if a party excludes a particular sector from the provisions of national treatment, but not from MFN status, investors can still be assured of equal treatment with respect to all other foreign investors, if not with respect to domestic industry. Essentially, the inclusion of the MFN article has enabled policy makers to be more precise in stipulating the kinds of exemptions which will be applied, and ensures that fewer sectors will be left completely "uncovered."

The Negative Lists of Reservations

The federal governments had completed their lists of reservations by the time the agreement was initialled on 7 October 1992. The Canadian provinces and U.S. and Mexican states, on the other hand, are given up to two years from the entry into force of NAFTA (likely on 1 January 1994) to itemize any measures under their jurisdictions to be exempted from various NAFTA provisions (Article 1108.1). Under the FTA *all* federal and sub-federal non-conforming measures in place prior to the agreement's negotiation were grandfathered.

Under the terms of NAFTA each signatory must choose those existing measures which it wishes to exclude from particular articles in the agreement and list these in a series of seven annexes dealing with particular sectors and types of exemption. In terms of each signatory's discriminatory measures, NAFTA is much more transparent than the FTA. The Annexes will be considered in greater detail in the next section due to the particular insights into the agreement which they afford.

Performance Requirements

With respect to the review of investments and their potential regulation, NAFTA prohibits:

1) export requirements
2) minimum domestic content
3) domestic sourcing requirements
4) trade balancing
5) technology transfer
6) "exclusive supplier" requirements

Of these, the last two were not prohibited by the FTA.

Completely new in NAFTA is a list of performance requirements which cannot be linked to subsidies. Under the FTA it was possible to link a subsidy to the fulfilment of any kind of performance requirement. The NAFTA list of prohibited performance requirements related to subsidies includes:

1) domestic sourcing requirements
2) domestic content requirements
3) trade balancing
4) linking access to the domestic market with export performance

Therefore, the performance requirements identified and banned from use in the FTA have been made more precise and added to in NAFTA. The ban of import substitution policies in the FTA has been replaced by bans on the use of policies which constrain imports or link imports to export performance. Instances in which a party can link subsidies to performance include for purposes of locating production in particular areas, for providing "a service" to "train or employ workers," to "construct or expand particular facilities," and to "carry out research and development" (Article 1106, para. 4).

Article 1107 is another new article with no counterpart in the FTA. This article stipulates that there should be no nationality requirements for senior management, but that it is permissible to specify that a majority of board members of a company be of a particular nationality.

It is interesting to note that all three parties maintain legislation which allows or has the potential to allow considerable discretion in the use of performance requirements, despite the limits upon the use of such measures as set out in NAFTA. In Canada this discretion takes the form of the criteria used by Investment Canada to determine the "net benefit" of reviewable investments entering the country. These criteria include the effects of a particular investment upon "employment, on the utilization of parts, components and services produced in Canada, and on exports from Canada," "the degree and significance of participation by Canadians in the investment," and on "technological development and product innovation in Canada" (Annex 1—Canada, p. I-C-3). Mexico applies similar criteria in its review process, considering as it does effects upon employment and training, "technological contribution" and contribution to industrial productivity and competitiveness (p. I-M-3). In the United States, Exon-Florio also holds the potential to be used much more extensively than it has been towards controlling investments entering the United States (See Graham and Krugman, pp. 97-100).

Discriminatory Treatment of Investments in NAFTA

Overall, the investment relationship between Canada and the United States leading into the NAFTA negotiations was already relatively unencumbered by protectionism and over-regulation. Further, the investment relationship between Canada and the United States and Mexico has been considerably liberalized both by NAFTA and by Mexico's overall liberalization program which began around 1985.

However, all three signatories continue to protect or restrict access to particular sectors of their economies and this favouritism has translated into a number of discriminatory measures which are written into the agreement. This discrimination is found primarily in the annexes which have replaced the grandfathering provisions of the FTA. Some sectors are identified in the main body of the agreement itself as being excluded from NAFTA, such as the exclusion of Canada's cultural industries in Chapter 21, while others, such as the United States' maritime sector, are excluded by means of extensive reservations in the annexes.

The following section will consider in greater detail the areas in which Canada, Mexico, and the United States have chosen to continue to maintain restrictions upon foreign investment. The NAFTA annexes afford readers of the agreement an opportunity to identify with relative ease some areas considered sensitive by the three signatories (transparency being one of the key motivations for replacing grandfathering with the annexes).

During the NAFTA negotiations it was realized that the grandfathering formula was no longer practical. The complexity and scope of the Mexican discriminatory legal regime mitigated against the reapplication of the grandfathering concept. Therefore the notion of the negative list was adopted. In addition, the negative list was viewed by the negotiators as an improvement over grandfathering insofar as it was more transparent.

The negative lists of NAFTA consist of a series of seven annexes for Mexico, and six each for Canada and the United States (Mexico has an extra annex to deal with constitutional derogations from the agreement). Each of these applies to particular rules and sectors. In each annex the signatories list those measures which do not conform to one or more provisions of NAFTA and which they wish to keep. Each element of these lists is referred to as a reservation.

The content of the annexes will be partial when the agreement comes into effect. This is because state and provincial governments can add their existing measures to Annex 1 up to two years after NAFTA comes into effect (Article 1108). The federal governments may add new or more restrictive measures to those areas identified in Annex 2 (see Article 1108(2) and the description of Annex 2 in the agreement).

Five of the NAFTA annexes can affect investment in a discriminatory manner. Annex 6 only deals with article 1208 on the cross-border provision of services. Annex 5 deals with non-discriminatory quantitative restrictions. Neither of these Annexes will therefore be discussed here. Annexes 1, 2 and 3 cover provisions from the investment and services chapters, Chapters 11 and 12 respectively. Annex 4 deals exclusively with the national treatment provisions of Chapter 11, and Annex 7 covers Chapter 14 on financial services, which extends its coverage to, "investors of another Party, and investments of such investors, in financial institutions" (Article 1401, para. 1b). It should be noted that any provisions on investment in Chapter 11 are over-ridden by any other provisions dealing with investments found elsewhere in the Agreement unless explicitly stated otherwise (Article 1112, para. 1).

Table 1 describes each annex in terms of the chapters of the agreement to which it applies, the specific articles which it covers, and the extent of the coverage. Annex 1 covers chapters 11 and 12, or those dealing with investment and services, respectively. The reservations in this annex can deal with any combination of five provisions in these chapters. These include: i) national treatment (Articles 1102, 1202), ii) MFN treatment (Articles 1103, 1203), iii) local presence (Article 1205), iv) performance requirements (Article 1106), and v) nationality requirements (Article 1107). Annex 1 lists existing, non-conforming measures held by federal, provincial, or state levels of government up to an indefinite period (although in some cases phasing-out schedules apply).

Annex 2 covers the same chapters and articles as Annex 1, but extends the coverage beyond the maintenance of existing non-conforming measures. Annex 2 lists "sectors, sub-sectors or activities" against which non-conforming measures are maintained by each Party, and against which each Party reserves the right to add more restrictive measures at any time.

Annex 3 is unique to Mexico, covering as it does sectors from which foreign investors are barred by the Mexican constitution. These areas include: i) petroleum and related petrochemicals, ii) electricity, iii) nuclear power and treatment of radioactive minerals, iv) satellite com-

Table 1: The NAFTA Annexes

Annex Number	Chapter(s) covered	Articles covered	Extent of coverage
1	Investment (11) and Services (12)	National treatment (1102, 1202), MFN (1103, 1203), local presence (1205), performance requirements (1106), and nationality requirements (1107)	Existing, non-conforming measures maintained (2 years for states and provinces to add their own restrictions)
2	Investment (11) and Services (12)	Same as above	Existing, non-conforming measures maintained and reservation of right to adopt new or more restrictive measures in sectors and activities listed
3 (Mexico only)	Investment (11) and Services (12)	Blanket coverage	Constitutional restrictions reserving complete control of certain sectors for the Mexican state
4	Investment (11)	MFN (1103)	Existing international agreements, any international agreements negotiated within two years, and any future agreements dealing with aviation, fisheries, maritime matters and telecommunications
5	Investment (11) and Services (12)	none	Existing, non-discriminatory measures which the parties commit to trying to liberalize (one year for states and provinces to add restrictions)
6	Services (12)	Cross-border provision of services (1208)	Commitments to liberalize particular pre-existing exceptions
7	Financial Services (14)	Cross-Border trade (1404), establishment (1403), national treatment (1405), senior management (1408)	Indeterminate maintenance of pre-existing exceptions

Source: Initialled text of the North American Free Trade Agreement, 7 October, 1992.

munications, v) telegraph service, vi) radiotelegraph services, vii) postal services, viii) railroads, ix) issuance of currency, x) control over inland ports, and xi) control of airports and heliports.

Annex 4 constitutes a reservation on the part of all three NAFTA countries to the application of Article 1103 (MFN treatment) to existing international agreements. The Annex covers both existing and future agreements in the areas of aviation, fisheries, maritime matters including salvage, and telecommunications.

Annex 7 deals exclusively with financial services. The main provisions affecting investment covered by reservations in the annex include "establishment" (Article 1404) and national treatment (Article 1407). This annex permits the maintenance of pre-existing, non-conforming measures.

Therefore, in sum, annexes 1, 2, 3, 4, and 7 contain discriminatory measures affecting investment. Of these, Annex 2 can be made more restrictive in the areas already listed insofar as each Party reserves the right to, "adopt new or more restrictive measures...(which) may derogate from an obligation relating to" one or more of articles 1102, 1202, 1103, 1203, 1205, 1106, and 1107 (refer to the descriptions of these above). Annexes 1 and 7 will have more measures, taken from existing legislation, added by the states and provinces within two years of the agreement coming into effect. It is not known whether the states and provinces will add a large number of measures.

Table 2 provides a breakdown of the number of reservations which each NAFTA country has included in annexes 1, 2, and 7. For each of these a breakdown of reservations by article is also provided. Annex 3 will be discussed as a special case later in this section, constituting as it does a list of highly discriminatory measures unique to Mexico. Annexes 4, 5, and 6 are not included in Table 2 as their discriminatory impact upon investments is either negligible (Annex 4), or non-existent (Annexes 5 and 6).

Under the name of each country are two columns. The first column starting on the left gives the number of times the country in question has listed a reservation to a particular article. The second column shows the distribution of reservations to articles in particular annexes among the total number of reservations taken by a particular country in Annexes 1, 2 and 7. In this way we see, for example, that reservations to

Table 2: Distribution of Investment Reservations Between Canada, Mexico, and the U.S. by Article

Annex	Article	Number of reservations by						Total no. of reser-vations per article
		Canada		Mexico		United States		
		Number	Share of Canada's total	Number	Share of Mexico's total	Number	Share of U.S. total	
1	1102	11	23%	31	35%	9	18%	51
	1103	3	6%	3	3%	5	10%	11
	1106	4	8%	8	9%	1	2%	13
	1107	5	10%	7	8%	1	2%	13
Annex 1 total		23	48%	49	55%	16	32%	88
2	1102	9	19%	6	7%	8	16%	23
	1103	5	10%	4	4%	6	12%	15
	1106	4	8%	0	0%	2	4%	6
	1107	7	15%	3	3%	5	10%	15
Annex 2 total		25	52%	13	15%	21	42%	59
7	1403	0	0%	12	13%	0	0%	12
	1405	0	0%	13	15%	8	16%	21
	1406	0	0%	1	1%	3	6%	4
	1408	0	0%	1	1%	2	4%	3
Annex 7 total		0	0%	27	30%	13	26%	40
TOTALS		48	100%	89	100%	50	100%	187

Source: Initialled text of the North American Free Trade Agreement, 7 October, 1992.

Article 1403 (Establishment of Financial Institutions) account for 13 percent of Mexico's investment reservations in the three annexes.

It is critical to note that the purpose of Table 2 is not to use a count of reservations in the annexes as a proxy for the economic significance of these. Rather, its purpose is to introduce the reader to the overall structure of the 3 annexes.

In terms of absolute numbers, Mexico has the largest number of reservations to investment Articles, with 89, followed by the United States with 50 and Canada with 48. The most frequently used annex is Annex 1, with 88 reservations between the three countries, followed by Annex 2, with 59 reservations, and then Annex 7, with 40 reservations.

Several patterns emerge in Table 2 which are worthy of consideration. The first concerns the concentration of reservations in Annexes 1 and 2 against national treatment (1102) and MFN (1103) by all three countries. Since these provisions constitute the cornerstone of non-discriminatory treatment in NAFTA, reservations to Articles 1102 and 1103 are more significant than reservations to the performance requirements provision (1106) or the senior management provision (1107). Almost 60 percent of Canada's reservations to investment articles in Annexes 1 and 2 deal with national treatment and MFN, 71 percent in the case of Mexico, and 76 percent in the case of the United States. What this suggests is that where Canada, Mexico, and the United States do have legislation or measures which are discriminatory, and which they wish to maintain, these are usually of a broad nature (as opposed to the specific forms of discrimination identified by articles 1106 and 1107).

Another interesting feature of Table 2 is the discrepancy, both in relative and absolute terms, of the use by Mexico versus the use by Canada and the United States of Annex 2. Annex 2 is much more restrictive than Annex 1 because it allows the parties to make the discriminatory measures already listed in this Annex even more restrictive at any time (the reservations in Annex 1 are fixed). Canada lists almost twice as many reservations in Annex 2 as Mexico, while the United States lists 62 percent more than Mexico. Furthermore, Canada and the United States each have more reservations to investment articles in Annex 2 than in Annex 1. Mexico exhibits the reverse pattern, with only 13 reservations in Annex 2. This difference may reflect a negotiating dynamic whereby Mexico, with several significant reservations in its unique and absolutely restrictive Annex 3, probably felt pressure to compensate for this by less liberal use of Annex 2 than either Canada or the United States.

Finally, Table 2 also includes Annex 7. This is the only annex of the seven which deals with a particular economic sector, the financial services sector. This reflects the significance of this sector in the negotiations. The summary of the Annex 7 reservations to provisions relating to investment in Table 2 indicates three things. First, this is an area of economic strength for Canada, as indicated by the lack of a single reservation by Canada to the articles listed. Second, Mexico's investment regime in financial services is still very restrictive as indicated by the numerous reservations to Articles 1403 and 1405, which concern establishment and national treatment. Third, we see reflected in the reservations for the United States a partially restrictive regime with no discriminatory restrictions against establishment but numerous reservations to the national treatment provisions (1405), reflecting the decentralized nature of the U.S. financial system.

Table 2 provides an overall guide to the character of annexes 1, 2 and 7, and the use which each country has made of them. However, counting reservations does not give a complete picture of the scope of the discrimination which has been carried over into NAFTA. This is due to the fact that the reservations range widely in terms of the economic value of their coverage. Some reservations will target a specific economic sub-sector while others will apply to "all sectors." Obviously, the former should not be given the same weight as the latter when it comes to analyzing their economic significance.

Table 3 gives a breakdown of the reservations against investment articles taken by each country in Annexes 1 and 2 by economic sectors. Note that the total number of reservations listed in Table 3 is qualitatively and therefore quantitatively different from the total listed in Table 2. This is because Table 2 dealt with reservations to particular articles, whereas Table 3 deals with reservations to particular sectors.

Table 3 highlights several interesting features of the Annexes. First, the existing discriminatory measures which Canada and the United States have carried over into NAFTA do not explicitly target either the manufacturing or the service sectors to any significant extent. In Canada's case 6 percent of its investment reservations target these areas,

Table 3: Distribution of Investment Reservations Between Canada, Mexico and the United States from Annexes 1 and 2 by Economic Sector

Sector	Canada		Mexico		United States	
	Total Number	Share of total	Total Number	Share of total	Total Number	Share of total
"All Sectors"	10	20%	6	9%	4	10%
Primary Sectors*	3	6%	4	6%	2	5%
Manufacturing	1	2%	9	14%	1	3%
Services	2	4%	10	16%	4	10%
Infrastructure**	12	24%	18	28%	15	38%
Energy	5	10%	2	3%	1	3%
Transportation	16	33%	15	23%	13	33%
Total	49	100%	64	100%	40	100%

*includes agriculture, fisheries, and mining.
**includes government services, such as postal communications, as well as private sector networks, such as telecommunications.

Source: Initialled text of the North American Free Trade Agreement, 7 October, 1992.

whereas for the United States, 13 percent of its investment reservations target explicit manufacturing and service activities. Mexico on the other hand directs 29 percent of its investment reservations from Annexes 1 and 2 towards these sectors. Closer examination of these reveals that many concern reservations to Article 1106 on performance requirements. In addition, many of these reservations are subject to "phase-out" schedules.

The above analysis, however, belies a distinction which needs to be made as between two broad categories of reservations in the annexes. On the one hand are reservations which are sector-specific, while on the other hand we find reservations which are better described as rules-based. The rules-based reservations are those which apply to the "all sectors" sector. These need to be considered carefully since, as part of their description suggests, they can apply to a range of economic activities. Canada holds ten such rules-based reservations, Mexico six, and the United States four.

To give the reader a sense of what these "all sector" reservations can cover, it is useful to look at the areas covered by Mexico's six "all sector" investment reservations. They deal with i) restrictions upon foreign ownership of border land; ii) review criteria upon which approval for foreign investments is based; iii) review thresholds and their relevant phasing-in schedules; iv) restrictions upon foreign participation in co-operative production enterprises; v) restrictions upon particular benefits reserved for certain types of Mexican enterprises; and vi) restrictions on the acquisition by foreign interests of Mexican debt securities.

Another interesting feature of Table 3 is the frequency with which reservations in the transportation sector appear. This accurately reflects the degree to which this remains one of the most restrictive sectors to investments in North America. The inclusion of the transportation sector in NAFTA is an improvement over the FTA which did not cover investments in this sector. Indeed, some advances were made in the negotiations to allow, for example, trucking firms to carry goods freely across any border within the free trade area. However, cabotage remains off limits to non-nationals in all transportation sectors, and the United States maintains highly restrictive control over its maritime sector. The latter is a multi-billion dollar reservation to national treatment which discriminates against Mexico and Canada.

Some sectors are highly protected but do not appear in Annexes 1 and 2. An important example is Canada's protection of its cultural industries which is carried over from the FTA as stipulated in Chapter 21 of NAFTA. Another example is Mexico's energy sector, which is highly restrictive due to constitutional limits upon foreign participation. These are described in Annex 3 which deals uniquely with Mexico's constitutional reservations.

Table 4 provides an overview of the sectors which are excluded from the provisions of the agreement, those in which investments in North America will remain restrictive, and those areas which will be substantially liberalized by the agreement. As the first column suggests, the Canadian and American investment regimes have not changed much in terms of sectoral liberalization. The Mexican investment regime, however, will undergo substantial opening up during the ten year phase-in period. Sectors which remain highly restrictive but which are covered by the dispute resolution provisions of the agreement are transportation, the maritime sector, various aspects of energy production in each country, and basic telecommunications. The third column lists areas excluded from the provisions of the agreement. All three countries exclude health and social services. Canada maintains its exclusion of its cultural industries (newspapers, television programming, etc.), as well as restrictions upon large scale water exports. The United States holds no absolute exceptions from the agreement except for health and social services, and Mexico's exclusions include those sectors listed in its Annex 3.

In sum then, NAFTA's actual gains in terms of a liberalization of the North American investment regime have been mainly limited to the opening of the Mexican investment regime. However, with NAFTA in place, the investment chapter's stronger rules suggest the potential for further liberalization down the road.

The Annexes are a useful addition to the agreement. They are more transparent and allow for phase-out schedules which were absent in the FTA due to the blunt nature of grandfathering. A word of caution is probably in order here, though. There is nothing inherent in the nature of a list to suggest that the passage of time will make it shorter rather than longer. The future merits of the annexes hinge to a great extent

Table 4: Liberalization and Protection of Investment Regimes in NAFTA

Country	Sectors to be substantially liberalized by NAFTA during the 10 year phase-in period	Sectors which will remain highly restrictive under NAFTA	Sectors which remain excluded from coverage under NAFTA
Canada	1) Specialty air services	1) Cabotage in all transportation 2) All maritime investment from U.S. 3) Fishing 4) Energy: uranium, oil, gas 5) Basic telecommunications	1) Culture 2) Health and social services 3) Aboriginal affairs 4) Large scale water exports
United States	1) Specialty air services	1) All maritime activities 2) Cabotage in all sectors 3) Energy: uranium 4) Basic telecommunications	1) Health and social services
Mexico	1) Auto parts manufacturing 2) Mining 3) Secondary petrochemicals 4) Construction 5) Enhanced telecommunications 6) Specialty air services 7) Busing and trucking 8) Financial services 9) Manufacturing in general	1) Culture 2) Cabotage in all transportation 3) Activities related to energy not already reserved to the state 4) Activities related to renewable natural resources 5) Basic telecommunications 6) Fishing	1) Health and social services 2) Petroleum, other hydrocarbons 3) Basic petrochemicals 4) Electricity 5) Nuclear power 6) Treatment of radioactive materials 7) Satellite communications 8) Telegraph services 9) Radiotelegraph services 10) Railroads 11) Control of air and maritime ports

Source: Initialled text of the North American Free Trade Agreement, 7 October, 1992, and "NAFTA: Investment Prospects in Canada," Alan Nymark, 22 September, 1992.

upon the willingness of the three signatories to adhere to a freeze of the lists, if not a negotiation of the lists down rather than up.

Furthermore, while the lists reveal a great deal about the protectionist regimes of Canada, the United States, and Mexico, they do not reveal everything. For example, high-tech consortia in the United States represent a growing threat to Canadian, Mexican, and other outside investors. Having failed to gain right of access to such consortia through the NAFTA negotiations, Canada and Mexico stand to find themselves marginalized from developments in an increasingly important sector of the U.S. economy. The success of the annexes, therefore, also depends upon the degree to which they highlight all discriminatory measures (not described elsewhere in the agreement). The power of transparency is diminished once it becomes selective.

Economic Implications of the Investment Provisions

On balance, NAFTA is an improvement over the FTA in terms of its treatment of investments. The considerable liberalization of the Mexican investment regime and the increased security and coverage offered by the NAFTA investment chapter will contribute to the current global trend towards heightened capital movement. Sectors in which NAFTA will be particularly important for investment flows will be those in which production is already dominated by multinational corporations. These industries and firms will be best placed to take advantage of the strategic opportunities offered by the fuller integration of Mexico's productive and market potential into the North American economy. A few of the sectors which have already started to adapt to these new conditions include autos, apparel, chemicals, and financial services. Closer consideration of how various sectors will respond to the changing North American investment environment is one of the pressing questions which should encourage further research. At an aggregate level, NAFTA will unambiguously serve to encourage foreign investment flows in North America. However, more detailed sectoral research is required if we are to attempt to predict exactly how particular industries and firms will attempt to take advantage of the more open and more diversified North American investment environment.[4]

What can be stated with certainty, however, especially in response to the more extremist positions, which sometimes appear in the political debate over NAFTA, is that the strategic decisions of multinational corporations are based upon considerations which are much more sophisticated than the "cheap labour" or "lax environmental standards" arguments used by their detractors. To suggest that factors such as these dominate the strategic decision to invest belies a fundamental misunderstanding of the current state of the global economy and of the nature of global production. More specifically, it overlooks the fact that the gains from cheap labour and lax environmental measures have been available to firms in Canada and the United States well before NAFTA, or the FTA for that matter, was ever negotiated. Ultimately NAFTA is as much a reflection of the growing importance of international investment in the global economy as it is a positive contribution to this trend.

Conclusions

The four most significant positive developments which NAFTA brings to the North American investment environment are i) expanded coverage of the NAFTA investment chapter over its FTA predecessor, ii) more sophisticated mechanisms for protecting foreign investments and resolving disputes, iii) greater transparency in the discriminatory measures held by each party, and iv) the liberalization of a wide range of sectors in the Mexican economy. There remain, however, some lingering problems.

First, as our study of the annexes suggests, not much progress was made in terms of further liberalization of the Canadian and American investment regimes. Sectors such as transportation, and in Canada, culture, remain highly restrictive. The financial services sector in the

---

4 Several interesting quantitative studies of the likely impact of NAFTA upon trade patterns can be found in the January 1991 issue of *The World Economy* (15:1). For an excellent overview of various attempts to model the effects of NAFTA refer to Sidney Weintraub, "Modelling the Industrial Effects of NAFTA," in Lustig et al. Unfortunately, none of these models addresses the investment issue adequately.

United States, while not highly discriminatory, is nonetheless characterized by inter-regional barriers.

Second, the institutional dynamic which will govern the evolution of the negative lists is not clear. Will the lists, for example, serve to freeze discriminatory measures, even in the face of protectionist political pressures, or will they rather encourage the use of ad hoc, informal discriminatory mechanisms which, due to their informal nature, do not appear in the annexes? The most prominent example of this sort of omission from the annexes is seen in the encouragement of high-tech consortia in the United States by the relaxation of anti-trust legislation (e.g. Sematech). Mexico and Canada attempted to negotiate access to such consortia under NAFTA but were unsuccessful.

Third, with a young and fairly open-ended investment review mechanism in place in the United States in the form of the 1988 Exon-Florio legislation and its administrative counterpart, the Committee on Foreign Investments in the United States (CFIUS), the potential exists for the discriminatory use of the review process. To date this has not happened. However, more explicit guidelines aimed at ensuring that review procedures remain non-discriminatory in all three countries would have been a positive addition to NAFTA.

References

Graham, Edward M. and Paul R. Krugman. *Foreign Direct Investment in the United States*. Institute for International Economics, Washington, D.C., 1989.

Lipsey, Richard G. and Robert C. York. *Evaluating the Free Trade Deal*. Toronto: C.D. Howe Institute, 1988.

Nymark, Alan. "NAFTA: Investment Prospects in Canada." Investment Canada, Notes of speech to the Seminar on NAFTA, Montreal, Quebec, September 22, 1992.

Rugman, Alan M. "Multinationals and the Free Trade Agreement." In Marc Gold and David Leighton-Brown (eds.) *Trade-offs on Free Trade*. Toronto: Carswell, 1988.

Rugman, Alan M. *Multinationals and Canada-United States Free Trade*. Columbia, University of South Carolina Press, 1990.

Safarian, A.E. "Foreign Direct Investment." In John Crispo (ed.) *Free Trade: The Real Story*. Toronto: Gage, 1988.

Safarian, A.E. "Free Trade and Foreign Direct Investment." In Earl H. Fry and Lee H. Radebaugh. *Investment in the North American Free Trade Area: Opportunities and Challenges*. Provo: Brigham Young University, 1991.

Steger, Debra P. *A Concise Guide to the Canada-United States Free Trade Agreement*. Toronto: Carswell, 1988.

Weintraub, Sidney. "Modelling the Industrial Effects of NAFTA." In Nora Lustig, Barry P. Bosworth and Robert Z. Lawrence (eds.). *North American Free Trade: Assessing the Impact*. The Brookings Institution, 1992.

The World Economy. Mini Symposium: Modelling North American Free Trade, 15:1, January 1992.

Trade Liberalization and the Environment

Steven Globerman
Department of Economics
Simon Fraser University

Introduction

FROM THE VERY START OF THE North American Free Trade Agreement (NAFTA) discussions, environmental concerns have been at the forefront of the surrounding public policy debate. Specifically, opponents of the NAFTA have consistently argued that further trade liberalization, especially between Mexico and the United States, would result in significant incremental environmental damage. Indeed, reflecting the strength of the early concerns raised in this regard, the Bush Administration agreed to carry on parallel negotiations concerning environmental issues alongside the trade negotiations in order to win Congressional approval for "fast-tracking" the NAFTA.

The signing of the NAFTA by Presidents Bush and Salinas and Prime Minister Mulroney on December 16, 1992, along with the election of Bill Clinton as the next president of the United States, have focused the free trade debate even more sharply around the question of whether the specific agreement does "enough" to recognize environmental concerns.[1] For example, President-elect Clinton has indicated that one of his concerns about NAFTA is that it does not go far enough in addressing environmental remedies and protection. In a speech given at North Carolina State University on October 4, 1992, Clinton expressed support for NAFTA, while at the same time he proposed the establishment of an environmental protection committee with substantial powers and resources to clean up water pollution and encourage the enforcement of each country's own environmental laws.

While government officials in Mexico, Canada and the United States lauded the NAFTA as being the "greenest" trade agreement ever produced, opponents are already claiming that it does not go far enough to recognize and remedy the damaging effect that increased trade will have on the environment. At this stage of the NAFTA debate, it seems fair to conclude that opponents of free trade will rely heavily upon the argument that the Agreement, as it now stands, will lead to substantial deterioration of environmental conditions, primarily along the U.S.-Mexican border.

The primary purpose of this chapter is to identify and assess the interactions between liberalized trade and the environment. Contrary to the standard argument that trade liberalization inevitably leads to further environmental degradation, this chapter argues that trade liberalization may well promote more careful use of environmental resources, as well as more extensive and widespread remedies for existing environmental pollution. It also argues that efforts to enforce environmental standards through trade policy measures invite a serious risk that importers will invoke spurious claims about environmental misbehaviour on the part of foreign exporters in order to protect domestic markets. In short, the NAFTA, if anything, may err in the direction of giving too much emphasis to environmental matters rather than too little.

The chapter proceeds in the following manner. First, environmental provisions in the NAFTA are identified and discussed. Then the chapter

---

1 See Government of Canada, *North American Free Trade Agreement*, Draft Legal Text, September 8, 1992.

lays out the major direct and indirect linkages between trade liberalization and the environment. It then discusses available evidence bearing upon the nature of these linkages. Finally, it assesses the overall environmental consequences of the NAFTA in light of both theory and evidence.

Environmental Provisions of NAFTA

Several important environmental provisions in the NAFTA are similar to provisions in the General Agreement on Tariffs and Trade (GATT). In particular, NAFTA allows the trade obligations of the NAFTA countries under specified environmental agreements to take precedence over NAFTA provisions. For example, NAFTA accords priority to three international agreements to which the U.S. is a party: the convention on international trade in endangered species of wild fauna and flora, 1973, the Montreal protocol on substances that deplete the ozone layer, 1987, and amended in 1990, and the Basel convention on the control of transboundary movements of hazardous wastes and their disposal, 1989, on the latter's entry into force for all three countries.[2] NAFTA affirms the right of each country to choose the level of protection of human, animal or plant life or health or of environmental protection that it considers appropriate. Moreover, each country may maintain and adopt standards and phyto sanitary measures, including those more stringent than international standards, to secure its chosen level of protection.

There are provisions in the NAFTA which establish standards subcommittees to work to make compatible standards-related measures in the areas of, for example, vehicle emissions and other motor carrier environmental pollution levels. The parties also agree to promote making compatible standards-related measures that are developed or maintained by state, provincial and local authorities and private sector organizations;[3] however, there is nothing in the agreement which

2 These agreements were cited earlier in Weintraub's chapter for this volume.

3 Ibid., Annexes 913 A–C.

obliges countries with "stricter" environmental standards to harmonize those standards with the "more lax" standards of other trading partners. On the contrary, countries are free to raise their environmental standards to whatever chosen level is desirable.

To be sure, disputes may arise over whether specific environmental provisions are merely disguised trade barriers.

In disputes regarding a country's standards that raise factual issues concerning the environment, that country may choose to have the dispute submitted to the NAFTA dispute settlement procedure rather than to procedures under another trade agreement such as GATT. The same option is available for disputes concerning trade measures taken under specified international environmental agreements. The panel hearing the dispute will presumably seek to determine if the action taken is credible on environmental (or related) grounds or whether it is transparently a trade protectionist measure. In dispute settlement, the complaining country bears the burden of proving that another NAFTA country's environmental or health measure is inconsistent with NAFTA.

In what is arguably a new departure for an international trade agreement, the NAFTA contains general statements that the signatories will work jointly to enhance the protection of human, animal and plant life and health and the environment. This ostensibly refers to earlier commitments on the part of the negotiators to carry on parallel discussions regarding environmental initiatives. The Agreement also embodies a general statement that no NAFTA country should lower its health, safety or environmental standards for the purpose of attracting investment. It is unclear at this time how effectively this latter clause can be enforced given that complaints would have to be handled through a dispute resolution procedure. Moreover, it is unclear what standards of evidence would be required to "prove" that investment patterns were changed by changes in environmental laws and standards.

Finally, as part of the parallel track negotiations, Mexico and the U.S. agreed in the spring of 1992 to a cooperative plan for improving the environment along the border. As part of this plan, the U.S. government pledged $379 million over two years for various activities, while the Mexican government's share is $466 million. Critics of the cooperative plan have focused on two issues in particular: (i) the failure of the plan to outline any new revenue-raising measures for border environmental programs; (ii) the absence of a binational enforcement group legally empowered to enforce pollution laws on both sides of the border.[4]

In short, the NAFTA embodies several unique, albeit general commitments to protect the environment and to ensure that environmental amenities are not sacrificed to attract capital investment. The latter commitment is an obvious obeisance to arguments raised by critics of NAFTA that "environmental dumping" will take place, whereby toxic firms relocate to Mexico to evade stricter enforcement of environmental standards in the United States and Canada. Precisely how and to what extent these commitments will be carried out in practice is unclear at the present time. Individual countries retain sovereignty over their domestic health and safety standards, although these standards can be challenged as unwarranted trade restrictions.

Economic Incentives and the Environment

It is clear that the NAFTA, *per se*, does nothing directly to weaken environmental standards and their enforcement in the member countries. That is, countries are free to strengthen their environmental laws and enforcement efforts as long as "legitimate" environmental objectives are being pursued. Hence, potential environmental objections to NAFTA must be based on the adverse impacts that trade liberalization has, directly or indirectly, on environmental amenities. In this section, we consider the potential for such impacts.

The relationship between economic activity and the environment can be made more explicit by noting that all economic activities involve the transformation of specific inputs into specific outputs. Some of the inputs utilized will be closely related to environmental amenities such as clean air and clean water. For example, the activities in question might utilize water as a direct input in the production process or they

---

4 For a detailed discussion of the border environmental plan, see Jan Gilbreath Rich, *Planning the Border's Future: The Mexican-U.S. Integrated Border Environmental Plan*, Austin: The University of Texas, LBJ School of Public Affairs, U.S.-Mexican Occasional Paper No. 1, March 1992.

might use water indirectly, e.g. by dumping waste byproducts into nearby waterways. It is difficult to be precise in defining environmental amenities, since what is included in the definition will depend, in part, upon the tastes and preferences of the individual offering the definition. For example, some might opt for a broad definition including clean air and water, the preservation of biodiversity, the preservation of wilderness areas and so forth. Others might opt for a narrower definition.

For purposes of this discussion, we do not need to define environmental amenities precisely; however, it is useful to be able to think of these amenities as being divisible and as being "used up" by specific economic activities to a greater or lesser extent. In this context, trade liberalization would damage the environment to the extent that it accelerated the rate at which environmental amenities are used up. By the same token, other economic activities can have the effect of increasing available environmental inputs, e.g. water treatment procedures which reduce chemical and other pollutants in waterways.

In this context, there are several ways in which economic activity can affect the environment. Most directly, an increase in the overall level of economic activity would presumably lead to an increase in the utilization of environmental inputs. Changes in the mix of economic activities can lead either to increases or decreases in the utilization of environmental inputs. For example, as real incomes rise, the demand for environmental amenities should increase. While the increase in demand may be relatively small at low levels of income, it can be expected to increase at a faster rate as a nation becomes wealthier. In more technical terms, the income elasticity of demand for environmental inputs is arguably positive and larger at higher levels of income.[5] If demand turns strongly in the direction of consuming more environmental amenities, it is quite possible that increased levels of economic activity (and resulting increases in income levels) may lead to overall decreases in the utilization of environmental inputs.[6]

---

5 Income elasticity of demand is defined as the percentage change in the quantity demanded of a specific good divided by the percentage change in real income.

6 That is to say, a shift towards a mix of "cleaner" activities might offset the

Ordinarily there will be several different ways to produce a given product. Put in other words, several economic activities may result in the same or similar products being produced. The activities differ in the sense that different mixes of factor inputs are used; e.g. some use more labour relative to capital, some use more capital relative to labour and so forth. In this context, some activities may use environmental resources more intensively than others. As noted above, as incomes increase, members of a society in their roles as both consumers and voters will likely spend an increasing share of their incomes on activities which use relatively small amounts of environmental inputs.

Different ways to produce any given product may persist for periods of time, even if some ways are clearly less efficient than others, because inefficient producers may be subsidized or otherwise protected by the government. Increased competition can be expected to change the mix of activities in use. Specifically, activities which are high cost relative to other activities producing similar products should be driven out of the economy. In this respect, trade liberalization can be expected to lead to such a rationalisation of production within a protected economy, at least on the margin.

One can fit the "environmental dumping" argument into the framework suggested in the preceding paragraph. Specifically, prior to free trade, it may be cheaper to produce a product in the U.S. than in Mexico, even if certain costs associated with environmental standards must be borne in the U.S., because of relatively high U.S. tariffs on Mexican imports. If these tariffs are eliminated, producers may find that it is cheaper to move from the U.S. to Mexico in order to avoid costs of complying with environmental standards.[7] In effect, a reduction in protection in the U.S. might lead to the substitution of one set of activities, i.e. production in Mexico, for another set of activities, production in the U.S., holding the product constant.

---

impact of an increase in the overall level of economic activity.

7 Note that it may not be less costly in a social sense if the costs of environmental externalities are properly attributed to production in Mexico.

It should be noted that a "reverse dumping" argument can also be made. Namely, trade liberalization might itself promote market oriented reforms in domestic economic policies including reductions in government subsidies and other pricing distortions. Such reforms, in turn, could result in a substitution of less environmentally damaging activities for more environmentally damaging activities. Probably the most relevant case in point here are subsidies extended by many developing countries to energy intensive activities such as transportation and heavy manufacturing.[8] If trade liberalization agreements lead to a reduction in trade distorting subsidies, an important byproduct might be reduced environmental pollution, since heavily polluting activities, which are often the focus of government subsidies in developing countries, would become relatively less profitable.

In the next section, we consider empirical evidence bearing upon these potential linkages. The foregoing discussion suggests that two potential linkages are particularly relevant: (i) trade liberalization leads to higher income levels which affect both the aggregate level of overall economic activity, as well as the mix of economic activities; (ii) the potential for pollution intensive activities to migrate to Mexico as a result of lower tariffs in the United States and Canada counterbalanced by the potential for market reforms in Mexico to discourage pollution-intensive activities either directly or indirectly.

Evidence on Linkages between Trade and the Environment

As noted above, one potentially important linkage between trade liberalization and the environment occurs through the impact of higher levels of economic activity. Specifically, trade liberalization can be expected to result in a faster expansion of the economies of the free trade

---

8 Observers have noted that in many developing countries, in particular, deliberate "underpricing" of petroleum products, chemical fertilizers and the like encourages the adoption of environmentally intensive production techniques. See Kym Anderson and Richard Blackhurst, "Trade, the Environment and Public Policy," in Kym Anderson and Richard Blackhurst, eds., *The Greening of World Trade Issues*, New York: Harvester Wheatsheaf, 1992, pp. 3-22.

area than would otherwise take place. As a consequence, there will be an even greater demand for all factors of production including environmental amenities.

At the same time, higher real income levels should encourage, at some point, increased private and public demand for greater environmental amenities, and the increased wealth associated with faster economic growth enhances the financial capacities of societies to invest in environmental protection and remedies.

The foregoing suggests that the relationship between real income levels and environmental pollution may not be linear. That is, over an initial range, the dominating influence is the overall level of economic activity. But beyond some point, the changing mix of activities towards less polluting ones will come to be the dominating influence. The "switchover point" is ultimately an empirical issue.

Available studies provide support for the hypothesis that the demand for a cleaner and healthier environment is strongly and positively related to higher real income levels, at least beyond some threshold income level. For example, Grossman and Krueger correlated the level of sulphur dioxide and smoke with per capita income and found that the level of pollution rises until income reached $5,000 per head (in 1988 dollars) and then starts to fall.[9] By way of background, Mexico's real income level per capita in 1991, measured as gross domestic product per capita in U.S. dollars, was below this threshold at $2,365. Income levels for Canada and the U.S. were well above this threshold.

In the absence of precise estimates of the impacts of trade liberalization on the three countries, it is impossible to infer the net impact of the NAFTA on sulphur dioxide emissions; however, analysts tend to agree that the major economic impacts of a NAFTA will be realized by Mexico. Hence, it is at least plausible to argue that sulphur emissions will increase as a result of the NAFTA, at least in the short run. However, to the extent that NAFTA accelerates the growth of the Mexican economy,

---

9 See Gene Grossman and Alan Krueger, "Environmental Impacts of a North American Free Trade Agreement," Paper prepared for a conference on the U.S.-Mexico Free Trade Agreement, Princeton University Press, October 1991.

it will lead to less sulphur dioxide pollution in the long run, since it will shorten the time it takes Mexico to reach the "crossover" income level.

It might be noted that estimates by the World Bank also indicate a curvilinear relationship between the average ambient level of sulphur dioxide and real income per capita; however, the World Bank places the switchover income level at closer to $2,500.[10] This estimate would suggest that the effects of the NAFTA are likely to be benign in both the short and long run, since Mexico will cross this income threshold in the near future with or without a NAFTA in place.

Some additional evidence on the relationship between income levels and environmental amenities is provided in a study by Walter and Ugelow.[11] Based on questionnaires sent to national officials in developed and developing countries, they found that while the strictness of environmental policies varied within each group, the level of strictness was nonetheless higher, on average, in the developed countries. This finding is also consistent with observations that urban sanitation tends to be an increasing function of income at all income levels, while ambient levels of particles tend to be a decreasing function of income over virtually all income levels.[12] This latter observation suggests that NAFTA will unambiguously reduce pollution related to sewage and ambient particles to the extent that it accelerates income growth in Mexico and, to a lesser extent, in Canada and the United States.

To be sure, some forms of environmental pollution increase with higher national income levels. For example, carbon-dioxide emissions tend to increase fairly uniformly with higher income levels, as does solid waste.[13] These observations qualify an unambiguous conclusion that the income effects of a NAFTA will either be benign or favourable for environmental amenities in North America. Nevertheless, taken on balance, one must conclude that the economic growth stimulated by a

---

10 See "The Environment: Whose World Is It, Anyway?" *The Economist*, May 30, 1992, p. 8.

11 Ingo Walter and J. Ugelow, "Environmental Attitudes in Developing Countries," *Resources Policy*, Vol. 4, 1978, pp. 200-209.

12 See *The Economist*, op. cit.

13 *The Economist*, op. cit.

NAFTA may well be positive, on balance, for the environment in terms of reducing the utilization of environmental amenities. The main effect here is the increased demand for a cleaner environment which is associated with a shifting away from pollution-intensive activities.[14]

Another important empirical relationship relates to the environmental dumping issue or the relocation of pollution intensive activities to Mexico. As noted earlier, one argument holds that a reduction in Canadian and U.S. tariffs will, on the margin, make it more attractive for polluting firms to relocate to Mexico in order to serve the North American market. A related concern is that increased competition associated with trade liberalization will lead domestic producers to "cheat" with respect to obeying environmental standards or that it will lead to increased and effective lobbying efforts to have environmental standards relaxed.[15]

The argument that firms facing the competitive pressures of free trade will abandon environmental responsibility and ignore codified (or uncodified) standards, i.e. use illegal, pollution-intensive production techniques, begs the question: why would they not also cheat prior to the implementation of a free trade agreement if they thought they could do so with impunity? Perhaps the risks of getting caught become worth taking when a firm is faced with the imminent prospect of bankruptcy; however, widespread increases in risks of bankruptcy cannot be realistically contemplated purely as a consequence of NAFTA.

Another scenario is that national governments will be less inclined to pass and enforce environmental standards given industrial dislocations and any short-term increases in unemployment associated with adjustments to trade liberalization. Indeed, governments might rely upon reduced regulation of business as a form of "adjustment assistance" for domestic industries. Equivalently, governments might relax domestic environmental standards in order to permit domestic firms to

---

14 Note that such shifting can reflect greater utilization of pollution abatement equipment or practices in activities which hitherto were relatively pollution intensive.

15 See Peter Emerson and Raymond Mikesell, *North American Free Trade: A Survey of Environmental Concerns*, San Francisco: Pacific Research Institute Policy Briefing, mimeo, December 1991.

compete on a "level playing field" with firms based in countries with weaker environmental standards and/or enforcement practices.[16]

Both the environmental dumping and the standards relaxation arguments are ultimately empirical issues. In both cases, empirical evidence provides little support for the arguments. Since the bulk of the available evidence relates to the environmental dumping issue, we shall review that evidence first.

One comprehensive review of the environmental economics literature concludes that domestic environmental measures have not induced industrial flight and the development of pollution havens. The primary reason seems to be that the costs of pollution control have not, in fact, loomed very large even in heavily polluting industries (i.e. on the order of only 1 to 2.5% of total costs in most pollution-intensive industries). Such small increments to costs are likely to be swamped in their impact on international trade by other effects such as differentials in labour cost.[17]

Specific studies can be cited to reinforce this conclusion. For example, Leonard found no evidence in overall statistics on foreign investments by U.S. companies and U.S. imports of manufactured goods that key high pollution industries have shifted more production facilities overseas in response to environmental regulations. Yet in a few high pollution, hazardous production industries, environmental regulations and workplace-health standards have become a more prominent and possibly decisive factor in industrial location and have led U.S. firms to move production abroad. Examples of such industries are those that

---

16 An alternative version of this argument might hold that standards in the U.S. and Canada will be "harmonized downward" to be made compatible with standards in Mexico.

17 See Maureen L. Cropper and Wallace Oates, "Environmental Economics: A Survey," *The Journal of Economic Literature*, Vol. XXX, June 1992, pp. 675-740. Another more focused literature review comes to the same conclusion, namely, there is no evidence to support the hypothesis that more stringent regulations in one country will result in loss of competitiveness, and perhaps industrial flight and the development of pollution havens. See Judith M. Dean, "Trade and the Environment: A Survey of the Literature," Background Paper, Washington, D.C.: The World Bank, 1992.

produce highly toxic, dangerous or carcinogenic products, such as copper, zinc and lead. For these latter industries, environmental regulations have combined with other changing location incentives and economic problems to speed international dispersion of capacity.[18]

In a similar vein, Walter reports that certain copper smelters, petroleum refineries, asbestos plants and ferro-alloy plants have reportedly been constructed abroad rather than in the U.S. for environmental reasons. Moreover, some recent Japanese pollution-intensive industries have reportedly been channelled to developing countries in Southeast Asia and Latin America; however, there is no evidence of a "massive" environment-induced shift in the location of production capacity. Moreover, a significant amount of the observed geographical mobility of production involves cases where major projects were absolutely barred for environmental reasons.[19]

Rubin and Graham conclude that during the decade of the 1970s, during which complex environmental regulations and high pollution costs were imposed on industries, the overall foreign investment and import trends of the mineral processing, chemical and pulp and paper industries did not differ fundamentally from those of U.S. manufacturing industries in general. The former industries are arguably among those that should have been most adversely affected by environmental legislation implemented in the U.S. In fact, only slight shifts at the margin could be detected in these industries. Specifically, only a few U.S. industries within branches of the chemical manufacturing sector have increased production overseas as a direct or indirect result of environmental regulations.[20]

---

18 See H. Jeffrey Leonard, *Are Environmental Regulations Driving U.S. Industries Overseas?* Washington, D.C.: The Conservation Foundation, 1984.

19 See Ingo Walter, "International Economic Repercussions of Environmental Policy: An Economist's Perspective," in Seymour Rubin and Thomas R. Graham, eds., *Environment and Trade*, Totawa, New Jersey: Allanheld, Osmun and Co., 1982.

20 See Seymour Rubin and Thomas Graham, "Environment and Trade" in Rubin and Graham, eds., op. cit.

Stafford examined whether traditional factors such as access to markets and differences in costs of labour and materials remained predominant in manufacturing-location decision-making, despite the added dimensions of environmental regulations introduced under the National Environmental Policy Act.[21] Personal interviews and mailed questionnaires were used to identify the most important factors in the location of 162 new branch plants of U.S. corporations. For most of the decisions investigated, environmental regulations did not rank among the most important factors considered. When such regulations were of some significance, uncertainties about when the necessary permits would be obtained were more important than spatial variations in direct cost. Stafford concludes that environmental regulations have had no consistent effect on the size of the search area, the number of sites considered, the sizes of the facilities built, or the decision to expand existing plants versus building new plants.

Bartik used a database of new manufacturing branch plants opened by Fortune 500 companies between 1972 and 1978 to determine if business location decisions are affected substantially by state environmental regulations. Two measures of state water pollution regulations and four measures of state air pollution regulations were used as variables. The study did not find any statistically significant effect of state environmental regulations on the location of new branch plants. Even sizeable increases in the stringency of state environmental regulations were found unlikely to have a large effect on location decisions for the average industry; however, for some highly polluting industries, the results cannot rule out the possibility of effects of environmental regulation on plant location.[22]

Finally, McConnell and Schwab estimated a statistical model to investigate the impact of a variety of country characteristics on the locations of 50 new branch plants in the motor vehicle industry during the period 1973-1982, a period when there were wide variations in

---

21 Howard A. Stafford, "Environmental Protection and Industrial Location," *Annals of the Association of American Geographers*, Vol. 75, 1985, pp. 227-240.

22 Timothy Bartik, "The Effects of Environmental Regulation on Business Location in the United States," *Growth and Change*, Vol. 19, 1988, pp. 22-44.

environmental regulations among regions. Most of the results indicate that environmental regulations do not exert an important influence on location decisions. At the margin, however, there is some evidence that firms may be deterred from locating where the ozone problem is severe and emission controls are correspondingly stringent.[23]

In summary, the evidence is quite persuasive that geographic differences in environmental standards and enforcement have a relatively small impact on the location decisions of firms. Indeed, any significant impacts appear to be concentrated in resource-based sectors that are arguably relocating from the United States for other reasons anyway. Moreover, there are other locations to which these activities can potentially relocate with environmental standards and enforcement that are substantially weaker than in the case of Mexico.

To be sure, critics might argue that differences in environmental enforcement between Mexico and the United States are much more substantial than those between different states within the United States or, for that matter, between different developed countries. In this regard, it should be noted that a number of the studies cited above consider potential relocation to other developing countries. Moreover, a study by the U.S. Trade Representative's Office concludes that the small share of costs ascribable to pollution abatement and the already low levels of U.S. tariffs in industries facing high pollution abatement costs argue against Mexico being a different case.[24]

There is less direct empirical evidence to appeal to regarding the potential for environmental standards or the enforcement of these standards to be relaxed in the developed economies as a result either of increased imports from other countries or of formal efforts to harmonize standards. It is certainly relevant to note that increased imports from developing countries in Asia with much weaker environmental regula-

---

23 Virginia McConnell and Robert Schwab, "The Impact of Environmental Regulation on Industry Location Decisions: The Motor Vehicle Industry," *Land Economics*, Vol. 66, 1990, pp. 67-81.

24 Office of the United States Trade Representative, *Review of U.S.-Mexico Environmental Issues*, Washington, D.C.: Mimeo, October 1991.

tions than those in North America have not provoked reversals of environmental legislation in the United States to date.[25]

The experience of the European Community (EC) suggests that when environmental standards differ across countries, convergence of standards will ultimately take place in the direction of the more restrictive set of standards. By mid-1991, the EC had adopted nearly 300 new directives and regulations dealing with environmental matters along with new measures applying strict liability standards in cases involving pollution. While many member countries arguably have not been aggressive in enforcing the EC environmental rules, pressure from those countries enforcing the rules and adopting their own tougher antipollution laws is apparently bringing about compliance by all members.[26]

The likelihood of NAFTA triggering a relaxation of environmental standards in the United States and Canada is reduced by the facts that Mexican imports are a relatively small part of total imports and, further, that environmental costs are a small share of all costs in virtually all industries. Furthermore, current pressures in the United States to reduce the burden of environmental regulations on companies is clearly driven by broader macroeconomic weaknesses in the U.S. economy rather than by import pressures in specific industries or from specific countries.

Overall Assessment of NAFTA and the Environment

The preceding sections suggest that existing arguments about NAFTA necessarily contributing directly or indirectly to a further degradation of environmental amenities are both simplistic and arguably incorrect.

---

25 A theoretical model developed by Rauscher concludes that the implications of a common market for environmental policy are uncertain. While there will likely be a relocation of emissions from one country to the other, total emissions may be higher or lower than in the initial state, i.e. prior to production factors being mobile. See Michael Rauscher, "National Environmental Policies and the Effects of Economic Integration," *European Journal of Political Economy*, Vol. 7, 1991, pp. 313-329.

26 See Rudy Portari, "Toughened Environmental Regulation Looms in the EC," *National Underwriter*, Vol. 95, 1991, pp. 52-53.

Increased pollution along the border between Mexico and the United States is frequently pointed to as a necessary consequence of increased cross-border commerce.[27] However, it can be argued in this regard that the economic activity generated by NAFTA will actually encourage less pollution along the border. This is because the incentives that maquila plants now have to congregate along the border will be blunted by a NAFTA which will make all Mexican exports, and not just those from maquila plants, eligible for tariff relief on their North American content.

Undoubtedly, the high degree of congestion along the border has exacerbated pollution problems (given limitations on the ability of the natural environment to absorb pollution), while limited enforcement of pollution standards, particularly by Mexico, has contributed to border-area problems highlighted by NAFTA critics. However, the relevant issue is whether NAFTA will exacerbate or mitigate existing environmental degradation.

As noted above, the NAFTA should mitigate environmental congestion problems at the border by encouraging the dispersal of economic activity away from the border region. Also, tariffs on pollution abatement equipment will be eliminated over time making this equipment substantially cheaper in Mexico. As a result, it will be cheaper for Mexican firms to meet environmental standards, although whether they choose to buy and install more equipment will depend, in part, on the efforts of the Mexican authorities to enforce existing standards. The freer movement of professionals in the environmental engineering area under the NAFTA should assist the Mexican government in its enforcement efforts given shortages of such expertise in Mexico.[28]

Finally, provisions in the NAFTA liberalizing cross-border trucking restrictions might indirectly encourage a reduction in vehicle pollution at major border crossing stations. For example, vehicles registered in

---

27 There are numerous discussions in the media documenting health and worker safety problems associated primarily with Maquiladora production along the Mexico-U.S. border. See, for example, Joel Simon, "Will Tijuana be a free trade tinderbox?" *The Globe and Mail*, December 19, 1992, D3.

28 The NAFTA includes provisions expediting the visa process for managers and many professionals including engineers.

most states currently face tighter emissions control procedures for licensing than do those registered in Mexico. Hence, to the extent that U.S.-owned vehicles displace Mexican vehicles in hauling traffic within the Mexican border, emission standards in Mexico will indirectly rise. On the other hand, Mexican vehicles entering the U.S. will presumably have to meet the same emission standards facing U.S.-registered vehicles. The opportunity to carry more traffic within the United States might therefore encourage Mexican fleet owners to reduce pollution from their vehicles.

These latter considerations add further weight to an argument that NAFTA will lead to improvements in environmental amenities rather than further deterioration, even if the relevant standards subcommittees fail to harmonize emission and other environmental pollution levels. Nevertheless, it might be argued that NAFTA is a promising vehicle for "leveraging" greater efforts from Mexico to deal with domestic pollution problems, as well as greater efforts on the part of all three countries to deal with trans-border pollution problems. In effect, one might argue that trilateral trade liberalization negotiations should be used to directly strengthen existing legislation and enforcement of environmental standards on a North American-wide basis.

One argument for directly linking trade liberalization to environmental protection measures is premised on the view that threats of trade retaliation on the part of trading partners effectively motivate a country to meet the environmental standards demanded by those trading partners.[29] In this regard, some observers argue that recent increases in Mexican budgets for environmental infrastructure and enforcement of environmental laws and regulations would probably not have come about if NAFTA negotiations had not provided the impetus.[30]

Another argument for an explicit and comprehensive linkage is that governments in high enforcement countries can and will invoke trade remedy laws, particularly countervailing duties, against exporters in weak enforcement countries. In this case, it might be more effective to

---

29 Equivalently, one can talk about the use of the "carrot" of trade liberalization as the motivating influence.

30 This point is made by Weintraub in his chapter for this volume.

have explicit agreements struck than to tolerate significantly higher risks of trade wars tied to escalating retaliation for specific environmental practices.[31]

A counter-argument against directly linking trade and environmental measures is that it is unlikely to be welfare maximizing for all countries to adopt identical environmental standards or environmental cost controls given that the point at which the marginal social benefit of abatement equals the marginal social cost of abatement will vary from country to country depending upon factors such as topography, climate, demography and so forth.[32] Another is that it is rarely welfare improving for countries to impose trade restrictions in response to their being "polluted upon" by another country's producers (or consumers).[33] Nevertheless, a theoretical case can be made for the "victim" country to use tariffs against the polluting country as a second best policy providing the importing country is large in world markets; however, the first best approach is the imposition of a coordinated "globally optimal" tax on trans-border pollution.

The latter observation, combined with the recognition that lobby groups will use environmental issues to extract protection against imports suggests the wisdom, on balance, of separating the treatment of environmental problems from the treatment of trade issues. The exis-

---

31 That this concern is becoming increasingly relevant is suggested by a report that Senator Max Baucus held hearings in December 1991 to discuss possible trade legislation requiring countervailing duties on imports from countries with less strict pollution rules than the U.S. to prevent environmental dumping. See Peter Fuhrman, "Strange Bedfellows," *Forbes*, December 9, 1991. Concern about this possibility is also expressed in GATT, Press Release: Expanding Trade Can Help Solve Environmental Problems, Geneva: Mimeo, February 3, 1992.

32 For a detailed discussion of these factors, see Charles S. Pearson, "Environmental Standards, Industrial Location and Pollution Havens," in C.S. Pearson, ed., *Multinational Corporations, Environment and the Third World: Business Matters*, Durham: Duke University Press, 1987, pp. 113-128.

33 For a full discussion of this point, see Peter J. Lloyd, "The Problem of Optimal Environmental Choice," in Kym Anderson and Richard Blackhurst, eds., *The Greening of World Trade Issues*, New York: Harvester Wheatsheaf, 1992, pp. 49-92.

tence of dispute resolution panels in the NAFTA promises to mitigate some of the more grievous abuses of environmental standards to blockade imports; however, this does not gainsay a general argument that the more the trade liberalization process is made contingent upon satisfying implicit or explicit environmental conditions, the more likely is trade protectionism.

In the last analysis, the level of inter-governmental cooperation to address border pollution problems is the single most important factor affecting environmental conditions in the member countries.[34] It is useful to repeat in this regard that eliminating explicit and implicit government subsidies, particularly to energy use, would also make a significant contribution to reducing certain emissions. Indeed, market processes can assist in rationalizing the harmonization of environmental standards. A case in point is the infamous American dolphin-protection laws which highlighted the issue of trade retaliation on environmental grounds at the GATT level. In one part of the eastern Pacific, herds of dolphin on the sea's surface signal the presence of schools of tuna farther down. Encircling the dolphins with purse-seine nets is one way of catching the deeper tuna, but at a high cost in dolphin deaths.

The most recent version of America's Marine Mammal Protection Act prevents American fleets from using this method of tuna fishing. Since 1990 the law has insisted that imported tuna must not be fished by methods that involve killing more than one-quarter more dolphin than are killed by the American fishing fleet. Mexico is one of three countries that failed to meet this target. A protest against an American ban on imports of tuna from Mexico led to a GATT ruling against the ban.[35]

---

34 See Office of the United States Trade Representative, op. cit. A number of studies conclude that the use of trade related measures will have at best a modest impact on natural resource activity which is a major source of environmental problems. See Peter A.G. van Bergeijk, "International Trade and the Environmental Challenge," *Journal of World Trade*, Vol. 6, 1991, pp. 105-115.

35 "GATTery v. Greenery," *The Economist*, May 30-June 5, 1992, pp. 12-15.

The GATT decision throws into doubt environmental laws that impose restrictions or penalties on foreign countries which may constrain in a substantial way the treatment of similar protests brought for dispute resolution under the NAFTA. A point which might be made is that with sufficient information, American consumers might have encouraged a reduction in the dolphin kill. Specifically, consumers could exercise their environmental preferences by buying more "American" tuna and less "Mexican" tuna. If consumers felt strongly enough about this issue, it would pay American producers to advertise their "dolphin-safe" methods of fishing. Certainly there are an increasing number of businesses that trade on a reputation of being "environmentally responsible" entities. Where individual consumption or production decisions impose no substantial third-party externalities, there is no compelling efficiency argument for government intervention, particularly given the risk that such intervention will be motivated by desires of domestic producers for protection and will likely lead to retaliation by other countries.

A contentious international trade environment is unlikely to promote an atmosphere of cooperation for inter-governmental agreements to address cross-border pollution including the harmonization of standards and the implementation of "globally-based, market-type" mechanisms to address pollution externalities.[36] Furthermore, the expertise needed to address trade issues does not necessarily overlap the expertise needed to negotiate international environmental agreements.

In summary, it seems wise to separate trade liberalization treaties from negotiations to create international environmental agreements which was essentially the procedure adopted by NAFTA negotiators. In a similar vein, it would arguably be a mistake to make trade liberalization contingent upon the trading partners resolving all major cross-border environmental problems. The NAFTA as it currently stands adopts basic GATT provisions allowing countries to exercise sovereignty in choosing environmental, health and safety standards as long as national treatment is extended to foreign producers, and the stan-

---

36 van Bergeijk, op. cit. briefly discusses the use of internationally tradeable emission permits.

dards are not defined and implemented in a way that is transparently protectionistic. In this respect, the NAFTA recognizes the likelihood that "optimal" environmental standards will differ from country to country, while at the same time recognizing that limits must be placed on the arbitrary use of domestic environmental legislation to disadvantage foreign producers.

In short, one can conclude that the NAFTA adopts a relatively effective position on environmental matters and that efforts to "strengthen" the environmental provisions will impose social costs that likely outweigh any associated social benefits.[37] Of course, this is not to say that inter-governmental negotiations to resolve trans-border environmental issues should be discontinued, or that efforts to harmonize standards which are impacting trade relationships should not be enthusiastically pursued. On the contrary, the successful implementation of the NAFTA will arguably facilitate successful negotiations in the environmental area in a setting where the sovereignty of the individual member countries has been formally acknowledged.

---

37 This caveat also applies to the provision in the NAFTA which proscribes a weakening of environmental standards to attract new investment. While it is unclear how this provision will be implemented, there is a grave risk of mischievous interventions on the part of governments that are driving away investment through policies that weaken the efficiency of markets. There is also a risk that governments may not be able to rescind environmental laws that are inefficient or even ineffective.